The Story of Medicine

BOOKS BY VERNON COLEMAN

The Medicine Men (1975)
Paper Doctors (1976)
Everything You Want To Know About Ageing (1976)
Stress Control (1978)
The Home Pharmacy (1980)
Aspirin or Ambulance (1980)
Face Values (1981)
Guilt (1982)
The Good Medicine Guide (1982)
Stress And Your Stomach (1983)
Bodypower (1983)
An A to Z Of Women's Problems (1984)
Bodysense (1984)
Taking Care Of Your Skin (1984)
Life Without Tranquillisers (1985)
High Blood Pressure (1985)
Diabetes (1985)
Arthritis (1985)
Eczema and Dermatitis (1985)
The Story Of Medicine (1985)
Natural Pain Control (1986)
Mindpower (1986)
Addicts and Addictions (1986)
Dr Vernon Coleman's Guide To Alternative Medicine (1988)
Stress Management Techniques (1988)
Overcoming Stress (1988)
Know Yourself (1988)
The Health Scandal (1988)
The 20 Minute Health Check (1989)
Sex For Everyone (1989)
Mind Over Body (1989)
Eat Green Lose Weight (1990)
Toxic Stress (1991)
Why Animal Experiments Must Stop (1991)
The Drugs Myth (1992)
Why Doctors Do More Harm Than Good (1993)
Stress and Relaxation (1993)
Complete Guide to Sex (1993)
How to Conquer Backache (1993)
How to Conquer Arthritis (1993)
Betrayal of Trust (1994)

Know Your Drugs (1994)
Food for Thought (1994)
The Traditional Home Doctor (1994)
I Hope Your Penis Shrivels Up (1994)
People Watching (1995)
Relief from IBS (1995)
The Parent's Handbook (1995)
Oral Sex: Bad Taste And Hard To Swallow (1995)
Why Is Pubic Hair Curly? (1995)
Men in Dresses (1996)
Power over Cancer (1996)
Crossdressing (1996)
How To Get The Best Out Of Prescription Drugs (1996)
How To Get The Best Out of Alternative Medicine (1996)
How To Stop Your Doctor Killing You (1996)
How To Overcome Toxic Stress (1996)
Fighting For Animals (1996)
Alice and Other Friends (1996)
Dr Vernon Coleman's Fast Action Health Secrets (1997)
Dr Vernon Coleman's Definitive Guide to Vitamins
    and Minerals (1997)
Spiritpower (1997)
Know Your Drugs (revised) (1997)

novels
The Village Cricket Tour (1990)
The Bilbury Chronicles (1992)
Bilbury Grange (1993)
Mrs Caldicot's Cabbage War (1993)
The Man Who Inherited a Golf Course (1993)
Bilbury Revels (1994)
Deadline (1994)
Bilbury Country (1996)

short stories
Bilbury Pie (1995)

on cricket
Thomas Winsden's Cricketing Almanack (1983)
Diary Of A Cricket Lover (1984)

as Edward Vernon
Practice Makes Perfect (1977)
Practise What You Preach (1978)
Getting Into Practice (1979)
Aphrodisiacs - An Owners Manual (1983)
Aphrodisiacs - An Owners Manual (Turbo Edition) (1984)
The Complete Guide To Life (1984)

as Marc Charbonnier
Tunnel (novel 1980)

with Dr Alan C Turin
No More Headaches (1981)

with Alice
Alice's Diary (1989)
Alice's Adventures (1992)

The Story of Medicine

Vernon Coleman

European Medical Journal

To Sue

Contents

Chapter 1: Medicine in Perspective

The influences and effects of historical events – Myths and prejudices as they affect the historian –The effects of medicine on such disciplines as agriculture and politics – To understand the present we need to know the past

In the past, medical history has usually been studied by medical historians and written about for the benefit of other academics with the same specific interest. This book is different in that I am not a medical historian and I have not tried to write a book for specialists.

My interest is much more in the present than in the past and in studying and describing the cause and effect of discoveries and events rather than in recording the minutiae surrounding them. I believe that, although lists of dates and details may provide a superficial impression of history, real medical history must consist of an account of the influences which have led to major discoveries and of the effects which those discoveries have had upon society. It seems to me that such an approach should interest a much wider readership.

My interest in cause and effect does not, of course, mean that I have been prepared to abandon factual accuracy. Indeed, on the contrary, it is particularly important to ensure that all names, dates, places and specific discoveries are detailed as accurately as possible when conclusions and analyses are to be based on those facts.

My aims have meant that I have had to look for the truth rather than the myths, legends, fantasies and misconceptions with which many history books are so richly decorated. Many characters who play an important part in Roman and Greek history, to mention just two specific eras when myths were part of daily life, probably never existed. Voltaire wrote that history is but a fable that has been agreed upon, and you do not have to read many history books to see what he meant. To illustrate and support their own theories and contentions, many authors introduce and use suppositions and poorly documented hearsay evidence. I have tried to eliminate these myths and misconceptions except where they themselves had an influence on medical care or social progress.

I have also had to be on the lookout for prejudice and bias, and one of my most difficult tasks was to try to recognise and limit as far as possible my own prejudices and those of the authors from whose works I sought information. The importance of bias is easy to underestimate but an experienced historian can make any event appear both inevitable and foreseeable. It is dangerously easy to look for and discover links between otherwise isolated facts if you are struggling to support a theory in which you have more than a passing interest.

Myths and bias are just two potential sources of inaccuracy. There are others. For example, much information reported as historical fact has to be regarded with suspicion when one realises that attitudes, knowledge and even language have changed over the centuries. These changes mean that reported material published ten centuries ago does not necessarily mean what it seems to mean today. The word 'plague' is used today to describe a specific disorder with well-recognised symptoms, but over the centuries the word has been applied to almost all of the diseases which have puzzled sufferers and observers – just as the word 'flu' is today used to describe a wide variety of viral diseases which have certain vague, poorly defined symptoms. Similarly, the word 'leprosy' has been frequently misused and an individual said to have had leprosy might have had any one of several diseases including syphilis, bubonic plague or smallpox or he might simply have been dirty, verminous or infirm.

Cynicism and suspicion are, I discovered, necessary qualifications for anyone writing a history book. I found, for example, that things do not happen quite as neatly and as suddenly as they might appear to do. There is not, of course, any sudden discovery which enables men to understand the working of the heart. What happens is that a number of isolated and, at the time, unrelated events result in a gradual increase in knowledge and understanding. Discoveries and inventions have very rarely had any immediate effect on ordinary life; rather they have been turning points or landmarks which have signalled a slow change in the direction in which thinking men have moved.

Another widely held misconception is that progress in medical care has been made by medical professions. The truth is that much progress in medicine has been made by people outside the mainstream of medical thought and practice. The contributions made by laymen include such specific innovations as the introduction of X-rays and such general contributions as the improvement of water supplies and sewerage facilities. Traditionally, medical history books have linked medical history to the medical profession and the acquisition and accumulation of medical knowledge, but improvements in health and reductions in mortality rates are related to far more than the origins of the Royal College of Physicians and the discovery of cellular pathology.

The truth is that the medical establishment has not always been right and the quacks have not always been wrong. Thinkers reviled and rejected by those influenced too much by greed, stubbornness, stupidity, jealousy and religious or philosophical commitments have often been proved right by later events. For many centuries members of the orthodox medical establishment provided care for only a small proportion of the total population. The majority of patients were looked after by informally trained midwives, medicine men, alchemists and apothecaries who together made formidable contributions to medical theory as well as medical practice.

Then there is the point that the role and influence of different treatments have been confused by the fact that the importance of the placebo effect has been easy to underestimate. For more than seven hundred years the kings of England and France were regarded by their subjects as able to cure physical illness simply by touch, and evidence of this faith survived in France until the reign of Louis XVI and in England until Queen Anne. Many other healers, who relied on pure belief and effectively acted as mediums for real or imaginary supernatural forces, have been able to influence the progress of disease significantly. The inter-linking relationship between mental state and physical illness is now known to be a strong and important one but at the time when traditional treatments were in common use this relationship was not widely recognised and was often attributed to unworthy influences. Nevertheless, although today we can relate modern knowledge and thinking to conditions and influences at all times in history, it is important to remember that, placebo response or not, the result was genuine. The King's Touch may have relied upon the placebo effect but it undoubtedly had real influence.

Another possible cause of confusion and error is the fact that history is a continuous, fluid process which cannot be divided into neat sections on either temporal or geographic grounds. Picking one area of medical care in the sixteenth century and describing it as typical of medicine at that time is as misleading as choosing an area of medical care today and claiming that general standards can be judged from that one example. The quality of care provided in a teaching hospital in London today is very different to the quality of care provided in an ordinary district hospital no more than a mile or two away.

Just as the quality of technical care has always varied from place to place, so disease patterns have varied, appearing and disappearing often inexplicably, being in turn epidemic and endemic, insidious and dramatic.

National boundaries have always been irrelevant as far as medical progress has been concerned. Diseases have never recognised customs barriers, and no country has had a monopoly on scientific advances for long. While making this point I should perhaps confess that in assessing the varied contributions made in different parts of the world I have been influenced by the availability of written information, a criterion which may have led to an apparent distortion in the advances made in individual countries. I hope that my awareness of this potential imbalance has enabled me to minimise its effect as a bias.

And so, aware of all these potential literary hazards, I began with the simple intention of studying the effects of medical progress on human history and the effects of general history on medicine. I discovered, however, that it is exceedingly difficult to separate medical history from any other type of history and that attempting to do so is rather like trying to complete a hundred jigsaw puzzles, all illustrating similar scenes, whose pieces have been mixed together; like trying to unravel a hundred balls of white string tangled by a nuisance of incorrigible kittens.

Close study of the history of all diseases, and in particular the communicable diseases, illustrates the intricate relationship between health and socio-economic status and the links between infection and malnutrition, uncontrolled fertility, an unhealthy environment and inadequate health services. General living standards, trading successes and advances in agricultural techniques have all contributed to health care, while disease and disorder have affected social progress. Malaria may have helped lead to the downfall of the Roman Empire, while haemophilia in the Russian imperial family in the nineteenth century may have contributed to the success of the Russian Revolution.

Agriculture may not seem to have any immediate relationship to medicine but, since the introduction of systematic digging and ploughing five thousand years ago, agricultural affairs have strongly influenced the lives or ordinary people. Famines have not only caused death directly but also led indirectly to disasters as varied as epidemics and wars. The underfed are not only easy prey for infections but also easily aroused to invade neighbouring countries in the search for food.

The need to improve the import and export of food supplies probably led the early settlers to begin developments by riversides and on estuaries. Major cities were built on rivers such as the Nile, Tigris, Euphrates, Indus, Ganges, Yangtze Kiang, Thames, Hudson, Seine, Rhine and Tiber, and those early town-makers could not have realised that there was to be a link between international travel and the spread of disease.

Industrial developments have had their impact too. The development of machinery during the Industrial Revolution led to improved agricultural techniques, which in turn led to the greater availability of food-stuffs. This produced an improvement in general health stands which meant that people were better able to fight infection. On the other hand, developments in industry changed the nature of other aspects of life, and the birth of large towns to act as dormitories for the growing factories put excessive pressure on facilities for the provision of clean water supplies. The squalor and unhappiness of town life that followed the Industrial Revolution undoubtedly contributed to alcoholism, tuberculosis and many other disorders.

The influence of religion on health and life in general has also been mixed. The Jewish leaders prohibited the consumption of pork in order to protect their followers from the dirty habits wrongly believed to be associated with pigs, but at the same time they encouraged communal bathing which did spread disease. The Moslems encouraged religious pilgrimages which took germs from one continent to another. In more recent times the Catholic opposition to contraception has undoubtedly exacerbated hunger, starvation and disease in many countries.

The conclusion has to be that a true social history of medicine cannot be divorced from a history of education, politics, religion, industry, economics, social class, military might or indeed any other aspect of human life. Medicine and disease have been affected by all these disciplines, which have, in turn, been affected by medical progress. Disease has influenced the general welfare and progress of man and the development of civilisation, and there is no reason to suspect that it will not continue to do so. The impact of scientific discoveries on health has invariably been far less immediate and dramatic than the impact of changes in general living conditions.

Goethe wrote that it is impossible to understand the present without a knowledge of the past, and I hope that the facts I have unravelled and the individual pictures I have managed to complete will provide some account of the lessons we can learn from what has gone before. Study of the social history of medicine reveals much about our contemporary problems because a true history of medicine is a history of people, deriving from and adding to our own attitudes and experiences as we see the same problems recurring time and again. History enable us to see the present in perspective, as a continuation of the past, and should, therefore, give us a chance to acquire some idea of the possible consequences of the present on the future.

Chapter 2: The Power of the Gods

The animal's natural instinct for survival – Man turns to the supernatural –The association between religion and medicine begins – The value of medical care provided by the priests

All living creatures have a natural instinct for survival which includes an ability to search for and use simple self-healing remedies. Injured animals lick their wounds, cats eat grass to make themselves sick if they have swallowed too much fur, black bears coming out of hibernation will deliberately search for berries which have a laxative effect, and many wild creatures know how to use spiders' webs to help stop bleeding. Birds will bathe in dust to get rid of lice, and there have even been reports from skilled naturalists of birds applying splints made of clay and stiff grass to injured legs.

It is not surprising, therefore, that human beings have a natural ability to use effective, simple remedies when they fall ill. Man has never been too primitive to treat himself, and there is good evidence to suggest that, even though *average* life expectancy during the Stone Age is thought to have been no more than fifteen years, many of the old-established, traditional remedies favoured were both effective and safe.

Nevertheless, however effective these remedies may have been, it was not long before primitive man began to wonder about the cause of diseases. Thinking men would undoubtedly have realised that prevention is better than any cure and they would, therefore, have sought some explanation for the occurrence of disease.

However, with no knowledge of human anatomy or physiology and no understanding of bacteriology, pathology and the other mechanisms responsible for the production of disease, it is not surprising that primitive man should turn to the supernatural for explanations and that consequently he would supplement his natural use of ointments, applications and herbal draughts with supplications to those gods who were recognised as the responsible forces behind all things good and evil.

These links between medicine and the supernatural developed in many different ways. Some observers simply associated bad spirits and devils with disease and good spirits and gods with good health and sought to release evil spirits from the bodies of those afflicted by disease. It was this idea which led to such forms of treatment as trepanning, where a hole is bored in the patient's skull so that the evil spirits can escape. Others regarded illness as punishments from the gods and tried to placate the offended deities by making sacrifices or supplications. The link between these different types of religious philosophy was the need for an intermediary, a man who could keep track of the needs, expectations and requirements of the spirits and who could, therefore, provide the community with advice about how best to avoid ill health and recover good health.

In this way the close link between the priests and the practice of medicine was born and was to remain strong and powerful for many thousands of years. The links were strengthened by the fact that priests often adopted folk remedies and used them as adjuncts to their spiritual solutions.

This association between medicine and religion had obvious shortcomings. For one thing there was unlikely to be any progress in medical understanding as long as supernatural explanations for physical disorders were accepted. If your headache is caused by the fact that a god is displeased with something you have done, the only solution is to look for ways to appease the offended god; searching for practical reasons and solutions for the headache will not help. Consequently, the links forged by primitive man ensured that medical progress would be delayed for centuries.

Despite these enormously important restrictions, medicine, as practised by the priests, often produced results. If it had not, it would not have survived for so long. The results were due to two things.

First, there is no doubt that many of the traditional folk and herbal remedies favoured by priestly physicians actually did work. Primitive people knew about the effectiveness of many drugs and the Peruvian Incas, for example, used curare to relax muscles and cocaine as a local anaesthetic many centuries before either drug was introduced into orthodox medical practice. One of the most extraordinary surgical techniques used by primitive man was the employment of black ants to suture wounds. This was done in South American, and the ants were first encouraged to bite the two sides of a wound; their bodies would then be twisted off, leaving the jaws in place as fixing clips.

Second, it is well known that symptoms can be alleviated by faith in either the treatment offered or the source or implement of that treatment. The placebo effect, whereby a patient may recover when given a pill consisting of nothing but sugar, is thought to depend upon the patient having trust in the remedy and in the person providing the pill, and it would undoubtedly work just as well for a cave man as for a twentieth-century patient.

Chapter 3: Medicine in Mesopotamia

The link between medicine and religion is weakened – A search for medical solutions to medical problems – The availability of medical care – Hammurabi's Code

The first slow, tentative steps towards the development of a scientific approach to medical care were taken in the part of the world now known as Iraq. At the time when those steps were being taken, some six thousand years ago, the land between the rivers Euphrates and Tigris was known as Mesopotamia, although during the ensuing centuries, the political maps of the area changed many times.

History books are full of contradictions about dates, rules and names relating to the Middle Eastern areas, and the inevitable absence of records has meant that there is much confusion about the precise dates of specific developments. It is clear, however, that early civilisations in that part of the world linked medicine, magic and religion just as closely as did other primitive peoples. It was widely believed that the air was full of demons which invaded humans as soon as the gods withdrew their protection and, consequently, treatments in early Mesopotamia involved either placating the gods or providing the patient with a remedy designed to drive the demons out. For many centuries no one really knew whether treatments worked because of any intrinsic value or because of effects they had on offensive demons or disgruntled deities.

What makes these powerful Middle Eastern countries so memorable is that it was there that these mystical links were first set aside as causes of accidents and injuries, and sources of infection and disease were first recognised. It is difficult for us to understand how difficult it must have been to separate medicine from religion and magic, but it was here that the first steps were taken towards the development of medical science as an individual discipline.

Progress in the world of medicine did not, of course, begin or continue without progress occurring in all other areas of society, and it is important to remember that the people taking these early steps towards the development of medicine were also building cities, trading with or conquering their neighbours, producing the first works of literature and of art and creating new mathematical theories. None of these disciplines developed without influencing or being influenced by other disciplines. For example, the custom of embalming and mummifying bodies must have provided the embalmers with a more extensive knowledge of human anatomy than had been acquired by any preceding civilisation. All the evidence we have does indeed suggest that, at the time, the store of knowledge available and the general standard of living in the cities was greater than it was to be for over fifteen hundred years after the coming of Christ.

Many centuries before the Greeks re-discovered the same thing, it was recognised that fresh air, sunshine and a good diet are necessary for good health. It was known that the human heart had an important role to play in the survival of the human organism, and it was accepted that a pump of some sort sent blood through vessels around the body. Physical examinations which would not have been out of place in a nineteenth-century hospital were performed, with pulses and temperatures recorded; and opiates were used for anaesthesia and alcohol as an antiseptic long before these essentials became accepted in northern Europe.

Once the links between medicine and religion had been weakened and it had been recognised that disease and disorder could have specific causes, the search for medical solutions increased its pace. In ancient Babylon, for example, the sick were taken into the market-places and left there. Anyone passing by was expected to stop, enquire about the patient's symptoms and offer any advice he thought suitable. Passers-by who had experienced the same symptoms and survived would be expected to offer a precise prognosis as well as an account of the remedies they themselves had found efficacious. This may sound laughable to us but it was undoubtedly not only an effective way of increasing the quality and quantity of medical knowledge but also of great help to the patients themselves.

As the centuries went by, more and more information was collected together. Fractured bones were set with splints or glue-soaked linen bandages, and gaping wounds were closed with strips of linen anchored to the healthy skin on either side with an adhesive. Sophisticated weighing machines were used to prepare drugs such as bicarbonate and calamine, and physicians learned to specialise and to limit themselves to looking after patients with particular types of disorder. Indeed, a physician who strayed outside his acknowledged sphere of experience and whose patient did not do well would find himself in serious trouble. There is even evidence that the first psychiatrists were at work, and it seems that several thousand years before Freud was a twinkle in his mother's subconscious it was recognised that guilt, fear and resentment could all have an adverse influence on human health.

The availability of medical treatment varied considerably from patient to patient. On military expeditions soldiers received free treatment from doctors paid by the state but, by and large, the better doctors were available only to the rich who could afford their fees. Slaves had the advantage that they might be treated by their master's own physician, but they also ran the risk of being used as guinea pigs if any particularly risky piece of medical work seemed necessary.

The greatest step towards the development of real medical profession was made not by a doctor or priest but by King Hammurabi, who ruled Babylonia about 2000 BC and who prepared a series of rules and regulations designed to protect both doctors and their patents. The Code of King Hammurabi included details of the fees which might be charged for the performance of specific services and included rather terrifying, but undoubtedly encouraging, rules about the penalties for professional misconduct or even for simple incompetence. Hammurabi ruled that a physician who caused a patient's death would have his fingers cut off. The penalties for not taking proper care of slaves were rather lighter but were nevertheless designed to encourage a high standard or practice.

As information was gathered together, so official texts dealing with such subjects as anatomy, surgery, gynaecology, pathology and ophthalmology were prepared. Doctors were expected to follow officially recommended treatments for at least three days before trying anything new, and an over-imaginative doctor who disobeyed this ruling would pay with his life if his patient died.

Once it was recognised that a fall can cause a fracture without any intervention from the gods, other cause-and-effect relationships were accepted and, for example, it quickly became acknowledged that eating infected food or drinking infected water could produce internal disorders. Consequently, health measures designed to protect the public were introduced in Babylon. Recognising that dirty habits could cause disease, legislators introduced punishments for those convicted of dropping bones or refuse on the ground. There were rules about how close to houses cattle could be kept, and clothes worn by people with infectious diseases had to be burnt. The dead had to be carried far away from populated towns, and strictly upheld regulations were designed to protect the water supplies from contamination.

While Europeans were still living in mud huts, the Babylonians were living in cities with access to lavatories, drains and clean water supplies.

Chapter 4: Our Debt to the Orient

Meanwhile in the Orient – Surgery in India – Medical practices in the East – Our debt to those early men of medicine

At the time when the people of Mesopotamia were formulating their first theories about causes and cures of disease, similar fundamental theorising was going on in India, China and other parts of the distant East. However, it might as well have been happening on a different planet: several thousand miles of rough country separated these various centres of the civilised world, and contact between different cultures must have been at best rare and of little influence.

And yet, at roughly the same time, the fundamental break with religion and mysticism was being contemplated. Our knowledge about exactly what went on in China and India four and five thousand years ago is inevitably sketchy and much of it is based on legend rather than fact, but there is evidence to suggest that even then amateur and professional physicians were recording the effects of treatment on human ailments. Good health was recognised as a sign that the elements which made up the body were in balance, while disease was a sign that the constituent elements had gone out of balance.

The type of care available in each country and the direction in which research and progress went were obviously dependent, to a large extent, upon the cultural and religious strengths and weaknesses of the countries concerned. In China, for example, where religious convictions prevented the drawing of blood or the mutilation of the human body, there was obviously no progress in the world of surgery. There were, however, important developments in other areas. It was in China that massage first became a respected and well-used form of treatment, and acupuncture, a treatment form rapidly gaining followers today in many Western countries, was first introduced in China many centuries ago. Many herbal drugs were known and there is even evidence to suggest that fingerprints were first used to identify individuals in ancient China. Great attention was paid to diagnostic skills; the Chinese listed ten thousand types of fever and when taking the patient's pulse would touch the radial artery in many different places in order to obtain the greatest amount of information.

Surgical skills in India, two thousand years before the birth of Christ, were remarkably well developed, and the ancient Hindus had scalpels, scissors, hooks, probes, forceps, catheters and syringes to help them. In all they had over a hundred different surgical instruments and used them for complex operations. In fact, today's plastic surgeons use a technique for operating on the nose that was first developed by those surgeons in India four thousand years ago. The operation was developed to deal with the disfigurement suffered by adulterous women who had had their noses cut off as a punishment.

The Indians' apparent understanding of infection and disease was an important factor in the success of their surgical endeavours. Operating theatres in India four thousand years ago were kept scrupulously clean, and surgeons had to keep their hands scrubbed, their nails short, and had to wear clean white clothing when operating. Sheets were steam-cleaned, instruments boiled, and operating rooms, though well lit and ventilated, were protected from dust and smells with the use of fragrant smokes and perfumes. The surgeons, who used anaesthetics and antiseptics some thousands of years before they were introduced into European hospitals, were even forbidden to speak during operations in case their breath contaminated the wounds. When convalescing from surgery, patients were encouraged to rest, to eat well and wisely and to enjoy plenty of sunshine and fresh air. Flowers, perfumes, and music therapy were used to make convalescence more enjoyable and successful. To prevent further infections, impure water supplies could be purified by boiling, heating in the sun or filtering through sand, coarse gravel and charcoal.

In addition to their surgical skills, the Indians had acquired other sophisticated medical skills. Before reaching a diagnosis, the Hindu physician would examine a patient and listen to his heart and lungs, and there are suggestions that the Indians knew how to protect against smallpox with inoculation and against malaria by using mosquito netting. These observations are all the more remarkable when it is remembered that it was not until the end of the nineteenth century that the association between malaria and the mosquito was first recognised officially by Western doctors. It even seems possible that the Hindus recognised an association between plague and rats. Like the Chinese and the Babylonians, the Indians used a wide variety of drugs, and one Hindu book alone describes the qualities of seven hundred plants, many of which are now known to have genuine effects.

Sadly we do not know precisely how these services and this knowledge was made available to the peoples of the Orient, whether the surgical skills and operating theatres were available to all or only to a select few. Nevertheless, it seems likely that the extent of medical knowledge in any country must have had some influence on the quality of medical care made generally available.

Of course, as far as we are concerned, the original thinking and the accumulation of information are of considerable historical importance. It was the ideas and information drawn from the Middle and Far East that contributed most to Greek and Roman medicine around the time of Christ. Although much of that knowledge was undoubtedly lost until the Renaissance several hundred years later, ancient medical discoveries and practices have undoubtedly exerted a powerful influence on modern medical practices. When we look back at what we used to know, we ought perhaps to be more conscious of the debt we owe to our scientific ancestors and of the ease with which learning can be lost if it is not used and looked after with care.

Chapter 5: The Great Men of Greece

The Greeks acquire information – Mixing fact and fiction –
The role of Hippocrates – The early medical profession

Like all successful powers the early Greeks were extremely good at collecting, collating and assessing information and ideas from the nations with whom they fought or traded. They acquired knowledge from other Mediterranean countries, from all around the Middle East and from the Asian continent, and they built their society and culture with the aid of the experiences, beliefs and practical skills of their neighbours.

When studying the history of the Greeks it is sometimes impossible to differentiate between fact and fiction, since they had a delightful habit of creating myths and legends to dignify most aspects of their society. In spite of this, it seems clear that the foundations of scientific medicine were laid in Greece. The blueprints may have come from Egypt and the bricks from Babylon, India and Crete, but it was the Greeks who brought these different elements together and created a scientific discipline based on proven facts and logical thought. It was the Greek philosopher physicians who first tried to analyse disease processes and to create treatment plans accordingly.

The man given credit for founding the principles of scientific medicine is Hippocrates, and he is said to have been born on the island of Cos in 460 BC. Inevitably, perhaps, there is much confusion about the identity of Hippocrates. Some of his work has been attributed to other contemporary physicians, and it is even argued that Hippocrates was not one man but several. To argue about the minutiae of a man's life is to risk missing the fact that the Hippocratic philosophies changed the course of life throughout the world.

At the time of Hippocrates' birth Greek medicine was still closely linked to religion, and it was in temples dedicated to Aesculapius, son of Apollo and the senior god of medicine, that most healing took place. These temples were usually built in peaceful spots, and patients were encouraged not only to pray and to make sacrifices to the gods but also to sleep, wash regularly, relax, exercise and eat healthily. Massage was usually available and mud baths were popular. These establishments were ecclesiastical health farms, and those attending them would undoubtedly have benefited from the psychotherapeutic effects.

The Greeks were really hedging their bets by continuing to pay homage to the gods because, even before Hippocrates, they had recognised that many disorders have psychological causes and that effective treatments often involve simple practical remedies. Many of the so-called priests seem to have had considerable faith in the innate healing power of the human body and were prepared to help things along with a judicious nudge from time to time. Recognising that cleanliness is next to godliness, the priests who attended the patients in the temples took care to keep their hands scrubbed and their nails short, while they used wine-soaked linen for bandaging and boiled water for washing wounds. Where prayer, exercise and diet were insufficient as a cure, they resorted to emetics, purges and blood-letting. They kept records of the treatments used, and over each patient's bed hung a marble tablet detailing his symptoms. It is fair to say that patients in these establishments were better cared for than those in London hospitals two thousand years later.

All this was taking place at a time when some of the greatest and most innovative thinkers the world has ever known were alive. In the fifth century BC Pericles, Sophocles, Euriphides, Aristophanes, Socrates, Plato, Herodotus and Thucydides were all making their mark. It was a time of thought, ideas and innovation, and the arrival of Hippocrates and the approach associated with his memory revolutionised medical thinking and practice.

The most important single thing Hippocrates did was completely to dissociate medical care from both religion and abstract philosophy and to establish it as a genuine scientific discipline. This may seem to us a simple and logical step but, at that time it must have taken enormous courage and intellect. Some of his observations were undoubtedly wrong and some of his conclusions certainly contradictory, but these small errors are of little significance when compared to his triumph in divorcing disease from religion. Hippocrates did for medicine what Galileo did for astronomy. We tend to remember Hippocrates for the Oath which bears his name but he (or they) played a crucial role in the development of medicine as a profession.

Hippocrates believed that the physician should look for a natural rather than a supernatural explanation for disease processes, and he encouraged other physicians to search for physical causes when studying illnesses. He made copious notes about the natural history of individual patients and collected many facts about specific diseases. He wrote accurate descriptions of puerperal septicaemia (the blood-poisoning that can occur around childbirth), malaria and dysentery, and he was the first to argue that the disorders of the brain, such as epilepsy, were caused not by divine wrath but by some disorder of the central nervous system. He recognised insanity as a disease rather than a sign of disapproval from the gods. He encouraged physicians to study individual patients so that they would have a better idea of the prognosis to offer others with similar symptoms. He classified diseases as acute, chronic, endemic or epidemic and believed implicitly in the importance of the individual patient.

From what he learnt from his observation of patients, Hippocrates concluded that the best way to help an individual recover good health was to support the body's own self-healing mechanisms in their battle against the specific factors responsible for disease. To this end he advocated a regime of fresh air, exercise, good food, hydrotherapy and massage which would find favour with most modern gurus of medicine. He applied the first logical approach to clinical problems and when, for example, the priests argued that epilepsy was caused by eating goat flesh or lying on goat skins, he wanted to know why the Lydians, who relied on goats for food and clothing, were no more likely to suffer from epilepsy than anyone else. He was enthusiastic about relating food intake to physical work, observing that those who are fat often die earlier than those who are thin, and took advantage of every opportunity to carry out clinical experiments. Although he used purgatives and diuretics, he reserved all drugs for use only when simpler remedies had proved ineffective. His knowledge of anatomy was poor since facilities for dissection were scarcely adequate, but he observed gymnasts and sportsmen and learnt what he could from the injuries and wounds he examined.

Medicine was not to return to such basic principles for nearly 2,500 years, and more than two thousand years later patients in Europe's capitals were lying on dirty mattresses in foul air and provided with poor food. Those with mental diseases were locked up, flogged and even murdered by those responsible for their treatment.

Hippocrates is also remembered for his role in the development of the medical profession. Although he published notes describing how a physician should dress and behave, he is best remembered today for the oath or code of conduct which bears his name. The oath may have been intended originally to help strengthen the emerging medical profession, since those who take it promise to support fellow physicians and to confine their teaching to those who are already familial members of the exclusive circle, but it also undoubtedly improved the lot of the individual patient. Incidentally, it was in the Hippocratic oath that the first clear division between medicine and surgery appears. Those who took the oath promised not to use the knife on their patients; the physician in ancient Greece considered himself above such crude forms of intervention and, with effective anaesthesia and aseptic techniques many centuries away in Europe, the distinction was probably a wise one.

After Hippocrates died, it was not long before the world of medicine subsided again. Aristotle, the great scientist who had studied under Plato and was tutor for a time to the young Alexander the Great, founded comparative anatomy and embryology, while Herophilus and Erasistratus dissected the bodies of executed criminals and together made the first recorded observations about human anatomy, but the Greek Empire was beginning to fall apart, and the plague which struck Athens during the Peloponnesian War undoubtedly led to the collapse of the Greeks as a world force.

Ironically, as the Greeks lost power and status, Hippocrates, who had made such a contribution to medical science by separating medicine from religion, was deified. It was as though this great step forward had never been made. Not for more than two thousand years would medicine attain such heights again.

Chapter 6: The Roman Legacy

The fall of Greece – The rise of the Roman Empire – Galen's importance – The theory of the four humours – The military and engineering skills of the Romans – The fall of the Roman Empire

As the Greek Empire declined, so the Roman Empire grew in size and strength. The two cultures were quite different, and while the Greeks had placed great emphasis on philosophy, art and science, the Romans had always been a practical people, more concerned with engineering and military problems.

Before the fall of Greece most Roman families did not both with doctors but looked after themselves. The head of each household kept a large home pharmacy of herbs and if a member of the family fell ill would hand out an appropriate remedy and call upon a suitable god considered to have jurisdiction over the particular disease, symptom or bodily function.

After the destruction of Corinth a number of Greek physicians fled to Rome, where, although they were treated as slaves and would be killed if they failed, they could earn good rewards if they proved popular and successful. Although trained in Greece, most of these physicians rejected the Hippocratic theories of natural healing and resorted to traditional treatments more in line with the Roman use of herbs and gods. As a result, many of the scientific advances made by Hippocrates and his successors were temporarily lost.

Slowly the physicians from Greece earned respect from the citizens of Rome; in 46 BC Julius Caesar granted citizenship to all practising doctors of medicine, and fifty years later Caesar Angustus issued a decree exempting all doctors from taxation. Augustus also introduced free clinics and free medical services. Unfortunately, the financial advantages associated with the medical profession meant that there were soon a great many second-rate doctors practising in Rome and, indeed, by AD 200 legislation had to be introduced to control the licensing of, and to provide some control over, physicians. It is perhaps important to remember that, although the medical profession was growing in size and stature, there were no other medical services. For example, civilian hospitals did not exist, and although some doctors in big cities would take rich patients into their homes for suitable fees, most patients were looked after in their own homes. The absence of hospitals was matched by an absence of nurses since proper training for women intending to care for the sick was not introduced until AD 400.

During the rise of the medical profession in Rome in the

first century AD three influential figures appeared. First, there was Celsus, who wrote *De Re Medica*, in which he detailed information about both medical and surgical practices. Then there was Dioscorides, a pharmacologist and botanist who described over six hundred medicinal plants and whose book was the basis of herbal therapy for the next fifteen hundred years. Drug therapy was considered an important aid to restoring health, and mixtures of a hundred different herbs in one remedy were not unknown. Unfortunately, dispensing was not always skilful: it has been recorded that some dispensing was done by prostitutes looking for an additional source of income. Finally, there was Galen, a physician whose thinking was destined to dominate medicine until the Renaissance.

Galen, like so many Roman physicians, was a Greek. Soon after qualifying he was appointed surgeon to a school of gladiators, a post which undoubtedly enabled him to learn something about human anatomy. Galen accepted the theory put forward by Aristotle that nature makes nothing without a purpose and tried to explain the function of all parts of the human body. He reached several remarkably accurate conclusions and taught, for the first time, that arteries are filled with blood which moves within the body as a result of the heart's pumping action. Like so many great men in medicine, Galen was a controversial figure for many years but gradually his research and his original ideas began to attract growing interest and support.

Sadly, as interest in his theories increased and as his stature as a medical teacher grew, so the number of people prepared to argue with him fell, and although many of his theories had little basis in fact and had never been proved, students of medicine tended to regarding everything he had written as inevitably correct. Research and original thinking in Rome seemed to stop after Galen's death.

Because of his historically important role, some of the background to Galen's theories about medicine is worth mentioning. While Galen's understanding of human anatomy was based on his experiences as a surgeon, his knowledge of physiology and pathology was based on the theory of the 'four humours'. It is difficult to decide exactly where and when this theory was first put forward. There is evidence that the Chinese, the Hindus and the ancient Egyptians all believed that the world was made up of a small number of basic elements and that human health depended upon maintaining a balance between them. The Indians believed that the human body, like the world around it, consisted of five elements: space, wind, fire, water and earth. The Chinese regarded the five basic elements as: wood, fire, earth, water and metal. The early Greek philosophers argued that the four basic elements were fire, air, water and earth and that each element had two qualities. Fire was hot and dry, air hot and moist, water cold and moist, and earth cold and dry. They translated these four qualities (dry, cold, hot and moist) into the four humours, claiming that the human organism consisted of blood (hot and moist), phlegm (cold and moist), yellow bile (hot and dry) and black bile (cold and dry).

Wherever the theory of the four humours originated and whatever its pedigree, it was certainly Galen who restored and dignified it. He, like many medical predecessors, believed that any illness was caused by an imbalance of these four humours and that consequently treatment should involve an attempt to restore the balance.

The Romans may not have been very advanced when it came to personal medical care but their military and engineering skills enabled them to advance public health facilities enormously. For several hundred years before the Roman Empire began to expand, the Romans had been enthusiastically building aqueducts, sewers and roads. The importance of providing these basic facilities cannot be overemphasised. Today, when World Health Organisation teams go into undeveloped countries, their first priorities are to provide clean water, efficient drains and passable roads. While Galen was struggling with the theory of the four humours, fourteen great aqueducts supplied Rome with 300 million gallons of drinking water a day. Houses had their own private cisterns and taps, and settling tanks were used to keep the water clean. Some of these aqueducts are still in use today, and there are few modern cities which can boast better water supplies than the Romans enjoyed two thousand years ago. Sewerage facilities were equally well advanced and the Romans had public lavatories and flushing water closets. Regulations ensured that public roads were kept clean, that only fresh food was available, that corn stocks were kept up as an insurance against famine and that dead bodies were cremated. Many Romans even enjoyed underfloor central heating.

The Roman army took their engineering skills with them when they travelled, and those countries and cities which came under Roman domination soon acquired similar facilities. When the Romans occupied London and other major cities in Britain, the Britons had bath houses and water-flushed latrines, while those who remained unbowed and unconquered still lived crudely and simply.

For several centuries the Roman Empire spread at a tremendous rate. It reached the Sahara in the south, Scotland in the north, the Spanish coast in the west and the Persian Gulf in the east. It grew so large that the corrupt and wealthy central society in Rome lost any real contact with the many peripheral societies and distant forces which made up the army. Distances were huge, travel was slow and there was little real opportunity for close relationships to develop between different parts of the Empire. In particular, there was one enormous problem associated with the growth of the Roman Empire which no one foresaw.

Rome was the hub around which the rest of the Empire revolved, and as a result there was constant traffic between the periphery and the centre. This meant that returning soldiers, merchants, politicians and diplomats brought with them diseases from foreign parts. They brought new diseases back to people who had no immunity to them and who were, therefore, extraordinarily susceptible. One of the diseases which helped to destroy Rome and its Empire was malaria, a disease which the Indians, several hundred years before, had attributed to the bite of a mosquito. In South America the Peruvian Indians were already treating malaria successfully with powder from cinchona bark but the Romans knew nothing of that. Their military might alone was not enough to protect them from this unseen enemy. Malaria, and other diseases such as smallpox and measles, weakened the people and undoubtedly helped to destroy the Empire.

The impact of the various plagues meant that the power of the traditional gods and herbal remedies were no longer regarded with such awe. As the Empire fell apart, the people who had been under its domination became desperate for new hope, a new medical discipline, a new religion. The answer they found was Christianity.

Chapter 7: The Influence of the Christian Church

The birth of Christianity – The decline of the medical profession – Cities in chaos – Plagues become endemic – Anatomy studies are halted by the Church – Monasteries open their own hospitals – Priests practise medicine – The emphasis on caring not curing – The King's touch – The local wise woman

The collapse of the Roman Empire left much of Europe in political, military and social turmoil. When the legislation and order imposed by the Romans on huge areas was withdrawn, regional control was available to those who were able to take it. The only organisation capable of providing anything like a central government, and of replacing the control of Rome, was the Christian Church, which had quickly developed a strong organisation and was capable of exerting authority and discipline upon its members.

The Christian religion offered new converts one tremendously important advantage over other forms of worship: an afterlife to be enjoyed by the faithful. At a time when plagues, disease and infections of many kinds were racing around the known world, a promise of life after death had considerable appeal. If death was unavoidable, at least you could take advantage of the offer of another life.

However welcome this discipline may have been to those yearning for strong leadership and some protection against local tyrants anxious for power at any cost, the Christian Church did little or nothing to improve the health or living standards of the ordinary people. Indeed, by abandoning many of the improvements in public health made by the Romans and by replacing technological improvements with prayers and superstition, the Church may well have contributed to the increase in mortality and decline in good health which characterised the early centuries of Christ's spiritual leadership of the Western world.

Details of the advances made by the Greek physicians, the Indian surgeons and the Roman public health experts were stored away in monastery libraries, and those Greek and Jewish physicians who still followed the teachings of the ancients were banned by the Church, which taught that all illness was produced by God and could only be alleviated by worship. The Church was hostile to all those anxious to study anatomy, physiology or pathology and so medical research came to a halt. The surgical art, which had reached such heights in India so many centuries before, fell into the hands of barbers, bath-house attendants, executioners and other half trained illiterates.

Towns and cities continued to grow in size but there were no longer drainage systems, fresh water supplies or laws about the keeping of food and disposal of refuse. Church leaders had no interest in providing such services, and without a concerned central government such facilities as already existed were allowed to fall into disuse and ruin. The official policy was to put all trust in God.

With growing, disorganised cities, plagues of one sort or another were endemic. Famine, too, was a major problem. The Romans had organised corn stocks to guard against starvation during lean years, but the Church did not make adequate provisions for such times, and many thousands starved to death when harvests were poor. The weakened people were then even more susceptible to infections.

The early Church undoubtedly did much to hold up medical progress. Anatomy, for example, remained a mystery, and scholars relied on Galen's notes about the anatomy of the pig and the ape since the Church, firmly believing in physical resurrection, totally disapproved of the dissection of human corpses. But although it is tempting to regard the Church's influence on medieval medicine as entirely destructive, it would be unfair to do so. There is little doubt that the Church provided most of the institutional care for the sick, disabled and the elderly. Those hospitals that existed were intended to provide succour for the soul rather than the body and offered spiritual comfort rather than physical care, but they provided shelter for the people who had nowhere else to go. Incidentally, lepers were excluded from some of those early hospitals, not because they were thought to have an infectious disorder but because they were thought to have sinned dreadfully for God to have punished them so severely. It was the risk of moral contagion rather than physical infection which led to their exclusion from society and to the building of special leper colonies and hospitals.

Many monasteries and abbeys had their own hospitals and infirmaries, intended either exclusively for the use of the inmates or for public use. These establishments were sometimes staffed by paid male attendants, although often the fitter convalescent patients also helped.

Local priests undoubtedly tried to play their part as well, and during plagues many churches were temporarily converted into hospitals. Some hospitals, which still exist today, were founded at that time through the auspices of the Church; for example, the Hôtel Dieu in Paris was founded by Bishop Landry in AD 561. Patients there were originally looked after by a small group of Parisian ladies who were connected with the Church, and when eventually those women were organised into a sisterhood by Pope Innocent IV, they probably became the first group of nursing nuns. Other hospitals were founded by trade and professional guilds who ran them for sick or aged members. Those who had no connections with any such organisation had to rely on finding space in a hospital founded by a generous patron.

However, it is important to remember that the emphasis in all these establishments was very much on care rather than cure and that their staff included few people with any real medical training. Even as late as the thirteenth century, when the Hôtel Dieu had been moved to a new site near Notre Dame, there were said to have been no more than six doctors in the whole of Paris. The absence of any real medical science or medical profession at this time meant that much healing was enacted on the basis of good faith, with great reverence accorded to the miraculous healing powers of the saints and of holy relics. The close relationship between medicine and religion that had been thrown on one side by Hippocrates was now back with a vengeance. Saints had replaced the Roman gods as the agents responsible for specific illnesses and organs. (For example, St. Blaise was in charge of the throat, St. Apollonia the teeth, St. Bernadine the lungs, and St. Erasmus the abdomen.) Prayers were offered to the saints considered most likely to be able to intervene, and holy relics were often worshipped like idols.

The widespread belief in the royal ability to heal by the laying on of hands also grew in popularity. Since kings were considered to be close to God, and since God was considered to be responsible for all illness, it is hardly surprising that this apparently sacrilegious belief should have proved so popular in both England and France. The King's Evil (scrofula or tuberculosis as it is now known) was the disease most commonly considered suitable for healing in this way. It was, after all, a disease which provided clearly defined physical changes, which did not weaken the patient so much that the journey to court would prove impossible and which sometimes disappeared spontaneously: three factors which made it eminently suitable for cure with the King's Touch. In England this apparently pagan practice is said to have started with Edward the Confessor. In France it was said to have been first tried by Clovis the Frank in AD 496.

With cities dirty, people almost permanently sick and no

proper medical profession, it is hardly surprising that increasing numbers of untrained people began to offer medical advice and help to those suffering and to those, such as women in childbirth, who simply needed some attention from a neighbour with experienced hands. The ordinary people sought support, advice and information from anyone with a little knowledge and experience. In each community, in each small village, there would be a woman whose knowledge and practical abilities were recognised and accepted locally. She would use such wild herbs as were available in the countryside and would help the labouring woman deliver her infant. The quality of care provided was undoubtedly poor, probably little better than that available to primitive men thousands of years before, but it was all there was.

The Christian religion, which dominated medical thinking, halted progress in Europe for the best part of a millennium.

Chapter 8: The Arabian Inheritance

Medicine is preserved as a science in Arabia – Rhazes and his influence – The Arabs learn from the Greeks but make their own contributions – The Crusaders

In AD 431 the Patriarch of Constantinople, Nestorius, decided that the Virgin Mary should be called the Mother of Christ and not the Mother of God. When this apparently inoffensive piece of pedantry resulted in his being banished for heresy, Nestorius and his followers went to Mesopotamia, where they spent many years translating the old Greek texts into Arabic. As a result, during the Dark Ages of Europe the science and the art of medicine were better preserved in Arabia than anywhere else.

The business of assimilating Greek culture into the Arabic world was continued by Chosroes, who not only kept a Greek physician at his court but also sent another physician off to India in search of more knowledge. The process of deliberately weaving bits and pieces of information together from around the world had begun, and by the middle of the sixth century a medical school had been founded in the city of Jundisapur in south-west Persia, where physicians of all nationalities and religions worked together.

As the Moslem Empire engulfed Persia in the seventh century, the existing medical societies were absorbed and the information was put to good use. Many great local physicians trained with the help of the classical texts, and the standard of medical care was undoubtedly higher in Arabia at this time than anywhere else in the known world. Rhazes were perhaps one of the most memorable individuals of the ninth century. He taught his students in wards and outpatient clinics and encouraged them to talk to and examine the patients. He believed that a fever was not a disease in itself but simply a sign that the body was working towards the destruction of some unseen disorder. He wrote accurate descriptions of smallpox, measles and scarlet fever and is perhaps best remembered for his advice when consulted about the site for a new hospital to be built in Baghdad. With remarkable astuteness Rhazes suggested that large pieces of dead animals be hung in potentially suitable spots around the city and that the hospital be built on the site where the dead animals decayed more slowly. This apparently simple but clever device suggests that he understood a good deal about the pathology of disease. However, his knowledge of medicines was perhaps not so sophisticated, and it seems that among the animal products he recommended as having medicinal properties were stag's teeth, elephant's teeth and lion grease; animal excrements were also considered to have their uses.

Not only were there proper hospitals throughout the Moslem Empire at this time but touring clinics were often sent round to country areas. There is even evidence that when large crowds gathered near mosques, first-aid stations would be set up to deal with those needing medical care. By the middle of the tenth century the Caliph of Baghdad had ordered that would-be doctors should take examinations and acquire licences. There was stiff competition in the hospitals for medical posts.

The Arabs may have acquired most of their knowledge from the Greek classics but they also contributed much that was new. It was in Arabia that the first alchemists began to look for the 'elixir of life' and found many useful chemicals as they did so. Arab scientists also expanded the science of astrology and developed the theory of the four temperaments (describing people as sanguine, choleric, phlegmatic or melancholic), which fitted well with the theory of the four humours.

By the end of the tenth century some European centres were beginning to follow the Arabian example. The Crusaders brought many medical practices and theories home from North Africa, and the medical school at Salerno, the first in Europe, was probably developed by Crusaders travelling homeward. Ironically, the old Greek texts had to be translated from Arabic into Latin before they could be used by European students.

It was perhaps fortunate for Europe that the Crusaders rescued much of this knowledge. They did so just in time: in 1256 the Mongols destroyed Baghdad and the Moslem culture, dismantling the library at Baghdad and using the stones to build a bridge over the River Tigris.

Chapter 9: The First Medical Schools

The medical school at Salerno – Roger of Sicily introduces rules about the practice of medicine – The Church leaders do not approve of priests practising medicine – Roger Bacon, a great original thinker – Bologna, Padua and Montpellier – The provision of medical care still largely in the hands of the illiterate and the unskilled

The Italian sea port of Salerno, just south of Naples, was both international and interdenominational. It was home for Christians, Jews, Greeks, Arabs, returning Crusaders and other travellers intent on moving around Europe. During

Roman rule Salerno had been a health resort, and in the centuries that followed it continued to attract men and women from all walks of life.

It was in Salerno that Western Europe began to regain some of its lost medical traditions and to revive the study of scientific medicine which had been retained almost exclusively by the Arabs for the best part of a thousand years. With the Church still the most powerful institution in Western Europe, and controlling almost all aspects of government, law, education and health care, it is perhaps not surprising that the first signs of a revival of scientific medicine should take place in a city with such a cosmopolitan population.

The revival of a truly scientific approach to medicine began in the ninth century. At first there was no formal establishment at Salerno and no formal training schedule, just a group of medical practitioners who began by passing on practical tips to any interested student. These humble beginnings were the spark which eventually led to the development of medical schools all over Europe, and those early practitioners in Salerno played a vital part in the redevelopment of medicine as a profession.

Gradually, the reputation of that informal teaching group spread and more and more students came to Salerno to learn their profession. Inevitably the students had differing opinions, which led to discussion and arguments, and what had begun as a series of simple, practical classes slowly came to deal with the problems on a much wider scale. In many ways it was not what was taught that was important so much as the fact that for the first time since Hippocrates diseases were being studied, patients observed and treatments devised in a rational attempt to deal with observed symptoms. Surgical practices were revived and, under the influence of the Jews, Arabs, Latins and Greeks, the scholars at Salerno once again severed the links which had for so many centuries tied medicine and religion so closely together. The teachers at Salerno may not have known much about anatomy or physiology but they were paving the way for a medical renaissance.

At Salerno students did not just learn the rudiments of good medicine, they also learned some of the tricks of the trade. One writer, for example, pointed out that when taking a patient's pulse the doctor should be aware that his very arrival might have produced a speeding up of the heart rate. Another Salerno author suggested that, if a patient did not pay his bill, the doctor should make some adjustment to his prescription to make the patient come out in spots. The additional, unexpected symptom was intended to result in prompt payment!

As the clergy still made up the majority of educated men in Europe, it is not surprising that many clerics and monks began to practise medicine in the Salerno style. By the eleventh century the principle of formal medical education had become widely accepted, and the School of Salerno, in particular, was widely respected throughout Europe. In 1140 Roger of Sicily ruled that anyone practising medicine had to be properly qualified, and other rulers made similar edicts. However, since Church policy was still that the endurance of suffering was saintly and that faith and prayers were far better aids to health than any pagan forms of intervention, Church leaders were not going to remain silent when it came to laying down the law. They resented the idea of the clergy's involvement in the business of health care for several reasons. They thought the practice of medicine potentially immodest and were worried about the implications for the Church should a clergyman be associated with the death of a patient. They were also worried that, with fat fees to be earned, many holy men were spending too much time on healing the body and not enough on healing the soul.

In the twelfth century several edicts were published which were intended to prevent monks and priests from practising medicine. Since the Church was still extremely powerful and since members of the Church were often the only people able to read, this ruling had a damaging effect on the development of a proper medical profession. The practice of surgery was considered particularly unsuitable for those who had taken holy orders, and the venom with which surgical practice was condemned by the

Church can be judged from the fact that it was several centuries before surgery became an acceptable art rather than a disreputable trade. The subsequent battles between physicians and surgeons can be traced back to this ecclesiastical disapproval.

Despite this official disapproval, some clerical practitioners still made major contributions not only to the quality of medical care available within each small community but also the quantity of medical knowledge more widely available. Roger Bacon, who lived from 1214 to 1298 was one of the most influential of these practitioners.

Bacon was an original thinker at a time when original thinking was rare and dangerous. Even at Salerno, Bologna, Padua, Montpellier and the other centres of academic excellence, most work was confined to the study and intellectual dissection of the ancient Greek texts. Bacon was a Franciscan monk who had been well educated both as a philosopher and as a natural scientist, and it was his work that made the Paris medical school famous.

One of the first to insist that chemicals could be used medicinally and that alchemy had a role to play in human pharmacology, Bacon found himself battling against the entire establishment. Galen had favoured herbal medicines, and the medical established revered the works of Galen. The Church strongly objected to Bacon's theories because it seemed dangerously sacrilegious for a monk to suggest that the will of God could be influenced with the aid of a handful of chemicals.

Not that Bacon confined himself to the study of drugs. He is said to have invented a telescope, a microscope and the first spectacles, and prophesied powered flight and underwater exploration. He performed a great many original scientific experiments. All this made him desperately unpopular with almost all sectors of established thought, and Bacon became the first of the scientific martyrs who were to litter the history of the Renaissance.

Outside the Church the medical profession continued to develop, and in 1224 King Roger II's grandson, the Emperor Frederick II, produced the first proper curriculum for the Salerno medical school. Students had to be aged over twenty-one and to have studied logic for three years. The course they were expected to follow was designed to last for five years, and graduates had to spend an additional year of practice under the supervision of a senior and experienced medical man. After graduation students took an oath similar to the one written by Hippocrates and agreed not to dispense or sell medicines but to limit themselves to the formal practice of medicine. It was the graduates from Salerno who first had the title of doctor. These regulations are remarkably similar to those in use at most modern medical schools today.

Sadly, Salerno did not survive as a major centre of educational excellence. Other schools were founded in the twelfth and thirteenth centuries, the earliest and most important at Bologna and Padua in Italy and at Montpellier in France. The latter, founded by Guy de Montpellier in the twelfth century, succeeded Salerno as the foremost medical school in the thirteenth century. Visited by returning Crusaders, as Salerno had been, word of the excellence of the medical attention available there gradually spread, and by the thirteenth century Montpellier was providing doctors for the households of popes and kings throughout Europe. Students from France, Spain, Italy and even Britain studied there, and John of Gaddesden, said to have been the model for Chaucer's doctor in the *Canterbury Tales*, is believed to have trained at Montpellier in the early fourteenth century.

These developments in medical education prepared the way for future progress, but it is important for us to remember that, even after the founding of academic establishments such as Montpellier, the practice of medicine was still largely in the hands of the untrained and the illiterate. The Church may have abandoned its tight hold on medicine but many Church leaders still retained the right to appoint medical practitioners, which they did with little regard for academic achievements. Many of the practitioners licensed by the Church were illiterate, and almost all surgery was performed by the technically, academically and culturally unskilled barber-surgeons. Even more important perhaps were the midwives, wise women and grocer apothecaries who provided what was effectively a general practitioner service for the community. For most people, real medicine still meant witches and midwives who had no formal medical training. The local women understood bones and herbs, while many scholarly physicians were dabbling in astrology, alchemy and an assortment of metaphysical therapies. Paracelsus, the sixteenth-century physician and alchemist, was later to claim that he learnt all he knew from sorceresses, and it seems that, although the academic world was making the break with religion, it had not yet learned to harness the knowledge gleaned over centuries by those 'general practitioners' with no formal training.

Mortality at this time is well illustrated by details of events in the first Crusade, which took place in the late eleventh century. It was estimated that half a million soldiers set out on the Crusade but that only 300,000 landed at Aleppo. After the long siege of Antioch only sixty thousand soldiers remained, and when Jerusalem was finally taken, it was an army of some twenty thousand men who half marched and half limped into the Holy City. Hunger, privation and disease had taken a far greater toll than the enemy could ever have done.

Chapter 10: The Black Death

The decline in the Church's power – The start of the Black Death – Mass flagellation – The inability of the Church to control the plague results in a loss of confidence – The economic effects of the plague – The first quarantine regulations

At the beginning of the fourteenth century there were medical schools scattered throughout Europe, and many scholars had revived interest in the teachings of the great Greek physicians. The Church's stranglehold on medical practices had been broken, and many thinking men were questioning the value of accepted medical therapies and beginning to experiment with new theories, diagnostic aids and chemicals. The revolt against the power of the Church had begun to take shape, and the artistic and scientific revolution which was to shake the world was beginning to develop.

Yet despite these theoretical rumblings the quality of care available in most areas of the world was still appalling. Public health facilities were worse than they had been during the Roman Empire; cities stank of refuse, excrement and death, water supplies were polluted and food supplies intermittent. Church and military leaders may have had access to clean hospitals and the medical skills of men who were, at least, literate, but for ordinary citizens health care meant the attentions of local woman with an armful of herbs or, if things went badly, a chance of a share of a dirty, stinking bed in a local hospice.

The absence of proper medical care and public health facilities meant that most of Europe was ripe for an epidemic, and in the fourteenth century it was to succumb to a major one. Epidemics have often changed the course of society, and the Black Death did just that.

For centuries plagues had undoubtedly played an important part in history. For example, it was a plague of some sort which led to the destruction of Greece in the Peloponnesian war. Although today the word 'plague' usually refers to a specific type of infection transmitted by fleas and rats, we have no means of determining exactly what caused those plagues that did so much damage in the past. Diagnostic skills were not well developed, and many of those reporting the spread of any particular plague were quite unskilled. Such plagues could have been bubonic plague, typhus, measles, smallpox or other infections.

The important point is that in small, isolated communities people tended gradually to acquire an immunity to most of the infective organisms which were encountered locally. Those who did not acquire immunity usually died. However, when contact is established between otherwise isolated communities, there is an exchange of infections and diseases. War, trade and other voyages of discovery have often led to the decimation of otherwise healthy nations. (Even in our century there is good evidence for this theory, one of the most dramatic being the islanders of Tristan da Cunha, who had no acquired immunity to the common childhood diseases regarded as trivial by most in the West. The islanders were decimated by simple measles because they had never met it before. This point is of recurring significance in medical history.)

It is now believed that the Black Death started at the trading station of Caffa on the Russian shore of the Black Sea. Merchants from Genoa had taken refuge there from attacking Tartars, who had brought the infection with them from the east, and the Genoese remained besieged in the Caffa for two years. According to legend, the plague entered the city of Caffa when the Tartars began to throw corpses over the walls, using huge catapults to aid them in this, the first recorded episode of biological warfare. When the Tartars gave up their siege and left, they took the plague with them to Russia, India and China, while the Italian merchants returned home, taking the plague to northern Europe.

From Genoa the Black Death spread quickly through Italy between 1345 and 1350. Florence lost between a third and a half of its inhabitants to the disease. From Italy the plague spread through France and Germany. It first arrived in England at Weymouth in Dorset in June 1348, and then quickly spread to London, where, because of the poor social conditions, it devastated the city.

The Black Death produced a state of panic in Europe. In Spain the clergy declared that the plague was caused by the opera; in England bishops claimed that it was a punishment handed down by God to a nation too enthusiastic about the theatre. Some clerics insisted that it was caused by witches, others that long-pointed shoes were responsible! One popular theory was that Jews were poisoning the wells and, as a result, in Burgundy alone fifty thousand Jews were forced to confess and then burnt to death. At Basle and Freiburg all known Jews were herded into a large wooden building which was set on fire, and at Strasbourg thousands were hanged. Many fled to Germany and Poland to reach safety.

One bizarre result of the plague was the spread of mass flagellation throughout Europe. Thinking that the plague was a divine chastisement and that by flagellation the penance might be diverted, many thousands roamed Europe whipping themselves. Even Pope Clement ordered public flagellations at Avignon in an attempt to stop the plague. Another sign of the unbalancing effect of the disease was the spread of other types of mass hysteria involving repentant sinners. The wild dance of St. Vitus, for example, spread rapidly across Europe in the wake of the plague, and the dancing mania caught up thousands.

In 1349 the war that England had been waging with France was temporarily halted while both sides got their breath. It was not resumed until 1355.

In southern France the Pope consecrated the River Rhône at Avignon so that corpses could be thrown into the river and considered buried. At sea, ships' crews were completely wiped out. In Britain the plague is believed to have reduced the total population from around four million to two million. Similar reductions in population are believed to have affected other countries, and at a rough estimate it seems likely that over twenty million people died from the plague within a period of a few years.

Whatever the cause of the plague, it soon became only too apparent that neither the medical establishment, the Church nor the local healers had any answer to it. Plenty of remedies were tried: dishes of fresh milk were left on the lips of the dying to absorb the plague poison; herds of oxen and cows were driven through the streets so that their good, clean breath might neutralise the action of the bad city air; goats were kept in bedrooms in the belief that the bad air in a house could be eradicated by a powerful smell; cold, moist, watery foods were blamed, as was excess excitement. Drunkenness was thought responsible by one set of experts, while others said that abstinence caused a greater susceptibility to the plague. Doctors wore cloth helmets and respirators stuffed with herbs in attempts to protect themselves, crosses were chalked on doors and bonfires built in the streets.

The obvious inability of the medical establishment to control the epidemic meant that faith was shattered, and, as the medical establishment and the Church were still closely linked, this also meant that the Church's powerful position in Europe was severely damaged. Loss of confidence in the Church continued and increased during the years which followed.

In Britain at the start of the fourteenth century the feudal system was strong, with the social scale consisting of king, lord, knight, landowner and peasant. The neat regime was brought down by the Black Death which increased the importance of the peasant, redistributed wealth and more or less ended the recurrent outbreaks of famine that had helped to keep peasant classes under control. The Church's influence decreased dramatically, and whereas the killing of Thomas à Becket was received with horror in 1170, the execution of the Archbishop of Canterbury in 1381 was received with cheers. During the next two centuries deviation from established Church thinking led eventually to the Reformation.

The Black Death put ordinary working men, for the first time, in a position of some power. In areas where the death rate had been high, there were gluts of food and shortages of labour. As a result, peasants could move from one area to another and demand better wages and conditions. To keep their land worked, landlords had to offer labourers attractive conditions, and the feudal system by which Europe had been ruled for hundreds of years was broken. Those who survived the plague benefited enormously. Its effects on the world were to last for centuries and to influence the whole history of Europe.

By 1374 the plague had become endemic, returning at irregular intervals to decimate populations just recovering from the previous round of death and destruction. Doctors, clergy and midwives had all proved helpless, and none of the preventive methods or curative techniques had been of any value. But in 1374 the first effective steps designed to control the spread of the plague were introduced. They were brought in not by doctors or others connected with the medical profession but by city administrators in the Venetian republic, which like all major ports was particularly vulnerable to plague attacks.

Regulations, drawn up by Visconte Bernabo stated that those who had contracted the plague should be taken from the built-up areas into fields and left there either to die or to recover; people who had nursed plague patients had to remain in isolation for ten days. The clergy were instructed to examine the sick and to report any cases of the plague to the authorities; anyone who failed to report a case of the plague was liable to be burnt at the stake. Powerful laws were introduced to prevent travellers bringing the plague into the town, and anyone who did so was liable to forfeit all his goods to the state. Ships approaching Venice had to be inspected, and any carrying the infection were refused entry.

These regulations proved so successful in Venice that other towns, cities and republics followed the lead and introduced similar laws. At Ragusa, on the eastern shores of the Adriatic, the local authorities went a little further and built a landing stage some way out of the city and ordered all immigrants and traders to land and remain there for forty days. This isolation period of forty days ('quaranta giorni' in Italian, from which our word 'quarantine' was derived) was soon copied by other port authorities in the Mediterranean area.

Chapter 11: Expanding Horizons

The first printing presses in the fifteenth century – The first international travellers – Magellan, da Gama and Columbus – The spread of information

Two developments in the second half of the fifteenth century had an enormous influence both on the quality and quantity of medical care and on the incidence and spread of disease. Both developments were concerned with communication: the first, printing, greatly influenced the availability of medical information, while the second, international sea travel, led to a devastating exchange of infections between Europe and America.

It is almost impossible to overemphasise the importance of the rapid progress made in the world of printing during the fifteenth century. Today we take it for granted that a major discovery made in one part of the world will be reported in all other parts of the world within hours. Printing processes are now so sophisticated that reports and photographs describing events in Australia can appear on the same day in newspapers in North America. On special occasions books can be on public sale within days of the event they report, and a steady torrent of information rushes around the world at such a rate that our problem today is not in obtaining information but in sifting the useful from the useless.

Before the printing presses began to make knowledge more easily available, the rate at which information could be shared depended on the speed and ease with which educated men could travel. These limitations meant that for centuries developments in Asia, Europe and America continued in isolation. Artistic and scientific advances remained regional or national resources rather than becoming available internationally.

By the fifteenth century students and scholars all around Europe were hungry for books and for the information they contained. One bookseller in Florence was said to have employed up to fifty scribes, and in monasteries throughout Europe monks were busy copying out volumes of all kinds. Printing techniques were not improved by accident; they were an inevitable result of a steadily increasing demand for knowledge and reading matter of all kinds.

It is sometimes said that printing was invented by Johann Guternberg, but this rather raw assertion suggests that before Gutenberg's time printing was unknown. In fact, material had already been printed and published for many centuries; the Chinese, for example, are thought to have invented paper about a thousand years before, using wooden blocks to enable them to print books. Gutenberg's great contribution was to make printing commercial and turn it from a country craft into a widely available industry. He did this by making up pages of type composed of individual letters instead of a single carved block. He used metal to make his individual letter punches, in much the same way as silversmiths and goldsmiths had made metal punches with which they could mark their products, and prepared moulds which enabled him to make an unlimited number of those individual letters with great ease. To print effectively, he had also to prepare a special ink that would work with metal.

These technical advances revolutionised printing and made it possible for those who followed to complete the task of turning a previously little known and little used art form into a basic means of communication for thousands of people. No longer was it necessary for a skilled craftsmen to carve every printing block by hand; Gutenberg's inventions had made it possible for printers to produce an enormous variety of printed material, easily, accurately and relatively inexpensively.

Gutenberg's inventions made a tremendous impact: within years printing presses had been set up in most European countries, and books on all subjects were readily available. As a result scholars could share their theories and discoveries without having to spend months travelling, while students could acquire in hours information that it had taken an author years to accumulate. Printed literature spread across Europe, and students of medicine found themselves able to study and question in detail the claims and assertions of all the established masters of their art. The development of those early printing presses had an enormous influence on both the quality and quantity of medical care available.

While Gutenberg and his successors were breaking down one barrier to international communications, such men as Magellan, da Gamma and Columbus were conquering physical constraint by making pioneering voyages of discovery to satisfy

53

commercial need for new trading partners. Until the fifteenth century Europe's only contact with the rest of the world had been confined to those parts of the East that could be reached by caravan. When, in the middle of the fifteenth century, the Turks sacked Constantinople and blocked the land route, ocean travel became the only alternative. Christopher Columbus sailed across the Atlantic and made his historic landing on American soil in 1492; Vasco da Gama opened a sea route to Asia in 1497, a little more than two centuries after Marco Polo had made his historic overland trip eastward in 1271; and in 1520 Ferdinand Magellan crossed the Pacific Ocean after sailing through the channel linking it with the Atlantic.

These journeys not only made the spread of information and theories international but also effectively destroyed the huge geographical barriers that had isolated different populations on their native continents. In terms of human health, such breaking down of barriers had one major disadvantage: infectious diseases which had become endemic and therefore relatively harmless on one continent could now spread to a new continent where they would meet a population composed entirely of previously unexposed and therefore vulnerable potential victims.

When Christopher Columbus landed in the New World, he could scarcely have imagined the effect that his voyage would have on the economic, physical and spiritual health of future generations. He had no way of knowing that by crossing the Atlantic Ocean he was destroying a massive barrier which had for centuries prevented the exchange of infective organisms between the eastern and western continents.

It is now known that the susceptibility of population to any particular organism or disease depends on a number of variable factors. Hereditary resistance and racial susceptibilities are obviously relevant but perhaps the most important single factor is the amount of exposure that a particular population has had to each disease-including organism. As I explained in a previous chapter continuing exposure to a disease can lead to the development of a valuable level of immunity. Modern epidemiologists have observed that diseases thought to be only mildly dangerous when caught by individuals living in a community where that disease is recognised as endemic, may be fatal when contracted by individuals from a community which has remained previously untouched by the disorder. For example, when Eskimos in the Canadian Arctic caught measles for the first time in 1952, seven in every hundred died. This is a phenomenally high mortality rate for a disease considered rather trivial by most of the populations in the so-called developed Western world. Similarly it has been shown that Indians living in North America suffer far less acutely from tuberculosis than their grandparents suffered a few decades ago. They have acquired a certain amount of resistance to the disease. Medical literature is full of other examples of islanders and isolated tribes who have suffered terribly when exposed to disorders which we think of as trivial.

Chapter 12: The Outcome of Travel

Columbus's voyage has some unexpected results – Syphilis and the trade in infectious diseases – Cortez, smallpox and the conquest of the Aztecs – Maize and potatoes change life in Europe – The international exchange of medical information begins with the introduction of quinine into Europe

By crossing the barrier that had previously separated the American continents from the European continent, Christopher Columbus and those who followed him opened the way for a huge exchange of infections. This 'trade' in bacteria and viruses was to become the most politically, socially and economically important result of the discovery of America.

The disease classically associated with Columbus's maiden voyage is syphilis. Before Columbus returned to Spain, syphilis was either unknown or, at least, mild and unimportant; after his return it became widespread and devastating. Its spread across

Europe was helped by the fact that, within a matter of months of Columbus' setting foot on the European mainland, the young French King, Charles VIII, led a campaign in Italy with an army of thirty thousand mercenaries from France, Germany, Switzerland, England, Hungary, Poland, Italy and Spain. Syphilis spread rapidly through the army and its entourage, causing so much damage that Charles had to abandon a siege of Naples and allow his soldiers to return home. Inevitably, they went back to their native countries and took their new infection with them. In the following few years other travellers took the disease to the equally unprepared populations of Africa and the Far East.

For a few decades the association between syphilis and sexual intercourse was not recognised. In Paris, for example, infected people were forbidden even to meet other citizens. The link between sex and syphilis was first recognised in Aberdeen, where the town council had strong things to say about the ways of loose women. Whether they recognised that the disease was infectious or simply considered that immorality inspired punishment from God, it is impossible to say. Whatever the view of the Aberdeen elders, however, the majority of the European aristocracy seemed to find a life of continence too high a price to pay for safety from infection. Members of the French, Spanish and English courts considered syphilis a sign of manhood and, although in an attempt to stem the spread of the disease some public bath houses were closed down (causing standards of personal hygiene to fall even lower), there seems to have been little attempt to stop the spread of the infection. One observer, Erasmus, is even quoted as commenting that any nobleman who did not get syphilis was either not very noble or not much of a gentleman.

Whatever the military and economic results of such widespread infection, the political effects were sometimes dramatic. Ivan the Terrible, the first Tsar of all the Russias is believed to have been suffering from tertiary syphilis when he rampaged through his homeland slaughtering peasants by the thousand. England's Henry VIII is commonly thought to have had syphilis, and it may be that his difficulty in siring an heir was a result of the infection. It is possible that the resultant constitutional troubles might have been avoided had Columbus and his men chosen to sail in some other direction.

The trade in infectious diseases which followed the first crossings of the Atlantic was not, of course, undirectional. The people of Europe may have suffered from the introduction of syphilis but the inhabitants of the Americas certainly suffered from the introduction of European diseases.

The travellers intent on colonising, conquering or emptying the rich lands of America took a whole range of disorders into a country which was relatively untroubled by infectious diseases and where, therefore, the population had had no opportunity to build up any resistance to infection.

Although measles and diphtheria were among the disease which crossed the Atlantic from east to west, the most important was probably smallpox, which is believed to have been taken across by Cortez. Smallpox was as important a factor in the conquest of Mexico as the fighting skill and bravery of the conquistadores, and the deadly nature of the disease spreading its way through a population with no natural immunity gave Cortez an enormous advantage. With an army of no more than six hundred men he conquered the Aztec Empire and saw his own culture and religion adopted by the natives. It is not surprising that the unhappy Indians should consider the God of the conquerors more powerful than their own when they saw the Spaniards immune to a disease which was causing death and destruction to their own race.

The effect of smallpox on the American population can best be judged from the fact that, before contact with the east was established, the total population of Mexico was probably between twenty five and thirty million. Fifty years later it was a tenth of that, and it halved again in the next fifty years. It is remarkably easy in such circumstances for a conquering army to impose a totally effective rule on a defeated nation.

Once it had been introduced from the continent, smallpox

spread from population to population. From Mexico it travelled to Guatemala, and from there it attacked the Incas, making them easy pray for the conquering Pizarro. Travelling armies from Europe soon realised that, while they themselves had considerable immunity to smallpox, the local inhabitants were extraordinarily vulnerable. Less scrupulous invaders would help spread the disease by handing infected blankets to local people.

Contact between Europe and the Americas did not just lead to changes in the socio-economic status of the American peoples; it also led to changes in European life. Two widely available products used as foodstuffs in American, maize and potatoes, were unknown in Europe and when they were imported they helped to change the dietary habits of millions. Both products enabled farmers to produce large quantities of high calorie foods from relatively small amounts of land. This inevitably had an effect on the health of the population and on the political composition of Europe. Changes in the types of food available also led to changes in the type of diseases seen. For example, it is clear that the incidence of dental decay in Europe increased rapidly following the import of plentiful sugar supplies from America.

Those fifteenth and sixteenth century expeditions also had one more important consequence: they led to the first international exchange of medical information. Quinine, extracted from the cinchona bark, was imported to Europe by explorers returning from Peru, where for years the natives had been using it to treat malaria. Quinine, quickly became established as a vital element in the pharmacological armamentarium of any self respecting physician but it also had a far more important effect on European medical practices. Until quinine was introduced, the practice of pharmacology had been an untidy mixture of folklore and witchcraft. The acknowledgement that quinine provided a specific solution to a particular problem was the key which opened the flood gates to the introduction of many other pharmacologically active compounds. Quinine was one of the first drugs to have a recognised beneficial effect and to be clearly associated with a specific set of symptoms. In the years that followed, many other drugs were suggested, tested, tried and accepted, and the practice of medicine slowly became a genuine science.

Chapter 13: The Rejection of Old Ideas

Controversial characters in the history of medicine –
Paracelsus perhaps the most colourful of them all – Vesalius
and the first textbook of human anatomy – It is recognised
that Galen might be wrong – Paré's contribution to surgery –
Treating the patient as a whole man – The rebirth of medicine

The history of medicine is richly peppered with fascinating, colourful and often controversial characters. The Renaissance was an excellent time for men who were more interested in scientific truth than in acknowledged prejudices, and the first half of the sixteenth century was a time of much controversy and original thinking.

The advances made during that period can be illustrated by describing the lives of three men, Paracelsus, Vesalius and Paré.

One of the most controversial and undoubtedly one of the most colourful characters in medical history, who may well have contributed as much as any other individual in the history of medical science, Paracelsus, was christened Aureolus Theophrastus Bombastus von Hohenheim when he was born in 1493. Better known as Paracelsus, this Swiss born citizen, who died in 1541, tore into the precepts of established medical thinking with all the zeal of an inspired missionary. He revolutionised medical thinking throughout Europe.

The most revealing of the many stories about Paracelsus reports him as having claimed to have learned more from his contact with witches and midwives than from a study of the ancient and previously well respected texts of such classical authors as Galen. Paracelsus believed that it was possible to learn only by experience and personal study, and he travelled widely in the search for useful medical information. He went to Spain, Portugal, France, Italy, Germany, Scandinavia, Egypt, Arabia, Palestine, Russia, Poland, Turkey, Holland and England to study, work drink and make friends. He wrote books, lectured, practised medicine and argued in Montpellier, Padua, Bologna, Basle, Vienna, Tubingen, Wittenberg, Leipzig, Heidelberg and Cologne – almost all the major medical centres of Europe. No idea or theory was too bizarre for his attention and no concept or belief too sacred to be rejected. He studied alchemy, astrology and herbal medicine in his search for information.

Unlike the established medical authors of the time, Paracelsus believed that a doctor's job was to understand the causes and symptoms of different diseases and to prescribe specific solutions where appropriate. He also believed in the importance of preventing disease and was one of the first members of the medical profession to recognise that there is often an association between a man's employment and his physical condition.

Paracelsus's writings make formidable reading, but it was not only his specific discoveries which made him such an important figure in Renaissance medicine: he was the first man to associate mining with certain chest diseases, to link cretinism and goitres with certain alpine areas, to use mercury in the treatment of syphilis, to advocate allowing wounds to drain instead of smothering them with layers of dried dung, and to argue that some foods contained poisons which had a deleterious effect on the human body. But all these important advances seem almost irrelevant when put alongside his philosophical contributions and his effect on the attitude of the men studying medicine in the sixteenth century.

Paracelsus was really the first 'people's doctor', and he proudly claimed that he pleased only the sick and not the profession. He bombarded medical students and scholars with a seemingly endless selection of almost blasphemous assertions, which encouraged them to think for themselves and to reject the previously unquestioned preachings of such authorities as Galen. He seems at times to have enjoyed humiliating the establishment, as for example when he welcomed barber-surgeons as well as official medical students to his lectures at Basle, but there is little doubt that this extraordinary man was the father of modern medicine and the sixteenth century equivalent of Hippocrates.

Andreas Vesalius, the second of this trio of Renaissance pioneers, was born in 1514 at about the time that Paracelsus embarked on his travels. Vesalius achieved contemporary notoriety and eternal fame as the author of the first textbook of human anatomy, *De Humanis Corporis Fabrica*. The end of the fifteenth century and the beginning of the sixteenth century in Europe had seen a tremendous upsurge in interest in human anatomy, and with increasing numbers of students and scholars able to study copies of the ancient texts produced by such men as Galen it was inevitable that the infallibility of these ideas was questioned. Once it was recognised that Galen could be wrong, many students began to offer original observations and theories. The inaccuracy of Galen's anatomical notes was made more obvious by the fact that, for the first time in centuries, human anatomy could be studied by practical dissection, now that the influence of the Church had declined. As a result artists and students of medicine were all anxious to dissect, study and draw human cadavers. Leonardo da Vinci was one of the many multi-talented Renaissance men whose interests included anatomy. Contemporaries such as Michelangelo, Raphael and Dürer all performed their own dissections and made drawings as they struggled to improve their knowledge of human anatomy.

Da Vinci had planned to publish a textbook of anatomical drawings, but Vesalius was the first to do so. His frank rejection of many of Galen's anatomical claims earned him considerable disapproval, since leaders of the medical establishment still firmly believed that Galen could not be wrong, even if the evidence proved otherwise. For more than a thousand years Galen had been considered beyond criticism, and his reputation was not to be easily overthrown.

Poor Vesalius was unable to cope with the outcry his researches in anatomy produced. He burnt his remaining manuscripts, abandoned the study of anatomy and took a job as court physician to Charles V in Madrid. But those who attacked him could not change the fact that Vesalius's book had revealed the fallibility of the ancient texts, and the study of anatomy continued in art centres and medical schools all over Europe.

The increasing amount of information about the anatomy of the human body led, quite naturally, to a tremendous improvement in the quality of surgical care. At the beginning of the sixteenth century, surgery was almost completely in the hands of uneducated wanderers who could be just as happy gelding a man's pig or cutting his hair as amputating his leg. The barber-surgeons were indeed barbers, who supplemented their income from work with the scissors by working with the knife.

However, once it became clear that anatomical understanding could make the preparation and execution of surgical operations more of a scientific endeavour than an exercise in butchery, more educated men began to take up the profession. In the early part of the sixteenth century in France and England, physicians at last acknowledged surgeons as professional colleagues.

Ambrose Paré was one of the best known and most successful of those early surgeons. He made several significant, practical contributions to surgical science, discarding the ancient but well established view that wounds should be treated with boiling oil and introducing such refinements as ligatures, artificial limbs and artery forceps.

Wise, ingenious and humane, Paré came from a medical family. His father, uncle and brother were all barber-surgeons. Because he had received little formal education Paré could not obtain a place at the Paris University to study the medical classics. Instead he worked and studied surgery at the Hôtel Dieu, the hospital which had served Paris for several centuries. Saved in this way from indoctrination, Paré acquired a sound basic surgical education which enabled him to obtain a post as an army surgeon. Fortunately for him, France was always at war for the next two decades and he was able to get plenty of practical experience. It was while working with the army that Paré made his greatest contributions to the available reservoir of information and achieved a reputation such that, when he retired from army work and set up in private practice, he became a royal surgeon.

Paré was one of the first surgeons to approach his work with sufficient skill and professional diligence to help demolish the dreadful reputation endured by previous members of his profession. He recognised that surgery could not be divorced from nursing care, nor from medical care in general, and by his own practical example Paré helped to establish the practice of surgery as a respectable medical speciality.

Chapter 14: New Ideas but Old Practices

In practical terms the medical revolution has had little effect – Astrology and medical practice – The importance of Nostradamus and Copernicus – The local midwife is the general practitioner for most families – The standard of obstetric care – The infant mortality rate

The theoretical advances and practical improvements introduced by such men as Paracelsus and Paré played an important part in the subsequent development of medical practice, but it was many years before the ordinary citizen noticed any real improvement in the quality of medical care available to him.

Despite the advances in printing techniques and the increasing numbers of Europeans travelling, talking and studying in foreign towns and countries, the old medical practices were slow to disappear. The dramatic new ideas introduced by men like Paracelsus were largely rejected by members of the medical establishment and totally ignored by the midwives and witches who between them provided advice and care for the great majority of the European population.

Surgery was practised by men who often doubled as barbers, pedlars, tinkers, conjurers and rat-catchers, and apart from the small number of practitioners of the quality of Ambrose Paré, most surgeons, whether they catered for the working people or for royalty, were both uneducated and incompetent.

Although a few physicians in practice had studied medicine at one of the great universities, in such centres as Montpellier, Padua and Paris, and would therefore have acquired a certain amount of traditional theoretical knowledge, most professional medical workers had practical skills which were based more on superstition and folklore than on a background of scientific information.

The orthodox physician relied heavily on such skills as astrology, palmistry and the study of urine as diagnostic aids, although the accuracy of such techniques was probably no more reliable then than it is today. Astrology, in particular, was widely used by leading members of the medical profession. Brought to Europe from Arabia, astrology had by the sixteenth century become a subject which fascinated all men who claimed to have any interest in learning. Medical men believed that different signs of the Zodiac ruled over different parts of the body and that, consequently, a study of the state of the planets at one particular time would help them to reach a conclusion about the health of a particular patient. Sagittarius, for example, was thought to have power over the human thighs. The study of astrology closely accompanied the study of medicine in the sixteenth century, and since a knowledge of astrology depended upon an understanding of astronomy, the three specialities were closely linked.

Nicholas Copernicus, the astronomer who demonstrated that planets rotate around their own axes and also around the sun, studied medicine at Padua in 1501 and spent the latter part of his life studying astronomy and practising medicine. Copernicus founded his diagnostic skills on the science of astrology and based his prescribing habits on the teachings of Galen. One of his prescriptions contained powdered gold, silver, emerald, sapphire, coral and a score of other substances.

Astrology reached its zenith in the middle of the sixteenth century when Michael de Notredame, better known as Nostradamus, was alive and prophesying. Nostradamus was the best known and most widely read seer of the Renaissance years and he, like Copernicus, also practised medicine. Nostradamus began making prophecies in 1547 and quickly proved himself so successful that he was appointed to cast horoscopes at the court of Henry II of France. He was also appointed as physician to Charles IX when he became King in 1560.

Even the preparing of prescriptions was considered by some doctors to need the astrology chart, and as late as 1660 John Locke, the philosopher and doctor, argued that medicinal herbs should be picked only at astrologically propitious times.

The power of the astrologer remained an important force throughout the sixteenth century, partly because the astrologers carefully protected themselves by arguing that if a prediction (and therefore a diagnosis) was wrong it was the fault of the patient, either for demanding too hasty an analysis or for feeding the astrologer with inaccurate information. It is difficult not to compare the fashion for consulting astrologers in the sixteenth century with the fashion for consulting psychoanalysts in the twentieth.

However, all this was of practical interest to relatively few people. Astrology and astronomy could be studied only by physicians who could afford the time and equipment. Most of the physicians who had studied at one of the great universities had to be content with bleeding or purging their patients or administering concoctions prepared with more imagination than scientific skill. Paracelsus might have been burning Galen's books, but the majority of physicians still followed the Roman's advice and prepared medicines containing a plethora of ingredients.

Indeed the total number of practising physicians in the sixteenth century was so small that the greater part of the population never saw a qualified or educated doctor. This fact is often forgotten by medical historians who describe in great detail the exploits of such men as Paracelsus and Paré and leave the reader with the impression that the ordinary citizen could expect a home visit or a surgery consultation with one or the other.

In reality most citizens relied on local women to provide them with medical help, as they had and would do for many centuries; the midwife was effectively the local general practitioner, treating all illnesses, major and minor, with her own selection of herbal remedies. Ironically, the quality of care which she provided may well have been better than that provided by the officially recognised physicians. Paracelsus recognised this fact and made a point of seeking out the local midwives on his travels to ask for details of their remedies, recommendations and recipes. Unfortunately, many well tried and effective herbal remedies were ignored for centuries, simply because the formally educated practitioners would not deign to interest themselves in the type of care provided by midwives for the ordinary people.

Midwives crossed social barriers only when it came to obstetrics, a speciality which was practised at all levels with an appalling lack of success. Difficult labours almost always led to the death of both mother and child, and even entirely normal labours were so dangerous that a pregnant woman probably had only a fifty per cent chance of surviving the experience. Babies and pregnant women are, of course, most vulnerable to unhygienic conditions, and it was the midwives' failure to understand the importance of cleanliness that contributed most to the appalling death toll of mothers and their infants.

The high infant mortality rate, which lasted for many more years, helped to keep the population of Europe relatively stable for a considerable time, and it still distorts the mortality statistics for that era. It is commonly believed that life expectancy at that time was no more than a few decades, but if we look at the ages at which memorable figures of the sixteenth century are reported to have died, we can easily see that this was by no means always the case. Paracelsus, who was killed in a brawl, was forty eight when he died, Vesalius reached fifty, da Vinci was sixty seven, Michelangelo eighty nine, Nostradamus sixty three, Copernicus seventy and Paré eighty.

For everyone, rich and poor, royal and common, the quality of general medical care in the sixteenth century was scarcely different from that in the Middle Ages. Philosophers and scientists had made the first steps towards improving the quality of life and the quality of available medicine, but their efforts were, as yet, unnoticed.

Chapter 15: The Decline of the Church

The power of the Church continues to decline – Henry VIII and Thomas Linacre – The seeds of a medical profession are sown – Hospitals are so dirty that it is safer to stay at home

For centuries the Church had maintained a stranglehold on medical care. The clergy often provided general medical services, the ecclesiastical authorities made medical appointments, and many hospitals were owned and run by monks, nuns and priests.

Then, in the space of a relatively short period, the power of the Church in Europe declined rapidly. This breakdown of ecclesiastical prestige to a large extent removed the care of the sick from the control of the Church.

It was in England that some of the most dramatic events occurred. Thomas Linacre, one of the physicians appointed to care for Henry VIII, managed to persuade the King to provide a charter for a body of physicians who would be entitled to examine and license would-be medical practitioners. Not to be outdone by a mere physician, one of Henry's surgeons, Thomas Vicary, obtained the King's assent a few years later to form a united company of barber-surgeons. The ambitious and rather unsuccessful aim of this new union was to keep surgery for the surgeons and to keep barbers in their place.

Henry VIII's attempts to regulate medical services in England may have looked good in theory but in practice they were something of a disaster. Neither of the newly formed colleges (both of which later became known as royal colleges and which are today official examining bodies for physicians and surgeons) could produce enough qualified practitioners to provide medical care for the whole population. By the end of the sixteenth century the College of Physicians had thirty-one 'fellows'. Unhappily, the legislation which had been passed made it illegal for anyone not qualified to offer advice or help.

The next, almost inevitable, step was the 1542 Quacks' Charter which allowed unqualified practitioners, usually known as apothecaries, to sell herbs to patients on the understanding that they would not charge fees for advice or information about their use. The brighter, literate and more ambitious apothecaries undoubtedly read some of the medical books that appeared on the market in the middle of the sixteenth century. These books, most of which dealt with the use of herbal remedies, were also popular among ordinary people who simply wanted to know a little about home medical care.

Change was not confined to the medical profession. In 1536 the City of London authorities pointed out to the King that hospitals which once provided beds for the poor and the sick now often housed priests and monks who wanted somewhere comfortable to live in the capital. Subsequently, many Church-run hospitals were dissolved, further reducing the power and wealth of the ecclesiastical authorities.

Not that the disappearance of hospitals was likely to have made much difference to the quality of care available for the sick. The lack of any effective, reliable ways to make diagnoses or to treat patients meant that for centuries hospitals had offered nothing more than a place where cripples, beggars, the sick and the weak could rest and die in some peace. Even one of the best European hospitals, the Hôtel Dieu in Paris, which had survived wars, plagues and political struggles, was dirty and overcrowded. The Augustinian sisters who tried to look after patients bundled together on piles of dirty straw had to contend with insufficient food and too many patients. They almost certainly found it impossible to keep the patients or the wards clean, although they are reported to have tried valiantly to keep their linen and bandages clean by washing them in the Seine. It is quite likely that an otherwise healthy individual with a single disease was better off being ill at home than in a hospital where infections could spread almost unimpeded.

Chapter 16: Scientific Advances

Progress in medicine influenced from without – The first medical equipment – Galileo, Sanctorius and Kircher – Microscopy adds a new dimension – Harvey and the circulation of the blood – The irrelevance of these theoretical advances to practical care

Progress in medicine has always been influenced by many factors outside the formal medical establishment. Many of the most important medical discovers and innovations introduced and accepted within the last two centuries were proposed not by physicians or surgeons but by politicians, engineers, physicists and chemists.

This apparent anomaly was as true in the sixteenth century as it is today. In some respects it was undoubtedly easier then for scientists who were not practising doctors to introduce theories designed to influence medical knowledge or practice. After all, there were no strict boundaries between different disciplines in those days, and it was common for one man to maintain an interest in a great many subjects. The lack of scientific journals and the paucity of solid factual material with which to fill textbooks made it comparatively easy for a man to become an expert in several apparently unconnected fields. It is probably also true to say that the general shortage of factual information produced a favourable climate for creative thinkers. An absence of acquired prejudices often makes it easier for someone with a superficial knowledge of a subject to see fundamental truths more speedily than would be the case for a devoted student who has listened to the ideas of all other existing experts.

Many people made notable contributions to medical science in the sixteenth century without apparently having anything more than a passing, natural interest in human health. For example, there were the scientists who helped to provide doctors with a system of measurements with which they could accurately assess and compare various anatomical and physiological qualities. Today we take it for granted that doctors routinely carry out a wide range of tests when performing a physical examination: many of those tests are designed to enable the physician to compare the patient's physiological performance with an accepted standard. So, for example, the humblest physician will usually be able to weigh his patient and to calculate his pulse rate. Taking note to these measurements enables the physician to assess the patient's condition in comparison with other patients and to compare his condition at that particular time with his condition at other times. Most of the diagnostic and therapeutic skills available to the modern doctor depend heavily upon the availability of simple measuring devices.

Galileo was one of the sixteenth century Italians who played a vital part in the design and building of the basic pieces of equipment with which these assessments are made. While attending a cathedral service he is said to have watched a lamp swinging on a long chain from the roof and to have used it to measure the beat of his pulse. One of his contemporaries, Sanctorius, designed and built the first weighing machine and the first clinical thermometer.

The microscope was, perhaps, the one instrument which made the most impact on the way in which medical science progressed during the seventeenth century. No single scientist can be given the exclusive credit for having invented the microscope, and it seems likely that early attempts to magnify with the aid of ground glass took place in different parts of Europe more or less simultaneously. Several investigators quickly realised its value as a scientific instrument. Athanasius Kircher, a Jesuit priest, was probably the first man to use the microscope to investigate the causes of disease; Robert Hooke, who worked in London, was the first to describe individual cells; Jan Swammerdam of Amsterdam used the microscope to help him dissect small organisms, while another Dutchman, Antonj van Leeuwenhoek, was the first person to describe red blood cells, spermatozoa and bacteria.

The equipment designed by these early scientists provided the basis for a new type of medical philosophy which was expounded by men like René Descartes, the seventeenth century philosopher, who regarded the human body as nothing more nor less than a complex piece of machinery. This crude (and inaccurate) approach may well have appalled the clerics but it undoubtedly took medical science forward in rapid strides. Once scientists had begun to regard the human body as a mechanical device, they could start to prepare accurate physiology texts. For example, three seventeenth century Italians, Giovanni Alfonso Borelli, Marcello Malpighi and Giorgio Baglivi studied, experimented on and wrote about muscles, lungs, stomach and kidneys. These discoveries about human tissues and physiology had little effect on practical medical care, but they provided the background information upon which future clinicians could work to develop diagnostic skills and therapeutic aids.

Both Galileo and Sanctorius worked at Padua, as did William Harvey, the English physician regarded by many historians as the most eminent and influential figure of that time. Like Malpighi and the others who based their approach on the understanding that the human body operates like a machine, Harvey first made a study of the existing theories and hypotheses and then examined them one by one by experimentation, using mechanical aids and mechanical arguments to help them.

71

Theories about the circulation of the blood had been proposed, argued and refuted by scientists and physicians of almost every era. Speculation had for many years been based on Galen's belief that the blood circulating in the arteries was different from the blood circulating in the veins, that both kinds of blood ebbed and flowed rather than circulated around the body and that blood permeated within the heart from the right side to the left. Galen's claims misled medical scientists for many generations. For some years before Harvey published his monograph *De Motu Cordis* in 1628, scientists had made educated guesses about the functions and actions of human blood. Theories were advanced in Italy by Columbo and Cesalpino, and in Spain by Michael Servetus, who was burnt alive in 1553 by the Protestant leader John Calvin for publishing a book which included the suggestion that a separate pulmonary circulation existed within the lungs, but Harvey was the first person to produce experimental proof for his theory. He realised that, since the heart was pumping blood along with every beat, it must be moving the blood somewhere. It seems obvious to us now that the blood had to be moving around the body in a closed circulatory system, but that single, simple conclusion earned William Harvey immortality.

Harvey's original thinking and his ability to prove his ideas led to many changes in medical research and practical care. His theory that blood is pumped around the body in a continuous cycle led directly to the discovery of many other basic physiological facts. It also slowly led to the realisation that blood loss during operations could be fatal and that blood-letting, by leeching or cupping, was not always an entirely logical procedure. It also refuted the theory that weakness and blood loss could be remedied by drinking human blood – a belief which had survived until the fifteenth century, when Pope Innocent VIII had been given fresh blood from three healthy young boys to drink.

All these men made enormously important contributions to medical science and provided small but essential pieces of information, which helped later researchers to acquire an overall understanding of human physiology, and equipment with which to test their theories. The watch and clock, the thermometer, the weighing machine and the microscope all enabled the inquisitive scientist to access and study the workings of the human body with some precision. In the centuries which followed research workers would be able to build on their theories and use the facts obtained to help improve both the quality and quantity of medical care available to the ordinary citizen.

Chapter 17: The Dawn of a New Era

Practical medical care in the hands of midwives, the apothecaries, the surgeons and the physicians – The roles and values of each group – Louis XIII and Molière – Thomas Sydenham revives the Hippocratic style.

While scientists such as Galileo, Malpighi and Harvey were performing experiments and providing theories to benefit future generations, medical care for sixteenth and seventeenth century Europeans was in the hands of four groups of often unskilled and ineffective 'professionals'.

For the great majority, medical care still meant a consultation with the local midwife, an often illiterate woman whose limited skills depended largely upon her knowledge of well tried herbal remedies. Many midwives had served apprenticeships with their mothers, from whom they had acquired their knowledge and practical skills, but occasionally, in an area where there was no recognised midwife, a woman thought to have the necessary practical experience would be appointed or elected to the post.

In spite of their lack of formal training, many midwives were popular, effective and well paid. In the seventeenth century 10 shillings would have been a good fee for a consultation with a physician, but it was not unknown for midwives to be paid more than this. In 1613 Margaret Mercer was reputedly paid 80 guineas for a single confinement in Germany, while in

1605 Alice Dennis received slightly more for attending the Queen. Two midwives who attended the court of James II were each paid 500 guineas. These enormous sums of money suggest that the ordinary midwife was by no means always regarded as an inferior member of the health care team.

The standards of care and hygiene practised by midwives are often considered to have been abysmally low but, although characters such as Charles Dickens's fictional Mrs Gamp (*Martin Chuzzlewit*) undoubtedly existed, in reality their conduct was governed by a number of regulations. The first were probably drawn up in Germany in 1452 but subsequently municipal and ecclesiastical authorities throughout Europe did what they could to ensure that midwives were honourable, honest and professional in their approach. From the sixteenth century midwives took oaths to be ready and faithful to their patients, and in England in 1646 midwives submitted a written complaint to Parliament stating that they were unable to maintain the necessary standards because of a lack of official recognition.

While the more literate and intelligent midwives were struggling for professional status and recognition, those members of the profession with the least knowledge and the most limited skills were often tempted to dabble in witchcraft. This was a risky but potentially very profitable exercise in the superstitious years of the fifteenth, sixteenth and seventeenth centuries. If a woman was accused of witchcraft and found guilty, she was likely to die; if she could manage to obtain a reputation for being a witch without attracting the attention of the authorities, she could enhance her prestige, reputation and income considerably. The damage done to the role of women in medicine by such activities was, however, enormous. Those midwives who did practise witchcraft effectively destroyed the cause of their colleagues by providing the authorities with much needed evidence to justify a war against women health professionals.

Witch-hunting was first organised in the fourteenth century by those members of the medieval church who controlled medical education and practice. It was, perhaps, the first illustration of the lengths to which the professional establishment will go in order to protect its own interests. In the fifteenth and sixteenth centuries thousands were executed all over Europe; women were burned alive at the stake in Germany, France, Italy and England. The official argument was a simple one: a woman was not allowed to study medicine, and if she claimed to be able to cure the sick in any way, clearly she had to be a witch, working with the aid of the devil. Those midwives who practised witchcraft gave such men as Matthew Hopkins, the English Witchfinder General, sufficient reason to continue their cruel campaign into the seventeenth century, although by this time the importance of midwives was beginning to be officially recognised.

The second important category of medical professionals was the apothecaries, who were legally allowed to sell prescriptions for herbal remedies but were not permitted to charge for advice. In practice, of course, the ambitious apothecary would charge a high price for the substances he sold and hide the price of his personal, professional services in the price of the drug.

In England in 1617, King James I granted a charter which gave apothecaries the exclusive privilege of selling and preparing medicines. A seven year apprenticeship was ordered and would-be members of the new profession had to find a position with an existing apothecary. Through their practical training they acquired a sound understanding not only of the drugs available but of the indications and hazards of drug therapies. By allowing the apothecaries an exclusive right to prepare and sell medicines, the established physicians had unwittingly lost the chance to retain exclusive control of the direction of the medical profession. The seventeenth century apothecaries were the predecessors of today's general practitioners, but in practice there were too few apothecaries to provide a service for more than a small percentage of the population. At the beginning of the century there were only just over a hundred apothecaries in England. The midwives, numerically far superior, still played a more important part in medical care as far as most people were concerned.

The third group of health care professionals were the surgeons. They were still considered far inferior to physicians and often operated under the strict instructions of the more formally educated members of the medical profession. A would-be surgeon had to serve an apprenticeship but, despite the advances which had been made in anatomy, physiology and all the experimental sciences, the ordinary surgeon was still relatively ignorant.

The sixteenth and seventeenth century physicians considered themselves superior to all other medical practitioners. In practical terms, however, the early members of the Royal College of Physicians, probably provided care inferior to that given by an efficient and caring local midwife. Because few physicians were officially trained, they were usually found only in large cities.

The French playwright and satirist Molière described the leading members of the medical profession as arrogant buffoons, and the evidence seems to support him. Doctors in seventeenth century France were still prescribing remedies which were more likely to do harm than good. Louis XIII, for example, was regularly purged with suppositories from the age of ten days, and in a single year it is said that he had 212 enemas, 215 purges and, just for good measure, forty seven bleedings. The young Marquis de Fors, who, in 1640, at the age of twenty, was wounded in combat at Arras, was bled twelve times by Cardinal Richelieu's personal physician. This was twelve years after Harvey had published his account of the circulation of the blood.

Medical care in other parts of Europe was little better, and old fashioned theories were slow to disappear. When Charles II of England had a fit in 1685 while being shaved, he was attended by fourteen leading physicians who treated him by taking blood and providing an emetic and a purgative. They also shaved his head and applied blistering agents to his scalp, put special plasters containing pigeon droppings onto the soles of his feet and gave him a medicine made from a human skull.

The one seventeenth century physician who is widely remembered for his good sense and the high quality of his care was Thomas Sydenham (1624-89). Sydenham was no researcher and he made no great contributions to medical science but he was a conscientious man who helped to raise the standard of general medical care available from the official establishment in Britain. Sydenham based his medical philosophy on that of Hippocrates, watching his patients carefully in order to take note of all those signs and symptoms which might provide a clue to the diagnosis. Preferring simple remedies to complex mixtures and sometimes bravely admitting that there was no suitable remedy worthy trying. Sydenham helped to take the medical profession into a new era. He prescribed iron for anaemia, quinine for malaria, and used opium to help treat pain.

His classical commonsense approach helped to prepare the medical profession for the flood of new information, ideas and treatments which would be produced by the medical scientists who had benefited from the breakthroughs inspired by such men as Galileo and Harvey. Thomas Sydenham established a new tradition of clinical observation and professional scepticism which was, in its own way, as revolutionary as the 'discoveries' of the experimentalists.

Chapter 18: The Nature of Infection

The nature of infectious disorders – The plague in Europe – Other infectious disorders cause havoc

During the Renaissance many attempts were made to explain the precise nature of infectious diseases. The most astonishing attempt was the work of Hieronymous Fracastorius, a Veronese nobleman who, in 1541, published a book entitled *De Contagione*. Fracastorius, whose foresight stands out even among the extraordinary intellectual explosions of the sixteenth century, suggested that contagious diseases were disseminated by small particles of matter which were able to multiply rapidly and which could be spread through the air, by simple, direct contact or from one individual to another through infected clothing. This valuable book was virtually ignored at the time because there was no real evidence to support the theory. It was almost another 150 years before the remarkable microscopist Antonj van Leeuwenhoek, who worked as a draper and city hall janitor in Delft and who had ground more than four hundred lenses and built more than two hundred microscopes in his spare hours, described bacteria for the first time.

Meanwhile, epidemics continued to affect Europe, and the mortality rate from infectious diseases was still as great in the seventeenth century as it had been in the less enlightened Middle Ages. The plague hit Italy in 1630 and killed 80,000 in Milan alone. In the Venetian Republic over half a million are said to have died. In Moscow in 1603 more than 120,000 succumbed, in 1679 Vienna lost 70,000, and in Prague in 1681 83,000 died.

Throughout the century the plague came and went, affecting France, Italy, Denmark, Germany, Sweden, Switzerland, Spain, the Netherlands and England. Individual attacks of plague were often followed by economic disaster and famine. London was affected in 1624 when 41,000 were killed, in 1635 when another 10,000 died and finally in 1664 when the total number of dead was nearly 70,000. Europe is still littered with statues and local customs originally created by citizens anxious to give thanks for having avoided the plague. In the English county of Derbyshire, for example, where the villagers of Eyam contracted plague through a parcel of clothes sent from London, many modern villagers still dress and deck their wells with flowers each year. The wells enabled the individual villages to remain tightly knit, closed communities and therefore helped to prevent the spread of the plague.

Attempts to prevent the plague spreading and to deal with those suffering from the disease varied from town to town and from country to country. Since no one knew exactly what caused the plague or helped it to spread, attempts to control it were not always devoid of hysteria and superstition. Terrified by this horrible disease angry mobs would kill any individual thought to have helped spread it.

Colbert, Minister to Louix XIV, issued regulations for the whole of France in 1683 which gave a considerable amount of power to the Board of Health and quarantine station in Marseilles. Houses where individuals had contracted the plague were burned to the ground. In Milan a writer who wiped his ink-stained fingers on the walls of houses he passed was stripped, shaved, purged and then tortured. His right hand was cut off, he was stretched on the wheel, his bones were broken and his body was burned. Finally his ashes were thrown into the river and his belongings were all burnt. A servant girl in Germany who infected herself and her master with the plague by bringing infected property into their home in Königsberg died, but angry, frightened townsfolk ensured that she was exhumed, hanged and then burned at the foot of the gallows.

However, several local authorities introduced useful regulations. In the English village of Faversham the local council appointed three wardens to examine people trying to enter the town and to exclude those who had come from well known plague areas. A woman was paid to search for dead bodies, which were then buried in lime filled pits. Infected clothing was burnt in huge fires which were never allowed to go out. In 1667 Sir William Petty introduced a plan to reduce plagues in London which was based on the far sighted economic argument for a medical service provided by the State. Petty suggested that the value to society of a healthy individual far exceeded the cost of providing a basic health service to the State and of organising a form of preventive medicine.

In the end, however, the plague died away not as a result of any human intervention but for reasons of its own. Epidemiologists are still puzzled by the way the disease seemed to disappear from Europe, making one last attack on Marseilles in 1720, when fifty thousand people were killed, and then disappearing until the end of the nineteenth century. Some historians argue that the plague was transmitted by fleas which lived on the black rat and that it disappeared when the black rat was driven out of Europe by the brown rat, which has a different flea and does not live so close to human beings. Others claim that the black rat was still common in London after the end of the plague. They suggest that the plague was spread directly from man to man and that its demise was due to an acquired immunity which helped to protect the population.

We shall probably never know why the plague finally died away. But whatever the reason it is unlikely to have had anything to do with medicine or the medical profession. (Nor, incidentally, is there much real support for the popular theory that the Great Fire of London cleansed that city.)

The disappearance of the plague was accompanied by other changes in the incidence of disorders that had previously been endemic in Europe. Leprosy (or the disease known as leprosy), which had at one time affected thousands throughout Europe, had more or less disappeared by the end of the sixteenth century, and syphilis, which had at first decimated the population in some parts of Europe, slowly began to fade in significance.

Other infectious disorders remained rife. Influenza was common on both sides of the Atlantic, smallpox was seen everywhere, while dysentery and typhoid killed millions. The death rate among mothers and infants remained high and half the newborn babies in seventeenth century England failed to survive.

Chapter 19: Conflict in the Profession

Jealousy between the apothecaries and the physicians – A struggle between the midwives and the surgeons – Obstetrics attracts interest – Forceps are introduced – The rise of the male midwife and the decline of the female

The conflict and professional jealousy between the apothecaries and the physicians in London continued to develop throughout the seventeenth century. The physicians were themselves very much to blame for the fact that the apothecaries had acquired so much power in such a comparatively short time. Membership of the Royal College of Physicians was limited to so few that any association prepared to license and regulate a body of professionals able to offer medical care and advice was bound to flourish. By the end of the seventeenth century still only a handful of qualified physicians were available for public consultation, whereas there were a thousand licensed apothecaries.

Undoubtedly worried by the fact that the apothecaries seemed to be encroaching upon their professional territory, the physicians made several attempts to regain professional superiority. In 1687 they offered to start treating the poor free of charge and in 1696 founded dispensaries to give free medicine in addition to advice. But still the apothecaries grew in power and popularity.

The conflict came to a head in 1703 when the physicians accused an apothecary called Rose of prescribing medicines without first referring to a physician – a breach of the Act of 1542 which allowed apothecaries only to dispense.

Although the physicians won their case against Rose, the House of Lords reversed the decision after an appeal and ruled that apothecaries could see, examine and prescribe for patients without consulting physicians. The House still maintained, however, that apothecaries could not charge for an examination, but only for the medicine that was dispensed. It is hardly surprising that subsequently most of the consultations between patient and apothecary ended in the handing over of a medicine. It may well be that the modern doctor's tendency to hand every patient a prescription dates back to that absurd ruling.

The Rose case was a major breakthrough for the apothecaries and a relative disaster for the physicians.

The seventeenth century also saw a struggle for power between the midwives and the surgeons.

Traditionally, obstetrics had been a speciality followed only by women. Midwives had had to compete with male dominance in all other areas of medicine but had ruled over the care of pregnant women and their newborn children without any real interference. All women, from the poorest peasant to members of the Royal families of Europe, relied on midwives when they were expecting babies. Since, in the absence of any form of effective contraception some women spent their adult lives pregnant, midwives had plenty of work.

In the seventeenth century, however, several men began to show an interest in the subject. In 1668 a Frenchman, François Mauriceau, wrote a textbook on the diseases of pregnant women, which included details of how to manage a normal labour, how to turn an unborn child within the womb and how to manage such problems as tubal pregnancy. A Dutchman, Henrik van Deventer, wrote a book in which he described the female pelvis and discussed how abnormalities of the pelvic bones can affect the course of pregnancy. Another Dutchman, Hendrik van Roonhuyze, was an expert at delivering babies by Caesarian section. Perhaps the most extraordinary male midwives were the members of the Chamberlen family. Peter Chamberlen, who attended Queen Henrietta Maria during a miscarriage in 1628, invented the first obstetric forceps. The invention, which revolutionised the way in which midwives and surgeons could help the pregnant woman with a difficult delivery, was kept a family secret for two centuries.

Traditionalists of all sorts joined with the established midwives to oppose the men who were beginning to take such an active part in the speciality and who argued that their technical superiority enabled them to provide women with a safer service. The midwives argued that most of the women who were delivered with the aid of instruments could be delivered more safely by hand. Laurence Stern joined in the argument in his book *Tristram Shandy*, in which he seemed to have little faith in the male midwife.

The midwives were not well organised to fight this new aggressive breed of obstetricians and surgeons. Moreover, they were reluctant even to try to use instruments. Slowly their authority diminished. The male midwives began to take over the responsibility for the care of the pregnant woman and left the traditional midwife to cope with the simple nursing.

Chapter 20: A Revolution in Medical Education

The scientific revolution begun by Paracelsus continues –
The University of Leyden – Modern medical education is
founded

By the end of the seventeenth century, the revolution started by Paracelsus and other early Renaissance scientists had inspired progress all over Europe. Many societies had been formed by academics who wanted to share their ideas with others, notably the Royal Society in London and the Academy of Science in Paris, both founded in the 1660s.

These scientific bodies took advantage of improved printing techniques to publish their own journals. The Royal Society of London, for example, published a great many important papers on scientific advances during the seventeenth century. Entitled *Philosophical Transactions*, the Society's journal published work by Isaac Newton when he developed his theory of gravity and his laws of motion, by Robert Boyle (whose work on gases is remembered by the laws which bear his name), by John Locke (whose *Essay on the Human Understanding* is considered to be a classical piece of philosophical writing), by van Leeuwenhoek (who sent his papers over from Holland) and by Robert Hooke who, working with Boyle, expanded the significance of Harvey's work on the circulation of the blood with a complementary piece of research which showed that the movement of the lungs draws air into the body.

More important, in practical terms, than the publication of these major papers was the effect of the scientific revolution on medication education and subsequently on the quantity and quality of medical graduates.

The impact of the new scientific era on the training of

doctors seems to have been greatest at the University of Leyden, which, by the end of the seventeenth century, had begun to rival Padua as the most important centre in Europe for scientists of all kinds.

Two men in particular helped not only to make Leyden an important centre of education but also to revolutionise medical education. Their major step forward involved no particular scientific discovery; they simply insisted that students should not confine themselves to a theoretical study of physiology and anatomy, as they had in the past, but should spend some time studying live human beings.

The first professor to introduce students to the idea of walking the wards was Franciscus Sylvius, who was also known as Franciscus de la Boe. Fielding H. Garrison, the eminent medical historian, points out that Sylvius did some original work of his own, but it was for allowing his students to accompany him on his rounds of his twelve bed ward in Leyden that he is probably best remembered. Following the logical pattern of scientific thinking that had been first produced in Padua, Sylvius encouraged his students to study symptoms, to listen to patients' complaints and then to try to produce reasoned explanations and rational treatments for probable diagnoses. It was not an original approach, since Hippocrates had taught much the same thing two thousand years previously, but it was, in the seventeenth century, as revolutionary an idea as any.

The other major figure at Leyden was Herman Boerhaave, who was appointed a lecturer there in 1701. Boerhaave encouraged his students to study primary sciences, such as physics, chemistry, botany, anatomy and physiology, and to try to correlate changes in the human body found at post mortem with symptoms recognised in life. Like Sylvius, he insisted that his students walk the wards and meet and talk to living patients. Through his students, Boerhaave's influence spread around the world; the medical schools in Vienna and Edinburgh were particularly influenced by his pupils. Since pupils from those two schools themselves later taught in other establishments on both sides of the Atlantic, it is no exaggeration to say that Boerhaave was the father of modern medical education.

Chapter 21: Medicine in Eighteenth Century America

America begins to feel its feet – Benjamin Franklin's rise – The first hospital in America – Medical education in America begins

In the years since Columbus had first crossed the Atlantic, the American continent had been under the economic and political control of the major European powers. No records exist of any significant original scientific work in America at that time, although the quality of medical care provided by the often untrained and illiterate medicine men was probably no better and no worse than the standard of general medical care available in Europe.

Contact between the two continents had undoubtedly led to permanent changes in the economic and political life of both New and Old Worlds, but it was not until the early part of the eighteenth century that the American people began to acquire their own medical establishment, hospitals and scientists.

The man most intimately associated with the early history of American medicine was Benjamin Franklin, a man of extraordinary talent who made a name as a printer and publisher, author, politician and diplomat, scientist and inventor. Born in 1706, Franklin was one of the men who helped to write the Declaration of Independence and the American Constitution. His accomplishments rival those of the Europeans who contributed to the scientific and artistic developments of the Renaissance.

The son of a soap and candle maker, Benjamin Franklin had no fewer than sixteen brothers and sisters – in itself a tribute to his mother's health and capacity for survival. Apprenticed as a printer, he quickly became a publisher, and his various business venues earned him enough money to spend the latter part of his life as a politician, diplomat and scientist. He is credited with the invention of bifocal lenses and the first flexible catheter; he wrote papers on such varied subjects as sleep, gout, deafness, infections and infant mortality, but perhaps his greatest contribution to the medical and social history of America was the part he played in the foundation of the first medical institutions on the west side of the Atlantic.

Franklin's contributions to American life really began in 1743 with the foundation of the American Philosophical Society, now America's oldest learned society. In his founding prospectus Franklin wrote that he intended to 'promote useful knowledge among the British plantations in America' and he stressed that the society should always include seven members: a physician, a botanist, a mathematician, a chemist, a mechanician, a geographer and a general natural philosopher. The society was modelled on the Royal Society in London where, for a while, Franklin had practised his trade as a printer.

A few years later, in 1751, Franklin helped to found the first real hospital in America.

The role of the Pennsylvania Hospital and other Philadelphia institutions in American history was vital. Until the 1750s any American doctor who wanted proper training had to go to Europe. Most went to Leyden or to Edinburgh, where the two most influential medical schools were situated, although many naturally also visited and studied in London for a while. The first American medical school was founded in Pennsylvania in 1765 by John Morgan, an Edinburgh graduate, and the links with the Scottish capital were strengthened by the appointment of other Edinburgh graduates to the teaching staff. One of the first professors to be appointed, Doctor Benjamin Rush, was one of the five physicians to sign the American Declaration of Independence in 1776. Both Rush and William Shippen, the Professor of Anatomy and Surgery at the new medical school, were Edinburgh graduates.

If Benjamin Franklin was America's first true intellectual and Renaissance man, Benjamin Rush was America's first physician to have a truly international reputation. Like the seventeenth century English physician Thomas Sydenham, Rush followed the Hippocratic school of learning and believed firmly in observing his patients carefully before coming to conclusions. He claimed that inflammation was an effect rather than a cause of disease, and he was ahead of many of his contemporaries in arguing that insanity was a disease rather than a divine visitation.

In the early 1700s medicine to most intelligent Americans was just another subject worthy of a little attention. Few educated men took more than a passing interest. Medical care was largely in the hands of midwives, salesmen promoting patent medicines, and quacks. By the end of the eighteenth century, however, medicine had become an acknowledged and respected profession. Numerous medical societies had been founded, and five medical schools had been established, in Pennsylvania, New York, Harvard, Philadelphia and Dartmouth College, the first diploma to a graduate completing a course of education in America being awarded in 1768 to John Archer at the University of Pennsylvania. A healthy medical establishment was booming and, although the quality of care available was still of doubtful value, America had caught up with Europe and was no longer dependent on the schools in Leyden and Edinburgh.

Chapter 22: Drugs and the Drug Industry

Pharmacology in the seventeenth century – The patent medicine manufacturers – Laudanum is introduced – The theriac – Heberden's disapproval – The therapeutic vacuum filled

The medical men who had led the advances in scientific thinking since the Renaissance had spent considerable time and effort on the study of human anatomy and human physiology; they had performed experiments with equipment such as the microscope and they had developed a number of useful surgical instruments.

One branch of medicine, however, had remained almost at a standstill throughout this period: pharmacology in the seventeenth century was still a confusing mixture of superstition and tradition.

When the first edition of the *London Pharmacopoeia* was published in 1618, it contained details of mixtures which included worms, dried vipers, foxes' lungs, powders of precious stones, oil of ants, oil of wolves, and butter made in the month of May. The 1650 edition suggested recipes for compounds containing moss from the skull of a victim of violent death. Later in the century practitioners were advised to use compounds containing human perspiration, the salvia of a fasting man, the sexual organs of animals, human urine, feathers, fur, raw silk, excreta of all kinds, spiders' webs, cast-off snakes' skins, swallows' nests and jaw bones from the skulls of executed criminals.

These ingredients were used by apothecaries and physicians as well as by lay people anxious to treat themselves. Indeed the seventeenth century official pharmacopoeia used by the College of Physicians included details of how to prepare compounds with crabs' eyes, live spiders rolled in butter and powdered Egyptian mummy.

The apparent inability of the leading members of the medical profession to distinguish between those remedies which had a useful effect and those which, in the light of modern experience, had little more than a placebo effect, does perhaps help to explain the popularity of the patent medicine manufacturers. After all, if leading medical scientists and practitioners were unable to differentiate between the pharmacologically active products and the compounds which relied for their effect upon fear, superstition and imagination, it is not surprising that the public fell for the claims and advertisements of the new breed of pill-pushers. Anderson's Pills, Dr Bateman's Pectoral Drops and Duffy's Elixir sold extremely well and made large sums of money for their manufacturers.

The first drug to be recognised in Europe as an effective

and specific remedy was quinine. Bernardino Ramazzini, the Paduan professor who founded the science of industrial medicine, claimed that cinchona bark (from which quinine is derived) did for medicine what gunpowder had done for war. He was almost certainly right, because the acceptance of quinine as an effective and powerful drug in its own right resulted in the dismissal of the centuries old Galenic teaching that the only useful medicinal preparations were those which contained dozens of different ingredients.

Very slowly the science of pharmacology began to take shape, and educated doctors began to put together a small accepted armoury of drugs recognised to have specific functions. In 1660 Thomas Sydenham had extracted laudanum from the opium poppy, which, like quinine, soon became accepted as a medicinal product. The real advances in pharmacology did not, however, take place until well into the eighteenth century, when such men as William Heberden began actively to promote the idea of a logical system of dispensing and prescribing.

The traditional medicine which particularly annoyed Heberden was known as the theriac, a sort of medicinal stew which contained just about anything that the man preparing it felt like dropping in. The theriac had been used as an essential medicine compound for the treatment of all kinds of illnesses and symptoms of just about every type for centuries. One of the first men to promote its use was a king of Pontus in Asia Minor, Mithridates VI, but Galen had a favoured mixture of his own, and his approval had more of less ensured the popularity of the idea. In cities such as Cairo, Constantinople, Genoa and Venice, which were important drug making centres, the theriac was prepared with great ceremony once a year and then used for the following twelve months. I rather suspect that any loose drugs found lying around the quay might have been found themselves in the pot.

The theriac sounds something of a joke today but in practice it was considered to be the most valuable tool of any physician or apothecary, since it contained just about every product thought to have any medicinal value at all. And before we laugh at the concept as hopelessly medieval, we should perhaps remember that Claude Bernard, a renowned physiologist of the nineteenth century, once recalled that, when he was apprenticed to a pharmacist, he was warned never to throw anything away but to keep it to pop into the theriac. Indeed, some modern medicinal compounds sold over the counter today contain almost as many ingredients as the ancient theriac, and there is about as much scientific logic behind their inclusion as there was behind the preparation of the theriac.

Heberden found the whole ideal of the theriac rather offensive and in his *Essay on Mithridatium and Theriacs*, which was published in 1745, he did a great deal to damage the professional popularity of this extraordinary mixture.

Fortunately, the therapeutic vacuum which could have resulted from Heberden's essay was quickly filled by the discovery of some new facts about some old medicinal plants. In 1763, for example, in a paper entitled *An account of the success of the bark of the willow in the cure of the agues*, a man mentioned at the top of the paper as Edmund Stone and at the bottom as Edward Stone informed the British Royal Society of the effectiveness of a compound prepared from willow bark. This compound was the forerunner of the modern aspirin tablet.

In 1776 William Withering, an English physician, described how he had learned about the effectiveness of the foxglove plant in the treatment of dropsy or ankle oedema, now known to be a major symptom of heart failure. Withering had learned about the usefulness of foxglove leaves from an old lady he had met on the way to Shropshire. The drug he described, known today as digitalis, is still one of the most important weapons in the treatment of heart disease.

It seems that the foxglove had been known to be effective in the treatment of dropsy for several centuries. Withering's contribution was to evaluate the product and to describe in some detail the potential hazards that might be associated with the drug's misuse. He had no way of studying the drug's full effect or of determining the precise way in which it worked, but his papers were among the first to include as precise an assessment as possible of a drug's potential pharmacological power.

Chapter 23: Power and Illness

The illnesses of individual leaders illustrated by
an account of George III, whose condition lasted for
many years of his reign

A history of the influence of medicine upon society would not be complete without some mention of the fact that many leaders, who had considerable authority over millions of people, may have been influenced not by logic or necessity but by disease. The difficulty in assessing the effect which specific disorders may have had on their particular victims is intensified by the fact that until fairly recently diagnostic skills were poor and medical records almost non-existent.

Henry VIII, for example, has been said to have suffered from syphilis, and some historians argue that it was this infection which made it difficult for him to produce an heir. Other medical experts disagree with this contention and claim that rhesus incompatibility was the cause of Henry's marital disharmony.

Napoleon is said to have suffered from piles and constipation, and it is sometimes claimed that at the Battle of Waterloo he was unable to sit on his horse because of the pain of his condition. With a little imagination it is possible to argue that Napoleon's piles led to his defeat and to subsequent changes of the map of Europe.

More recently it has been discovered that Queen Victoria was a carrier of haemophilia, the bleeding disease which affects only men but which can be carried by women.

It seems that Queen Victoria's third child, Alice, also carried haemophilia, as did Alexandra, daughter of Alice and Louis IV of Hesse-Darmstadt. Alexandra married Nicholas II, Tsar of all the Russias, and had a son, Alexis, who suffered badly from the disease. It can be argued that it was entirely because of her son's condition that Alexandra became dependent on Rasputin, the mad monk about whom so much has been written, and partly because of it that the Russian imperial family failed to provide the Russian people with the compassionate leadership they needed. On the basis of this conjecture it has been suggested, only partly in jest, that Lenin owed his success to Queen Victoria.

Speculation of this kind can hardly be classified as historical fact since it is based to some extent on rumour and imagination, but it is undoubtedly true that at many times the health of individual leaders has had an important effect on the health of millions of their followers.

One of the best documented accounts of the effect that one man's health may have on history concerns George III, who ruled Britain for sixty years, from 1760 to 1820, during one of the most important periods in the country's history. During his reign, Britain was fighting France, Spain and America abroad, while at home there was considerable political upheaval.

And yet, according to many contemporary accounts, during much of this time of turmoil and conflict George, who had considerable authority and influence over Parliament, was quite mad.

It now seems likely that George III had inherited the rare disease porphyria, which did not immediately threaten his health but undoubtedly had a powerful effect on his mental state. Although it is impossible to say precisely what effect George's condition had on his attitude to people and to world affairs, it is certainly possible that his personality played an important part in influencing the Americans to declare war on Britain and that his objection to Pitt's proposals for Catholic emancipation may have been coloured by his illness.

Historical events rarely follow a logical pattern, but it is interesting to ponder the possibility that the health of rulers, politicians and military leaders may have influenced events which not only had a powerful effect on people at the time but may subsequently have altered the political, social or economic status of their countries.

Chapter 24: The Industrial Revolution

*The Industrial Revolution – The economic advantages and
social changes – Industrial diseases become more
important – The effects of industrial progress on the health
of children – Alcoholism and tuberculosis: two major
problems – The effect of the Engineering Revolution
on health*

Harvey had provided practical proof of the circulation of the blood, and Vesalius had sparked an international revival of interest in human anatomy; Leeuwnehoek had described blood corpuscles and bacteria, and Boerhaave had introduced bedside teaching into medical education. But by the beginning of the eighteenth century living standards in all parts of the world were still primitive. The theoretical advances made by some of the greatest anatomists and physiologists had not yet led to any practical results. Ill health and early death at the end of the seventeenth century were hardly any better than they had been before the Renaissance had begun. Practical progress seemed to be at a standstill.

Then suddenly, in the eighteenth century, the world was changed by the most dramatic and far reaching revolution in the history of mankind. It was a revolution inspired not by medical scientists, soldiers or politicians but by engineers and businessmen.

The Industrial Revolution, which started in Britain and quickly spread around the western world, changed living standards, disease patterns and all other facets of society within a few dramatic decades. Countries which had depended upon agriculture, local crafts and livestock were suddenly dominated by machines and the work they could do.

The population of Britain in the early eighteenth century was a mere six million – a third the size of the French population at that time – and yet it was no chance occurrence that Britain became the original home of the machine age. As a small island

Britain had few of the transport problems which faced the large European landmass, since no inland town was more than a hundred miles or so away from the coast. Land travel at that time was slow and difficult but it was relatively simple to transport goods by sea. A good natural supply of such basic resources as coal, china clay, iron and fresh water gave Britain an important additional advantage.

Even before the Industrial Revolution these fundamental advantages had helped to give the British a relatively high standard of living. In contrast to other European countries, the good things in life were spread fairly evenly across the land. There was a wealthy upper class, of course, but there was also a huge affluent middle class group of people. This widespread affluence produced an enormous and apparently insatiable need for manufactured goods. Consequently, many businessmen found that the demands for their products often exceeded the supply. The only answer was to improve the rate of production, which they accomplished by introducing machines to do work previously done by men or animals. As a result, the beginning of the eighteenth century saw the first steam engines, which, with the fuel saving improvements made by James Watt later in the century, soon became indispensable to almost all branches of industry. Other innovations, including, for example, a technique that improved the rate at which iron could be produced, enabled the Revolution to pick up speed.

These developments affected the wealth and health of the ordinary citizen in several ways. To begin with, there were the inevitable economic advantages of living in an era of unprecedented growth in trade. As machines helped to make manufacturing processes cheaper, Britain could compete very much more effectively in world markets. Greater export sales gave industrialists more money to spend on wages, and for a while this undoubtedly led to a period of comparative prosperity for the ordinary working man and woman.

However, not all the changes produced by the Industrial Revolution were to the advantage of the population in general.

Craftsmen, instead of working at their own pace on tasks that required skill and provided considerable satisfaction, found themselves working with machines which were dirty, boring and often dangerous. When improved farm machinery became available, labourers discovered that they were no longer needed. The inevitable protests were regarded as reactionary by the progressive enthusiasts who stood to gain most from the Revolution, while the protesters, who at best could expect to find work in poorly lit, badly ventilated factories, had little reason to share the enthusiasm of their employers.

Social changes were as dramatic as the ones affecting employment possibilities. The building of huge new factories inevitably meant that entirely new communities had to be developed, and so new towns grew up at an unprecedented rate. People moved in huge numbers from the south of England to the north, where many of the big factories were being built. Villagers moved into towns, and women and children were, for the first time, dragged into heavy employment.

Thousands of people who had lived in small cottages in rural surroundings where they could tend their own small gardens and enjoy the relatively clean fresh air of the country, had to move to rows of terraced houses, where they were denied the chance to grow their own vegetables and were condemned to breathing polluted air. The overcrowding that resulted from the Industrial Revolution led directly to a rapid and savage deterioration in the quality of life and health. The new housing estates springing up all over Britain had no clean water supplies, no sewerage facilities and inadequate space or arrangements for play and recreation. In these conditions infectious diseases spread rapidly. As the Industrial Revolution spread throughout the world, so too did its harmful effects on health, although the full impact of the Revolution on the health of the British people did not become apparent for more than a century.

One direct and immediate result of the Industrial Revolution was the increase in the incidence of disease related to various manufacturing processes.

The first firm and formally recognised association between occupation and disease had been made back in the sixteenth century by the ubiquitous Aureolus Theophrastus Bombastus von Hohenheim, who had written abut the relationship between mining and certain disease processes. At about the same time George Bauer, who was also known as Georgius Agricola, published a volume called *De Re Metallica*, a set of twelve books which included details of the diseases and accidents which most commonly affected miners. He included in his books advice on how these disorders could be best avoided, suggesting and describing in detail ventilating machines which he said could be used to replace stagnant air underground. He also suggested that miners should wear masks to protect their lungs. Inevitably, perhaps, these imaginative and far reaching solutions were ignored by the medical establishment, which was more concerned with treating people when they had become sick than with keeping people healthy, and by the mine owners, who were able to find an inexhaustible supply of fresh miners for considerably less than the cost of installing expensive machinery.

The official father of industrial medicine, however, was Bernardino Ramazzini, who was a Professor of Medicine at the University of Modena and then at Padua in the late seventeenth century and early eighteenth century. It was while living in Modena, which at the time contained a large number of tall, overcrowded houses, that Ramazzini watched a man clear out a cesspit. The man was, perhaps not surprisingly, working as fast as he could in order to get out of the pit and breathe some diluted polluted air instead of having to make do with the concentrated stuff. Ramazzini realised as he watched the man that some occupations are associated with their own specific hazards.

Inspired by this thought, Ramazzini visited local mines, shops and factories and studied the type of work being done by miners, bakers, grooms, printers, blacksmiths and other labourers and craftsmen. As a direct result of his observations, he suggested that workshops should be ventilated, that working temperatures should be controlled as much as possible and that men doing repetitive tasks should be allowed to rest at intervals and change their posture to avoid future trouble with their health. He gave credence and authority to the philosophy that men should be able to earn their living without sacrificing their health.

Unfortunately Ramazzini's observations and theories were not put into practice and, by the time of the Industrial Revolution, it was common for workmen in all branches of industry to suffer from diseases which were often unique to their occupation. Hargreaves' spinning jenny, Arkwright's frame, Crompton's mule for cotton spinning and James Watt's steam engine all revolutionised major industries but all produced specific hazards. It was not until the second half of the eighteenth century that industrial medicine was revived as a speciality, with Percival Pott describing the association between chimney sweeps and scrotal cancer in 1775, and Thomas Beddoes' reporting in 1799 that brassworkers and stone cutters were particularly susceptible to consumption.

Even then progress was still remarkably slow. New industrial processes continued to produce additional hazards. New paints, dyes and alloys became associated with new diseases, and each fresh machine seemed to bring with it an extra hazard for the man who would operate it. To us, disorders such as miner's elbow, wool-sorter's disease, knife-grinder's phthisis, painter's colic, weaver's bottom, hod-carrier's shoulder, brass-founder's ague, grocer's itch, glass-blower's cataract, hatter's shakes, Billingsgate jump, tailor's ankle and so on sound faintly comical. To the men who suffered, and sometimes died, from occupational disorders, they were far from amusing.

Legislative help and practical support from the medical profession was not forthcoming until the beginning of the nineteenth century.

The direct effects of industrial progress on the health of workmen, women and children were severe enough. There were other less obvious influences too.

Moving great numbers of country folk into heavily populated urban areas changed living conditions enormously in a relatively short time. The increase in the incidence of infectious disorders associated with poor community services became an obvious problem a little later, as the primitive facilities available within these communities began to break down under the excessive load. But the change in lifestyle produced several obvious effects very quickly. One of the most dramatic of these was the increase in the incidence of alcoholism and the cruelty, violence and privation associated with it.

Alcohol had, of course, been around for many centuries. In Britain, before the Romans, fermented brews made from barley, honey or apples had caused a considerable amount of fighting. In the sixth century things were so bad that the church decreed that drunken monks would not be given any supper. But widespread regular drunkenness did not become a big problem until the eighteenth century, when living conditions changed rapidly and many people found that they had little to do with their little free time but try to forget the miserable conditions in which they were working and living. Inevitably, perhaps, children were beaten, badly fed and often neglected by drinking parents. In his *Gin Lane*, published in 1751, Hogarth described vividly the effects that drink could have on an ordinary, respectable family.

As the incidence of alcoholism increased, so did the number of people suffering from tuberculosis (consumption). The damp, cold English climate suited this disease perfectly, and the overcrowding produced by the Industrial Revolution helped to spread the disorder rapidly. The incidence of tuberculosis was no doubt enhanced by the window tax, introduced in 1696, which encouraged landlords to brick up windows in order to reduce their liability for tax. This effectively resulted in thousands of people being deprived of air and light. A similar situation existed in France, where a window tax was also in force during the eighteenth century.

In the sixteenth and seventeenth centuries the revolutionary ideas of the Renaissance scientists had begun to give life back to medicine and the medical profession. Nevertheless, although the Industrial Revolution may have had little or nothing to do with health care specifically, James Watt, Jethro Tull and the other men who led the Industrial Revolution from the front had a far greater effect on mortality and morbidity rates in the eighteenth and nineteenth centuries than any of the medical scientists who had been at the heart of the Renaissance. The trouble was – they were not improving health standards; they were making them worse.

Chapter 25: An End to Scurvy

The damage done by scurvy – James Lind experiments, but no one takes any notice – Lemon juice is introduced just in time to save Nelson

In 1535 Jacques Cartier had sailed from St. Malon in France with a total crew of 110 men, intending to explore the coast of Newfoundland, but within six weeks one hundred of his men had developed scurvy, a disease caused by the absence of Vitamin C from the diet. In the early stages the symptoms are simple enough – the patient usually notices that his gums bleed rather easily. Later on, however, the disorder begins to affect the whole body, resulting in considerable pain before death intervenes.

Luckily for his men and his expedition, Cartier discovered from a native that the complaint could be cured by drinking the juice from the fruit of local trees. His crew recovered within days.

Wise sea captains quickly followed Cartier's example and, to maintain a healthy crew, ensured that each man was provided with a regular supply of either orange or lemon juice. In a book called *The Surgeon's Mate*, published in 1636, John Woodall actually recommended that these juices be used to prevent the development of scurvy. Few captains who read his book needed to suffer the agonies of Vasco de Gama, who lost a hundred of 160 men on his voyage to India, although no one knew why these juices prevented scurvy.

Then, remarkably and inexplicably, captains stopped providing men with citrus fruits, and the scurvy began once again to decimate crews on long voyages. When Anson's fleet circumnavigated the globe between 1740 and 1744, he lost three quarters of his men to scurvy.

It was not until 1747 that the idea of preventing scurvy by giving sailors lemon or orange juice to drink was reintroduced. The man who suggested it was James Lind, an Edinburgh graduate, who performed the first proper clinic trial in his successful attempt to prove that, by using one or other of these fruits, scurvy could be prevented. He published the results from his study in 1753 and described how he had given some sailors vinegar, some cider, some oranges and some lemons. Only those sailors who had been given fruit avoided scurvy. It was Lind's work which enabled Lieutenant Cook (later to be promoted) to sail around the world between 1769 and 1771 without a single case of scurvy.

Surprisingly, the Admiralty took no notice of Lind's research. In 1779 the Channel Fleet had 2,400 cases of scurvy after a ten week cruise. Sir Gilbert Blane, however, cured an outbreak on twenty eight ships in 1782 by using fruit and eventually succeeded in convincing the Admiralty chiefs that the proposal was worth following. In 1795, a year after Lind's death, lemon juice became a compulsory part of every sailor's diet. To make sure that the sailors took their lemon, it was added to their grog ration. When, in later years, limes were used instead of lemons, the Americans gave British sailors the nickname 'limey' to commemorate the fact.

Since, in the Seven Years' War, from 1756 to 1763, approximately half of the 185,000 sailors involved had died of scurvy, it was perhaps just as well that the Admiralty acted when it did. It is unlikely that even Nelson's tactical skills could have made up for a navy decimated by scurvy, and the wars with Napoleon which were to follow might have had a rather different outcome.

Chapter 26: A New Weapon Against Disease

Smallpox has killed millions – By the early eighteenth century it is still spreading – Inoculation becomes fashionable – Dimsdale makes his fortune – Jenner publishes his famous paper – The prophet is ignored in his own country, but the news spreads around the word – The American President is pleased

Over the centuries, smallpox has been responsible for many millions of deaths. Modern historians have traced the disease back to ancient Egypt, where Pharaoh Ramses V seems to have died of smallpox in 1160 BC. Since then smallpox has been the most widely distributed of all the serious infectious diseases. Plague, cholera, yellow fever and malaria have all killed many millions but none of these diseases lasted for so long or affected such a large part of the world as smallpox.

During the Elephant War of AD 569 in Arabia, a smallpox epidemic among the Abyssinian troops besieging Mecca saved the city, and in the following centuries the disease spread over the whole of Europe and Africa. Whenever smallpox was introduced into a new area, it proved devastating. In the sixteenth century the Aztec Empire collapsed when three and a half million Mexicans died of smallpox, brought by Cortez's small army, and later smallpox was used to help defeat native American armies; Amherst and Colonel Bouquet, for example, used infected blankets to spread the disease among the Indians. By the beginning of the seventeenth century smallpox was endemic in America; nine tenths of the population on the Massachusetts coast were killed by the infection, and small towns were sometimes almost completely wiped out.

During the early eighteenth century smallpox was still common and spreading; in 1707, when smallpox reached Iceland, 18,000 died from a population of 57,000. In Europe at that time it was estimated that one in every five children would die of smallpox, which was also said to be the leading cause of blindness. About sixty million Europeans died of smallpox in the eighteenth century. Advertisements for servants would often include a note warning that applicants would have to produce evidence of having had the disease before they would be allowed into a household. It was known that people who had had smallpox could not catch it again and therefore spread it further.

The disease had a devastating effect on almost all aspects of life. It attacked and killed members of most royal families. During the Franco-Prussian war 200,00 soldiers contracted the disease, of whom more than 25,000 died, while, at the same time, the disease killed 18,000 French citizens in Paris.

Naturally, many attempts were made to control the disease. No effective form of treatment had been discovered (and non ever has) but there was one way of preventing smallpox which had first been tried in China and India twenty-five centuries before. It had been discovered that, by putting material from smallpox scabs or pustules into the nose or skin of a healthy individual, a less severe attack of the disease could be produced, which would subsequently provide the patient with protection against the more serious and potentially fatal form. In China, for example, where a proverb cautioned that you should not count your children until they had all contracted smallpox, physicians collected the scales from drying smallpox pustules, ground them to a power and blew them into the nostrils of people who wanted protection. They also tried placing healthy individuals in contact with patients suffering from mild forms of smallpox in the expectation that the healthy people would contract the mild form of the disease and then remain protected.

However, it was not until the beginning of the eighteenth century that this effective form of preventive medicine first became popular in Europe. An Italian, physician, Dr Emanuel Timoni, working in Constantinople in 1714, discovered that the Turks used inoculation to protect their citizens from smallpox, and sent a paper on the subject to the Royal Society in London. Meanwhile Giacomo Pylarini, a Greek doctor working in Smyrna at about the same time, took some thick material from a small-pox pustule and rubbed it into a scratch made with a clean needle on the arm of a healthy volunteer. An account of this experiment was sent to Doctor John Woodward in London, who published the details in the *Philosophical Transactions* of the Royal Society. It is possible that Pylarini based his theory on the knowledge that mothers often encouraged their offspring to mix with other children who had smallpox, as long as the infection seemed to be in a mild form. It seems very possible that, for many years before Timoni and Pylarini published their papers, local wise women were effectively practising this type of preventive medicine.

Inoculation became fashionable in Britain and in Europe when Lady Mary Montagu, the wife of the British Ambassador to Turkey, had her daughter publicly inoculated against smallpox. Experiments with prisoners from Newgate Prison seemed to prove the relative safety of the technique.

Unfortunately, this type of inoculation carried some risk, and after a few deaths had resulted from the practice, it soon lost popularity in Europe. In American, however, inoculation continued apace. Both Benjamin Franklin and George Washington advocated the method, and as smallpox spread across the American continent, so did the use of this often effective form of protection. In the 1740s Dr Kilpatrick in Charleston, who inoculated by making a very shallow, superficial scratch, showed that the practice could be comparatively effective and safe. He inoculated between eight hundred and a thousand people in 1743, only eight of whom died.

One man who made a fortune from inoculation was Thomas Dimsdale, a leading British practitioner of the technique, who, in 1786, was invited to go to Russia to inoculate the family of Catherine II. In return for this comparatively simple contribution, Dimsdale was made a baron, a councillor of state and a major general. He was also given his expenses, a fee of £10,000 and an annuity of £500. Dimsdale may have done well out of this particular family but he did understand the shortcomings of inoculation. When a Society for the Inoculation of the Poor was formed in London, Dimsdale objected on the grounds that, in the overcrowded conditions in which the poor of London lived, inoculation would simply spread smallpox and produce artificial epidemics of the disease. This was a valid argument, because inoculation did not protect the patient against smallpox but rather gave him a minor attack of the infection so that his body could prepare its own defences and so that he would remain immune if exposed to more serious attacks of the same disease. In Dimsdale's opinion there was no guarantee that individuals who caught the infection from an inoculated patient would not allow the spread of a more dangerous version of the disorder. One doctor reported, for example, that a single inoculated child had infected a total of seventeen people, eight of whom had subsequently died. Inoculation, it seemed, might be very good for the rich but for the majority of the population, who lived in close contact with one another and who could not all be inoculated at the same time, the method was fraught with danger.

Throughout the eighteenth century, smallpox continued to recur and to kill many hundreds of thousands. Indeed, one of the greatest epidemics of smallpox to affect London occurred in 1772, half a century after inoculation had first been introduced; in that one year nearly four thousand people died. The disease was still spreading across Europe in that decade, and in 1774 it claimed the life of King Louis XV of France.

1774 also saw a vital breakthrough in the fight against smallpox made by a Dorset farmer called Benjamin Jesty. Frightened by the latest news of a local outbreak of smallpox, Jesty vaccinated his wife and two sons with cowpox (a similar but mild disease contracted by cows) to protect them against the more dangerous disease. The difference between inoculation and vaccination is an important one. Vaccination involves giving the person a harmless disease in the expectation that, in preparing its defences against the mild disease, the body will also prepare defences against a similar but potentially lethal disease. The theory, of course, depends very heavily on the similarity of the two infections concerned. Jesty had undoubtedly noticed that girls working on his farm who had contracted cowpox did not seem to get smallpox. Jesty's experiment was, however, ignored by the medical profession for two decades.

The idea was revived by a general practitioner called Edward Jenner, who is probably responsible for saving more lives than any other medical practitioner in history. The son of a clergyman, Jenner worked in Gloucestershire, England where it had long been known that dairymaids who developed cowpox did not get smallpox. Jenner slowly collected evidence from his patients and the local people until, in 1796, he was certain enough of his theory to repeat the experiment first tried by Jesty in 1774. With enormous professional courage Jenner inoculated material from a cowpox pustule on the hand of a dairymaid, Sarah Nelmes, into the arm of an eight year old, James Phipps. The real test of Jenner's nerve came seven weeks later, when the time had come to inject the boy with material from a genuine smallpox pustule. To Jenner's undoubted relief, the boy remained healthy.

With the remarkable pig-headedness that has characterised the scientific medical establishment through the ages, the Royal Society did not think Jenner's account of his experiment worthy of publishing (although they had been happy to publish one of his earlier papers describing the natural history of the cuckoo).

Undeterred by the lack of interest shown by the profession's leaders, Jenner continued with his experiments and within two years had performed twenty-two similar vaccinations. He described his work in a booklet which he published himself in 1798. Like Harvey, Jenner had based his research upon a solid foundation, beginning with a thesis (admittedly based on what might have been dismissed as an old wives' tale) and turning it into a proven scientific fact.

Within a remarkably short time, news of Jenner's work had spread around the world. In some areas an infected cow would be led from door to door so that material could be scraped off and used to vaccinate the waiting citizens. In France, the Emperor Napoleon ruled in 1805 that all his troops who had not had smallpox should be vaccinated at once. Jenner was not quite so popular in his own country, however. The theory of vaccination met considerable opposition from jealous members of the medical profession who argued that there was a risk of transmitting syphilis and by others who claimed that preventing smallpox was interfering with the will of God. It was even suggested that, by limiting deaths from smallpox, vaccinators would put a burden on family men who might otherwise have expected their liabilities to be limited! However, Jenner's supporters slowly outweighed his opponents, and eventually the British Parliament awarded him a grant to continue his experiments. By the time they did, however, the technique had already been accepted in most parts of the world.

Getting the material for vaccination to America and other distant parts was not quite as easy as spreading it around Europe. The technique was first introduced in America by Dr Benjamin Waterhouse of Boston, who was Harvard's first Professor of the Theory and Practice of Physics. Waterhouse had been sent a copy of Jenner's booklet by a friend, John Coakley Lettson, who was a leading figure in the Society for Inoculation of the Poor in London and who had quickly recognised the superiority of Jenner's method of vaccination over the established form of inoculation. In 1800 Lettson sent Waterhouse some cotton threads that had been soaked in cowpox, with which Waterhouse vaccinated seven of his own children.

Waterhouse proved Jenner's theory to his own satisfaction by arranging for one of his vaccinated children to be left in a room with a patient suffering from a naturally acquired dose of smallpox. When the boy remained healthy, Waterhouse proceeded to protect the American people and to make his own fortune by vaccinating as many as he could. Later, Thomas Jefferson, the American President, persuaded a deputation of North American Indian chiefs to take supplies of the vaccine back to their people. Mass vaccination programmes were there-

106

fore in operation on both sides of the Atlantic within a few years of the publication of Jenner's experiment.

Transmission of the cowpox vaccine to Central and South America was organised by King Charles IV of Spain, who, in 1803, put twenty-two unvaccinated children on a frigate and two more who were vaccinated immediately before departure. When the vaccinated pustule developed on the original two children, two more were vaccinated with the material obtained from them. This process continued until the frigate arrived in Venezuela, where more children were picked up. In this way the cowpox vaccine was taken to Central and South America, the Philippines, Macao and eventually to China, where the original form of inoculation had first been used so many hundreds of years before.

Meanwhile, Russian doctors were vaccinating people on their border with China. It had taken only a few years for Jenner's discovery to affect the whole world. During the following two centuries vaccination, first against smallpox and then against other diseases, would prove to be a most effective weapon for controlling dangerous infectious diseases (although the weapon was subsequently overused).

Chapter 27: Quackery and Genius

The shortcomings of the medical profession – The quacks do well – The piss prophets – Mesmer: charlatan or genius? – Mesmer's influence on medicine and medical thinking

The lack of any solid scientific foundation upon which diagnostic skills could be based and the absence of reliable, safe, effective forms of treatment for anything more than a handful of assorted symptoms meant that orthodox eighteenth century medical practitioners, whether physicians or apothecaries, were just as vulnerable to critical comment as their predecessors had been. Medical schools had been built and students were being given a rudimentary introduction to subjects such as anatomy and physiology, but the educational programmes in these establishments were more suited to the training of theoretical scientists than to the preparation of practising doctors. Learned societies and august journals provided philosophers and experimental scientists with a good variety of opportunities to discuss and explain their work, but the theories and philosophies they shared were largely irrelevant to the ordinary citizen.

With all these shortcomings it is not surprising that orthodox medicine did not have a monopoly on the care of the sick. Indeed there were a great many charlatans and confidence tricksters in practice. One of the most successful of the many relatively sophisticated quacks to make their fortunes in the eighteenth century was Sir William Read, a tailor, who set up in the Strand in London as an eye specialist in 1694 and who even managed to number Queen Anne among his patients. Read was knighted by Queen Anne and later became oculist to George I. Another well known and successful quack, Joshua Ward, had tried politics earlier in his career but eventually found medicine more to his taste, making his fortune by selling pills, drops, powers and such wonders as 'liquid sweat'. Having succeeded in correcting the dislocated thumb of George II, Joshua Ward found himself a successful society practitioner and was consulted by Chesterfield, Walpole and Gibbon. Ward's success was so great and his influence so strong that he was not only given a coach and six horses and the right to drive through St. James's Park but also specifically excluded from the restrictions of the Act of 1748 which was designed to stop unqualified people preparing pills. Dr Samuel Johnson, incidentally, described Ward as the dullest man he ever knew, while Alexander Pope noted that he had become a 'famed physician' without 'the least pretence to skill'.

Quacks did not operate only in London, nor did they confine their attention to the rich and powerful. Many worked in country districts, selling their remedies as they travelled around. The more successful had horses and carriages while the less successful had to travel on foot. Often these quacks joined up with travelling fairs and shows and sold elixirs and magic potions with the semi-hysterical rhetoric of traditional fairground hawkers.

Some of the most successful practitioners were women. Mrs Sally Mapp, a bonesetter who lived in Epsom, is said to have had liveried servants and to have treated many members of fashionable society. Mrs Joanna Stevens earned herself a fortune by preparing and selling a special remedy which she claimed would get rid of bladder stones. Her cure was apparently so successful – though no evidence exists to prove its value – that, when she offered to sell the secret recipe to the nation for £5,000, Parliament actually voted to give her this enormous sum of money. When she duly handed over her secret, her recipe was found to be a mixture of snails, soap, egg shells and various vegetables.

For centuries fully qualified and highly respectable physicians had often claimed to be able to diagnose illness by studying, and tasting, the urine of their patients. Chaucer, Shakespeare and Molière had all written rather derisory comments about such doctors but their opinions had done little to damage public faith in this apparent mystical skill. Since even the most eminent member of the medical establishment had no real way of knowing what a patient's urine did or did not show, there was obviously no reason why quacks should not take advantage of this touching faith and offer to provide prognoses based on a study of urine samples.

Often known as 'piss prophets', these specialist quacks would plant a colleague in with patients as they sat in the waiting room and then wait for the bogus patient to elicit information about each individual in turn. Later, the piss prophet would study phials of urine and announce to each startled patient the truth about his family, relatives and friends. With faith established in this simple way, the doctor would be able to sell a bottle of his expensive mixture without too much trouble. By the time the patient discovered that the medicine had no useful effect, the doctor would be miles away in another town or village.

One of the most colourful eighteenth century quacks was Dr James Graham, who took advantage of the early electrical experiments of Franklin, Galvani and Volta to offer his patients the first electrical treatments. Graham made his fortune with the aid of his 'celestial bed', which he hired out to anxious couples for massive fees. The bed, which was designed to guarantee conception to the childless, used magnetic and electrical power in a way unequalled before or since. The magnificent celestial bed in the temple of health just off the Strand is said to have cost Graham £10,000 to build, while hiring it for the night cost a minimum of £50. Incidentally, one of the young girls who was said to have helped Graham illustrate his lectures on sex was later to acquire fame and fortune as Lady Hamilton, the mistress of Lord Nelson. When the celestial bed's popularity faded, Graham turned to mud baths and gave lectures while buried up to his chin in earth but unfortunately this gimmick did not prove quite so popular.

The craze for electrical devices did not disappear when the bed was dismantled. Later, quacks introduced and successfully marketed many medical cures which depended upon electricity for their effect. An electrical eye bath was said to cure weak vision, and electrical towels and hairbrushes were sold to anyone prepare to hand over the right amount of money. A Yale graduate called Perkins made a considerable amount of money on both sides of the Atlantic by selling 'electric tractors'. These were metal rods which were said to remove pain when rubbed on the body, but their effect undoubtedly depended upon faith rather than electrical power.

A great many of these quacks were, like Perkins, nothing more than confidence tricksters relying upon the fact that people who are ill want to get better and will be particularly ready to believe in a potential cure if they are in pain. In addition, the quacks knew that the person who has paid out hard earned money for a cure will be more than ready to believe that he has bought something worthwhile. The placebo response works well when the patient has to put up with a little discomfort – and it did not matter particularly whether the discomfort involved an evil tasting medicine or a little damage to the wallet.

It would be a great mistake to dismiss all these unqualified practitioners merely as grasping charlatans, for they could only get away with selling their unproven cures because the qualified practitioners had nothing better to offer. If the physicians, surgeons and apothecaries had been able to provide effective and safe forms of treatment, the quacks would not have flourished. As it was, there is little doubt that many of the men and women described as quacks undoubtedly contributed a great deal to the health of the people they treated. As far as the individual patient is concerned, of course, it does not really matter whether relief is obtained from a consultation with a highly qualified practitioner, who has a thorough knowledge of human anatomy and physiology, or from an illiterate scoundrel.

In addition, many of the so-called quacks who practised in the eighteenth century contributed a great deal to medicine in general. The medical establishment has always been loath to give credit to those who have not acquired the regularly accepted qualifications; even today there are many orthodox practitioners who refuse to admit that such people as osteopaths can be of any use to patients.

Of the many quacks who made major contributions to medical science, the one who probably stands above the rest was Franz Mesmer. He graduated in Vienna in 1766 and aroused the sort of controversy that had first surrounded Paracelsus two centuries earlier. Mesmer began his academic career by studying the power and influence of the universe on human beings. His first theory was that some unseen power from the planets influenced human behaviour in just the same way as the moon influences the sea. At first Mesmer believed that the power was transmitted through ordinary magnets, since his experiments suggested that by moving a magnet he could control the flow of fluid from a patient being bled, but gradually he began to realise that the magnet was not really necessary and that the same effect could be obtained with nothing more mysterious than his own hands. 'Hypnosis', in its various forms (the word 'hypnosis' had not then been invented), had been the subject of study and experimentation since the days of ancient Egypt; Athanasius Kircher, a seventeenth century microscopist, had done some significant work on the subject, but Mesmer was the first man to seek to use the influence of mind over body

Mesmer claimed that the explanation for this new power source was something called 'animal magnetism', a powerful basic force derived from the planets or from some other unknown body in space, which could be utilised by human hands and controlled in such a way as to have an effect on individual patients.

Mesmer was enormously successful and the Austrian medical establishment quickly started a campaign to discredit him. When he cured a young blind girl, they accused him of being a cheat and a charlatan. Thrown out of Vienna, he moved to Paris, where he soon established an even more lucrative private practice. Undoubtedly quite a showman, Mesmer would dress up for his seances and influence his patients with music, staring eyes and a wand. For a while he continued to use magnets as part of his consulting room technique, although he realised and openly admitted at an early state that they were not entirely necessary. His success with patients suffering from disorders which we would now describe as 'psychosomatic' or 'stress induced' was tremendous.

Inevitably, Mesmer's success in Paris once again aroused considerable controversy, and many members of the medical establishment, inspired no doubt more by jealousy than other motives, set up a special commission to investigate his claims. The commissioners, who included Benjamin Franklin, the chemist Lavoisier and a Dr Guillotin, who invented the instrument which bears his name, decided that there was no justification for any such force as animal magnetism and instead claimed that Mesmer's effects were produced by imagination.

Whether or not the commission's findings would have affected his practice we have no way of knowing, for Mesmer was not to practise in Paris for much longer. The King, Louis XVI, and his court had been enthusiastic supporters of Mesmerism, and when the French Revolution became a reality, Mesmer left France.

Although he died in obscurity in Switzerland in 1815, Mesmer's influence on medical care and, in particular, on the treatment of the mentally ill remained important. His ability to control, influence and cure the mentally ill helped to lead to reforms in practical psychiatry, and such men as Sigmund Freud owed a great deal to his work. Mesmer's influence was not, however, confined to the care of the mentally ill. Many surgeons used mesmerism as a form of anaesthetic.

Although the medical establishment may have considered him to be a quack and a showman, Franz Mesmer was probably one of the most influential and important figures in the history of eighteenth century medicine. His influence as a practitioner matches his influence as a philosopher, which, at that time, was rare indeed.

Chapter 28: The Evils of Institutional Care

Institutional care in the eighteenth century – Tenon's report – The care of the mentally ill – Practical improvements led by Pinel in France

The quality of institutional care in the eighteenth century was no better than the quality of general medical care. The general standards in most hospitals were low, and death rates were high. The Foundling Hospital in Dublin, for example, admitted 10,272 infants in the years from 1775 to 1796, and of these only forty-five survived.

In 1788 Jacobus-René Tenon published a report describing the hospitals of Paris which must have shocked even the most complacent city officials. He described how the Hôtel Dieu contained 1,220 beds, in each of which between four and six patients were crammed. Patients in many parts of the hospital lay about on dirty straw, and no attempt was made to keep infectious patients away from those suffering from non-infectious diseases. The stench in the hospital was said to be so foul that people entering it would often do so only when holding a vinegar-soaked sponge to their noses. Patients who had surgical operations invariably died, and relatively few patients ever walked out of the hospital. Most healthy pregnant women confined in the Hôtel Dieu died in childbirth.

The same things were true of almost all other hospitals throughout Europe. When Tsar Paul came to power in Russia in 1796, he was so horrified at the state of the hospital in Moscow that he ordered it to be rebuilt. In Frankfurt physicians considered working in hospital equivalent to a sentence of death. Another reforming writer of the eighteenth century, John Howard, toured European hospitals and prisons at about the same time as Tenon made his report, and his studies were equally startling. It was the same story almost everywhere: dirty straw as bedding, no fresh air, no sunlight, no bandages and a milk and water diet supplemented with weak soup.

If the standard of care in ordinary hospitals was low, that in mental hospitals and psychiatric institutions was almost beyond description or comprehension. At the Blockley Hospital in Philadelphia, for example, a report published in 1793 showed that, since it was almost impossible to hire nurses, insane women patients were looked after by just three male keepers, who exhibited their patients as a sort of side-show, opening the wards to the public and allowing visitors to poke fun at the more obviously insane patients. There was no heating in the hospital because the authorities had decided that insane patients were unlikely to suffer from extremes of temperature. Dr Benjamin Rush, thought to have been one of the most enlightened medical practitioners in America, is reported to have kept disturbed patients awake and standing for twenty-four hours at a time.

At the beginning of the eighteenth century Daniel Defoe, best remembered for his account of the exploits of Robinson

Crusoe, had written a bitter complaint about the number of private mad-houses where for a decent fee patients could be hidden away from the world. 'Is it not enough to make anyone mad,' he asked 'to be suddenly clap'd up, stripp'd, whipp'd, ill fed and worse us'd? To have no reason assigned for such treatment, no crime alleged or accusers to confront? And what is worse, no soul to appeal to but merciless creatures who answer but in laughter, surliness, contradiction and too often stripes?'

But no one in Europe took much notice of Defoe, and medical practitioners continued to treat mentally ill patients in the belief that physical punishments would cure their troubles. At the Bethlem Royal Hospital, known better as Bedlam, half-naked patients were kept chained in irons, were allowed only straw bedding and were cruelly mistreated. Physicians bled their patients at the end of May or the beginning of June each year, and after being bled each patient would be made to vomit once a week before being purged. For the more troublesome patients there was a tranquillising wheel on which individuals could be strapped and spun round until they lost consciousness. Until 1770 visitors could pay a penny to see the 'fun' at Bedlam.

John Wesley, the founder of the Wesleyan Church, suggested that a useful treatment for lunacy might include rubbing the patient's head several times a day with vinegar in which ground ivy leaves had been infused. More seriously ill patients, described by him as suffering from raving madness, would receive more dramatic remedies, and he pointed out that, since all madmen were cowards, binding them sometimes did as much good as beating. Wesley, who seems to have considered himself a benefactor of the mentally ill, also suggested pouring water onto their heads and giving them a diet of nothing but apples for a month. Between these treatments mental patients would usually be confined to over-crowded quarters where urine-soaked and excrement-laden straw would serve as bedding. Wesley, incidentally, was one of the first men to use electricity in the attempted treatment of mental illness.

While Tenon, Howard and others were writing about the

inhumane and degrading conditions in ordinary hospitals, other observers were making similar protests about the conditions in lunatic asylums. One of the most powerful indictments of the ways in which the mentally ill were cared for was made by Dr Philippe Pinel, a physician to Bicêtre and Salpêtrière prisons in Paris where many lunatics were housed. Pinel decided to offer to free a number of prisoners from their chains if they promised to behave like gentlemen. To the surprise of the less imaginative officials, the prisoners were not violent or disorderly when their chains were removed.

Like Hippocrates so many years before, Pinel argued that the mentally ill are sick and not responsible for their own condition. Pinel amplified this simple theory in a textbook written in 1801, which was effectively the first treatise on psychiatry and in which he described how mental illnesses can be temporary or permanent and either relapsing or persistent. He also argued that domestic crises, unhappy love affairs and similar stresses can all produce types of mental illness.

Unfortunately, not everyone agreed with Pinel, and the humane theories he had expressed were not widely accepted for many years. At the beginning of the nineteenth century, mental hospitals, like many general hospitals, were still quite unsuitable for the care of people needing medical attention.

Chapter 29: The Birth of the Pharmaceutical Industry

Pill-making by hand has its problems – William Brockeden's pill-making machine – The pharmaceutical industry is born.

The observations and experiments conducted by men like William Withering had extended the range of useful pharmacological compounds available, but the business of preparing and dispensing medicines had hardly changed since the days of Galen. Weighing scales had made the process of preparing medicines slightly more scientific, but the apothecary in practice at the start of the nineteenth century still used a pestle and mortar to mix his compounds. Finished medicaments were sold as mixtures, powders or pills, and the rate at which an apothecary could stock his shelves depended entirely upon his own dexterity and that of any assistants he might have. Even pills were made by hand: the active ingredients were first ground together with a pestle and mortar, then rolled like a piece of pastry before being divided into short sections and rolled into spheres. If a pill was bitter-tasting and likely to be difficult to swallow, it might be given an outer coating; if the pills were intended for an upper-class clientele, they might be coated with silver or gold.

Without machinery to standardise the preparation of pharmaceuticals, it was difficult to ensure that each dose of each medicine was identical to all others. Pill-rolling by hand inevitably meant that some pills contained more active constituents than others. It was also difficult for any one manufacturer to gain an advantage by increasing his output. An apothecary who wanted to double his output of hand-rolled pills would have to hire twice as many apprentices, so any extra potential profit would inevitably be reduced.

These two problems were overcome in the early nineteenth century by a man who was destined to become the most important single influence in the foundation of the enormously powerful pharmaceutical industry. Born in Devon, England in 1787, William Brockeden trained as a watchmaker but also earned money as an author and artist. It was in his capacity as an artist that he made the discovery that was to revolutionise the preparation of medicines and enable apothecaries to replace pill-rolling apprentices with efficient, reliable tablet-making machines.

Infuriated by the fact that he could not obtain drawing pencils which were free from grit, Brockeden had the idea of compressing pure powdered graphite in a die between two punches. Realising that his invention could have other uses, he then took out a patent for a device for 'Shaping of pills, lozenges and black lead by pressure in a die'.

In 1844, a few months after Brockeden's patent was granted, the *Pharmaceutical Journal* announced: 'We have received a specimen of bicarbonate of potash compressed into the form of a pill by a process invented by Mr Brockeden and for which he has taken out a patent. We understand the process is applicable to the compression of a variety of other substances into a solid mass, without the intervention of gum or other adhesive material.'

The invention was immediately successful on both sides of the Atlantic, and in America Jacob Durnton experimented further with Brockeden's idea. He discovered that the die and punch faces could be kept clean by adding small amounts of cocoa butter or mineral oil to the basic tablet ingredients, to act as lubricants.

Inevitably, there were experts who dismissed machine-made tablets as nothing more than a passing fancy, and one disgruntled apprentice wrote to the *Pharmaceutical Journal* asking whether he had trained for three years only to spend his future writing out labels and wrapping up bottles of factory-made tablets. Even at the end of the nineteenth century the *Pharmaceutical Journal* published an editorial stating that, 'Tablets have had their day ... and like every other form of drug preparation that has preceded them, will pass away to make room for something else.'

However, the profession and the public found tablets attractive and too simple to resist. They were easier to take and to carry around than powders or mixtures, and customers soon realised that the efficacy of individual tablets did not vary much. When machines began to turn out tablets by the thousand, the popularity of the tablet was confirmed. Within a few years of the registration of Brockeden's patent, small companies making compressed tablets had sprung up all over the world, and apothecaries had discovered that it was easier and cheaper to buy their finished tablets from a specialist supplier. Thus, the Industrial Revolution had its first direct effect on the medical profession and upon the medicines its members prescribed.

Chapter 30: Surgery Gains Status in France

Surgery progresses in France – The physicians object – The military influences on surgical developments – Larrey's contributions.

In most European countries, surgery was still in the hands of semi-literate incompetents but in France some progress had been made. The event which had enabled French surgeons to rise above their contemporaries in other parts of the world had been the effective treatment in 1686 of King Louis XIV's painful fistula by the surgeon Charles François Félix. Félix obviously dealt with the King's unfortunate condition to everyone's satisfaction, because his work earned him a farm, a title and a fee three times as great as the honorarium paid to the royal physician. Since physicians had always considered themselves to be superior to surgeons in social status and learning, this small operation was clearly of enormous significance both to Félix and to French surgeons in general.

Needless to say, the popularity of surgery as a speciality at the royal court did not meet with the French physicians' approval, and when another royal surgeon persuaded Louis XV to create five chairs of surgery at St. Come, the Paris faculty of physicians protested publicly and marched to St. Come through snow and sleet. The citizens who watched the extraordinary protest were not impressed by the physicians, and the march apparently ended in disarray. It had no effect on the King's decision.

The status of French surgeons was strengthened in 1731 with the founding of the first Academy of Surgery, and it was confirmed in 1743 when Louis XV ruled that barbers and wigmakers could no longer practice surgery and that all surgeons had to study and pass the requisite examinations. An illustrious surgeon from Montpelier, François de la Peyronie, who together with Félix's successor as royal surgeon, Georges Maréschal, had helped to found the Academy of Surgery, was one of the main forces behind this restrictive ordinance, which lasted until the

French Revolution some fifty years later.

While the French were establishing the basis of a power-ful surgical profession, physicians in other countries were still helping to ensure that surgery remained a subordinate craft. In Germany, in the eighteenth century, surgery was largely in the hands of the strolling bonesetters and barbers. In Britain, the surgeons had managed to separate themselves from the barbers in 1745, but the restrictions on unqualified surgeons applied only within a seven-mile radius of London. In the greater part of Britain surgery was still open to anyone who felt fit or able to practice it.

The French King's fistula had given surgery in France a head start over the profession in all other European countries. The French Revolution, and the wars that followed, helped to ensure that those studying and practising the art of surgery were able to obtain a good deal of experience. The same type of ex-perience was, of course, available to the surgeons of other ar-mies, but only the French seem to have had the basic training and education to benefit fully from it.

One man in particular, Dominique-Jean Larrey, is remem-bered for his reputation as a surgeon who succeeded in match-ing practical skills with a genuine affection both for his work and for the soldiers he was paid to look after. In general, mili-tary surgeons were not well loved, but Napoleon described Larrey as the 'most honest man and the best friend to the soldier that I ever knew' and explained that Larrey 'tormented the gen-erals, and disturbed them out of their beds at night whenever he wanted accommodations or assistance for the wounded or sick'. 'If the army were to raise a monument to the memory of one man,' Napoleon concluded, 'it should be to that of Larrey.'

To Larrey we owe the development of flying ambulances, clearing stations, base hospitals and efficient systems for deal-ing with battle casualties, but perhaps his most important con-tribution was his ability to make his soldier patients aware that he cared for them. He treated casualties according to their sur-gical need rather than their rank or nationality and made many friends throughout the army.

Larrey's popularity with the ordinary soldier can be judged from the fact that members of the Imperial Guard saved his life on several occasions, sharing their rations with him, wrapping him in their own clothes when he was cold and rescuing him when he was surrounded by Cossacks. Even when captured by the Prussians, Larrey's reputation as a generous and gentle surgeon led Field Marshal Blücher to provide him with an escort back to the French lines.

The history of surgery belongs almost exclusively to the French. The profession was founded during the Renaissance by Paré, it was given status and respectability in the seventeenth century by Félix, and its popular acceptance as a medical speciality was ensured by such men as Larrey at the end of the eighteenth century.

Chapter 31: The Apothecaries Gain Control

Changes in France following the Revolution – Laennec and the first stethoscope – Progress in all fields of medicine, but blood-letting continues – Robert Knox obtains anatomy specimens from dubious sources – Political changes within the medical profession – The Apothecaries Act in Britain

Many social, military, economic and cultural changes took place in the early decades of the nineteenth century. The establishment in Europe and America had been severely shaken by the events of the previous few years, and the long series of wars had produced great changes in living conditions.

As a direct result of all these changes the quality and availability of medical care changed dramatically in both the New and Old Worlds. Critical observers, such as Tenon, Pinel and Howard, helped to encourage the ordinary people to demand better health-care facilities, and for the first time angry citizens questioned those administrators whose regulations had in the past caused so much discomfort.

Things improved faster in France than anywhere else, probably because there the changes in the relationship between the official, political establishment and the general public had been greater than anywhere else in the world. Just before the French Revolution conditions in France were roughly as bad as they were anywhere else in Europe. Directly after the Revolution they were probably better in France than in most other European countries. However, improvements in the quality of medical care and the standard reached by medical practitioners changed quite dramatically all over Europe during this short period.

One reason for the dramatic improvements in France was that many of the men who had served in Napoleon's armies as surgeons later became important and effective members of the medical establishment. The fact that so many military surgeons made important contributions to the development of medicine as a useful, caring profession is a tribute not only to the democratic nature of the new post-Revolution French society but also to the quality of Larrey's fellow surgeons.

Marie-François-Xavier Bichat, for example, who died at the age of thirty-one in 1802, began his career as an army surgeon and yet produced some of the most notable early books on the importance of human anatomy to clinical surgeons and physicians. His influence spread around the world. Another former surgeon, René Théophile Hyacinthe Laennec, not only became a successful, well-respected hospital physician but also earned himself immortality by inventing the stethoscope, the first purely clinical instrument to have been designed solely to aid the diagnosis of disease.

Like other physicians of the time, Laennec had learned to listen to his patients' hearts and lungs by placing his ear directly on their chests – a technique that was not only invariably ineffective, occasionally impractical and sometimes embarrassing but also often quite unhygienic. While struggling to listen to the heart of an extremely fat patient, Laennec is said to have remembered watching two young children playing among a pile of logs in the Bois de Boulogne. The children had been tapping out signals to each other, one child tapping the log and the other listening by placing his ear against the other end. Attempting to copy this trick with a tube of rolled-up stiff paper, Laennec placed one end of the tube on the patient's chest, directly over the heart, and the other to his own ear. When he found that this simple instrument enabled him to listen to the human heart more effectively and more comfortably than before, he had a slim wooden cylinder made. This cylinder, the first stethoscope, was an instant success and was adopted by physicians all over Paris.

Men such as Bichat and Laennec, who had learned their profession through close contact with the ordinary people and who had considerable practical experience, were among the first of a new breed of caring, imaginative clinicians who helped to give the medical profession a much better reputation.

Like other clinicians in practice in those early years of the nineteenth century, they were, for the first time, putting the theoretical studies of the great medical scientists to practical use. Physicians throughout Europe and America were beginning to realise that they could use such instruments as the microscope to help them understand the pathology of specific disease processes. Two eighteenth-century scientists, Leopold Auenbrugger and Giovanni Battista Morgagni, had produced original work which had at the time had little effect on medical practice. Auenbrugger, a physician in Vienna, had discovered in 1751 that by tapping the chest it is possible to discover the presence of any fluid. He got the idea for his experiments in human percussion after watching wine merchants tapping barrels to see how much wine remained in each one.

Morgagni was the first real pathologist. In his book *De Sedibus et Causis Morborum* he showed that the study of dead bodies could provide real help for those concerned with the care of the living. In the early nineteenth century the work of these two men bore fruit and became generally accepted. Auenbrugger's percussion method was used alongside Laennec's stethoscope to aid in diagnosis, and Morgagni's teachings helped clinicians to judge the importance of post mortem findings.

The success of those early nineteenth-century clinicians can be judged from the fact that so many of them gave their names to diseases which had until that time remained a mystery. Richard Bright, Thomas Addison, Thomas Hodgkin and James Parkinson were just four members of the British medical profession to give their names to specific diseases. Many members of the profession made important contributions to medicine which are still of value today. One of the most extraordinary pieces of clinical research was done by William Beaumont, an American army surgeon who, in 1833, published a description of studies on the human stomach. The victim of his research was a French Canadian called Alexis St. Martin, who had received a gunshot wound which, on healing, had left part of his stomach on view to the outside world. Beaumont was able not only to watch St. Martin's stomach dealing with food but also to measure the quantity and quality of gastric juice produced. Beaumont began his studies in 1825 at an isolated military post in the forests of Michigan and studied Alexis St. Martin for several years. He showed that different foods have different effects on the stomach lining and that the production of stomach acid can be influenced by things other than food.

Despite these advances, the sagacity and acumen of the men who led the nineteenth-century revolution in clinical medicine must not be allowed to disguise the fact that the medical profession which provided general care for the public was not made up of an endless series of Laennecs and Beaumonts. There were many hundreds of doctors still practising medicine in the same dull, ineffective and dangerous way that it had been practised for centuries.

For example, blood-letting was still a principal therapeutic tool favoured by the majority of practising doctors. The fact that when blood was removed a patient would be quieter and have a lower temperature was considered a point in its favour by many practitioners. As far as the doctor was concerned, the main advantage of blood-letting was that it enabled him to do something which had an obvious effect on the patient and which did not cause any immediate and obvious harm. It was also easy to perform. Some practitioners would cut into a vein, some would deliberately cut into an artery, while others favoured cupping, a procedure which involved making a cut into the skin and then placing a cup-like instrument over the opening. A vacuum created within the cup by sucking out the air caused the blood to flow from the wound. Finally, there were the men who used leeches. The popularity of these creatures as a means of bloodletting increased rapidly during the nineteenth century: in 1824 two million were imported into France; by 1832 this figure had risen to fifty-seven million.

Medical education at this time was not always pursued without opposition, conflict or controversy. For example, the dissection of human cadavers had become an essential part of medical training, not only for the student anatomist but also for the clinician anxious to learn more about the pathology of human disorders, but while, in many parts of Europe, there was a plentiful supply of corpses for doctors to dissect, the ready availability of human material was not universal.

Until 1751, in Britain the only legally available corpses were the four criminals annually allocated to the Barber Surgeons' Company in London. After 1751 the law was changed to make the corpses of all executed criminals available to the dissectionists, but the old-fashioned habit of gibbeting corpses meant that there was still a shortage. This led to the growth of a night-time industry dedicated to supplying the medical profession with corpses.

One of the first men to follow Bichat's example and link anatomy with clinical science was the Edinburgh physician Robert Knox, who had also worked with Baron Larrey in Paris and whose attractive lecturing style kept the lecture theatre full – he is said to have had a regular class of over five hundred students. Unfortunately there was a shortage of cadavers at that time in

Edinburgh, and the unhappy Knox became involved in one of the great medical scandals of the century.

Bodies were obtained by people like Knox in a number of ways from a variety of sources. Poor people sometimes sold the bodies of their dying relatives, and corpses were sometimes removed from coffins by unscrupulous undertakers, who buried an earth-filled coffin and sold the corpse. A more dramatic method of obtaining fresh corpses was simply to dig them up. It is said that in Britain in the 1820s, a total of some two hundred men were busy digging up bodies and removing them from churchyards. Some of these early 'resurrectionists' were undoubtedly medical students or anatomy lecturers looking for material for themselves, but many were common criminals who would steal anything for a good price. Corpse-stealing had been an offence since 1788 but relatively few people were caught and, when they were, sentences were usually light.

There was, of course, one way to obtain corpses for dissection which did not involve skulking around in churchyards at the dead of night. Murder was the technique favoured by two Irishmen, Burke and Hare, in 1827. They began their careers on the fringe of medicine by selling the body of a dead lodger which was about the carted away for a pauper's funeral. Encouraged by the ease with which they made this sale, the two unemployed men then suffocated two more lodgers who seemed ill and apparently likely to die. Business continued to be profitable, and eventually Burke and Hare took their total number of victims to sixteen. All these bodies were happily bought by Dr Knox and his assistants.

When the two men were eventually caught, Hare turned King's evidence and as a result was allowed to leave Edinburgh, while Burke was hanged and later dissected by Professor Alexander Monro, who held the chair of anatomy at Edinburgh University. The unhappy Knox was virtually ruined by the scandal, since the body of one of the victims was found in his private dissecting room. The medical profession, which contained many men as guilty as Knox, managed to keep clear of the scandal.

The Burke and Hare murders resulted in the passing of an Anatomy Act in 1832 which ruled that all unclaimed dead bodies should go to the medical schools for dissection.

* * *

At the beginning of the nineteenth century, practising clinicians in Britain fell into one of four categories. First there were the university-trained physicians who had usually studied at either Oxford or Cambridge and were Fellows of the College of Physicians. These practitioners had usually acquired Fellowship of the College on the basis of their academic studies. They dressed immaculately and fashionably and wrote and spoke in 'dog Latin', but they were ignorant of the more practical side of clinical medicine. The physicians, who were few in number, provided most of the medical care for the London establishment but were not, at that time, considered to be specialists or in any way professionally superior to the apothecaries, who provided a similar service for the great majority of the population. Socially, however, qualified physicians were far superior to surgeons and apothecaries, and they were the only members of the medical profession who could expect to enter a large house through the front door – apothecaries and surgeons had to enter through the servants' or tradesmen's entrance.

The second group of medical professionals included the surgeons, who, since 1801, were also able to describe themselves as belonging to a Royal College. A licence from the College entitled a graduate surgeon to operate anywhere in Britain but did not allow him to prescribe remedies designed to deal with internal ailments.

In the third, and most important, group of medical professionals were the apothecaries, who provided medical care for the majority of people able to afford professional care. Although traditionally they had been trained to dispense medicines and although, by law, they were still not permitted to offer advice, in practice the apothecaries became Britain's general practitioners. In Italy, France and Germany the apothecaries were the forerunners of the pharmacists; in Britain they were the predecessors of today's family doctors and provided the main driving force behind the development of the modern medical profession.

Not all the people professionally involved with the care of the sick were qualified, of course, and even as the three established branches of the British medical profession grew in strength, so too did the stature and popularity of the fourth group: the quacks. Harley Street, for example, began its long association with the medical profession when an outrageous quack called St. John Long began to practise there. The demand for quacks was inevitable, since there were still relatively few qualified people available. In Lincolnshire, at the turn of the century, for example, it was reported that there were in practice five qualified physicians, eleven surgeons and apothecaries who had served their apprenticeships, twenty-five druggists who had received no training at all but who were engaged in the dispensing of medicines, sixty-three unqualified and untrained midwives, and forty quacks who had received no education at all. It is probably fair to estimate that less than a quarter of the medical practitioners in the north of England had any medical training.

However, the Industrial Revolution had increased the number of people who could afford to buy professional medical care, and many of these people were not satisfied with the attentions of an unqualified, uneducated quack. They wanted to be seen by someone who had been officially recognised and who had acknowledged qualifications.

Health professionals in all three branches of medicine were themselves eager to belong to a universally recognised association. They, like some of their patients, did not approve of quacks being allowed to practise unimpeded. Consequently, several new laws were proposed, designed to regulate the status and legal rights of those within the medical profession.

In 1806, for example, the Royal College of Physicians published a piece of proposed legislation in which it was suggested that Britain be divided into sixteen districts, each of which would be under the control of a resident physician who would award qualifications to people wishing to practise in his area and then charge each practitioner an annual fee. The Royal College of Physicians clearly wanted to take control of the entire British medical profession.

A second scheme, proposed by Dr Edward Harrison and supported by the Presidents of the Royal Society and the Royal College of Physicians and the Master of the Royal College of Surgeons, suggested that there should be a medical register for all physicians, surgeons, midwives, apothecaries, chemists and druggists. The scheme was abandoned, however, when the College of Physicians opposed it on the rather dubious ground that the new register would damage the supremacy of its members.

Finally, in 1815, the Apothecaries Act was passed. This most important piece of legislation made it compulsory for all new apothecaries to serve a five-year apprenticeship, study anatomy and physiology, walk the wards in a recognised hospital for at least six months, and pass an examination and obtain a licence before practising their profession. These regulations governed the whole country, and the apothecaries succeeded in outmanoeuvring the College of Physicians, whose members could now be prosecuted if they practised as apothecaries without an apothecary's licence. Qualified surgeons, who were members of the newly formed Royal College of Surgeons, formed an agreement with the apothecaries, and many of the more ambitious young practitioners sought qualifications from both the Society of Apothecaries and the Royal College of Surgeons.

Within fifteen years of the Act being passed, the Society of Apothecaries had won for its members the right to charge a fee both for providing advice and for dispensing medicines, and had therefore broken the dominance of the College of Physicians. Many of the newly registered apothecaries grouped together in the areas in which they practised to share scientific and medical experiences and to provide each other with professional and political support. One of the first of these societies was the Worcester Medical and Surgical Society, founded in 1816 by Charles Hastings. Hastings later founded the Provincial Medical and Surgical Association, a professional organisation which was to become better known as the British Medical Association.

The Society of Apothecaries soon began to take over the general control of medical care in Britain. The College of Physicians was reluctant to allow too many new fellows to be registered but the apothecaries were happy to meet the public demand for more doctors. By the 1840s, when the College of Physicians was still granting licences to only a handful of doctors at a time, the apothecaries were granting licences to hundreds of young men and carving for themselves a major slice of the medical profession's responsibilities in Britain.

Chapter 32: Killer Diseases Force Social Change

Smallpox, tuberculosis and cholera continue to threaten – The cholera epidemic in Europe produces improvements in public health – Chadwick's proposals – Dr John Snow and the Broad Street Pump – Potato blight in Ireland

At the beginning of the nineteenth century infectious diseases were still rife. Three of the most prevalent were smallpox, tuberculosis and cholera.

In the years since Jenner had published his inquiry into the *Causes and Effects of the Variolae Vaccine*, the number of people dying of smallpox around the world had fallen. But, although there was already powerful evidence to support the theory that vaccination saved lives, there were still many groups of people unprotected.

As the century began, there was a growing body of opinion opposed to vaccination in principle. Some opponents honestly felt that vaccination was a dangerous practice and pointed to occasional deaths as evidence. Other opponents of Jenner's scheme felt that compulsory vaccination programmes were an infringement of human rights, although they could not disagree with the thesis that one member of a community who refuses to

130

have a vaccination may provide a harbour for a virus which would otherwise be unable to survive.

In America, President Thomas Jefferson had suggested with considerable imagination that smallpox vaccine would not only provide those using it with protection but help to eradicate smallpox from the earth. But in Jenner's home country the argument raged for many years before mass vaccination programmes were introduced. It was a three-year epidemic which killed 41,000 people that finally produced the 1840 Vaccination Act – legislation which sounded the first peals of the death knell for the disease in Britain. Progress in the fight against smallpox elsewhere in Europe was intermittent. Napoleon had insisted that his soldiers be protected against smallpox, but later French leaders were not so enthusiastic, and in the Franco-Prussian war of 1870-71 more than 23,000 French soldiers died from the disease. The German generals who had insisted that their men be vaccinated lost only 278 men to smallpox.

As smallpox came under control, however, tuberculosis continued to kill or disable thousands. Caused by a bacterium which some believe to be the oldest living creature on earth, tuberculosis exists in two main forms – bovine and human. The bovine type is contracted by drinking milk from tuberculous cows, and since children drink more milk than most other members of society, bovine tuberculosis mainly affects children. The human type of tuberculosis, which spreads from person to person and affects the lungs, is also known as phthisis or consumption, and it was consumption which was largely responsible for the large number of deaths involving young adults in the nineteenth century.

In the rural areas of Europe during the fifteenth and sixteenth centuries, bovine tuberculosis (also known as scrofula or the King's Evil) was the commoner of the two types and affected many hundreds of thousands of youngsters. By the late seventeenth century, however, consumption was becoming more important as towns grew in size and the poor living and working conditions facilitated the spread of the disease. John Locke wrote in 1685 that a fifth of all the deaths in London that year were due to consumption. The Industrial Revolution made Western Europe and America a perfect breeding ground for the tubercle bacillus, and by the nineteenth century the disease was endemic. Consumption is said to have killed more people in nineteenth-century Britain than smallpox, scarlet fever, measles, whooping cough and typhus fever put together.

Even though men such as John Coakley Lettsom, who practised in Margate, England at the end of the eighteenth century, claimed that consumption could be prevented or cured by good food, sunlight, fresh air and rest, the social changes which accompanied the Industrial Revolution meant that the disease was allowed to continue to spread unchecked, and although there is some evidence to support the theory that, by the beginning of the nineteenth century, the disease had been around for so long that many families had acquired genetic resistance to it, consumption was still a major killer in all developing countries.

The third of this important trio of diseases, cholera, became important in Europe only during the nineteenth century. As trade with the East continued to expand, the cholera bacteria were transmitted from central India to China, Japan and Asiatic Russia, reaching Poland, Austria, Germany and Scandinavia by about 1829. During the next few years cholera travelled slowly but persistently across the whole of Europe. The natural history of the disease in Britain was typical of its progress in most European countries.

When cholera first arrived in Britain in 1831, it found an ideal environment: no large town had water safe to drink, and most of the rivers were polluted. The growing population in most towns crowded into the tiny back-to-back houses, and the average two-roomed house often had twenty people crammed into it, all using unhygienic privies which frequently overflowed into the yards and streets. The better-off families might have had fewer problems with their sewage disposal, but they had to take their fresh water supplies from the same polluted sources as everyone else. The lessons which had been learned had been long since forgotten, and the modern, growing towns were all run on exactly the same lines as medieval villages.

The cholera epidemic of 1831 obliged the authorities to consider what could be done to improve the general state of public health. Although the poor, who suffered more from cholera than the rich, sometimes claimed that the disease was due to deliberate poisoning, and the religious insisted that cholera was a punishment for immoral behaviour, most observers seemed to recognise that the epidemic was related in some way to the poor water supplies and sewerage facilities.

Of the many men who struggled to do something to improve the quality of public health care in Britain, one of the first and most far-sighted was the civil servant, lawyer and journalist Edwin Chadwick, whose ideas and innovations influenced events in America as well as Europe. Dismayed by the number of people killed by the cholera epidemic, Chadwick, who had been invited by the Government to help with Poor Law Reform, argued that proper sanitation facilities would not only improve the quality of life but also be of value in economic terms. This deliberate equation of good health and economic strength was not a new philosophy, as it had already been put forward in the seventeenth century by Sir William Petty. But, whereas Petty's arguments had gone more or less unnoticed, Chadwick's did not. The changing political climate in Britain in the early part of the nineteenth century, which had accompanied the drive for equality initiated by the working people as they became better off and better educated, meant that there was a genuine need for change. Since more working-class people now had political power, politicians were under more pressure to do something about the foul conditions in which the town dwellers usually lived.

Chadwick prepared and studied maps which showed where the worst death rates due to disease occurred. His figures showed that the average age at death was forty-three for gentlemen, thirty for tradesmen and twenty-two for labourers crowded together in the cities, and on the basis of these statistics concluded

133

that disease was spread by atmospheric pollution caused by over-crowding, poor water supplies, bad drainage and dirty towns. In his report entitled *A Report of an inquiry into the Sanitary Conditions of the Labouring Population of Great Britain*, which was published in 1842, Chadwick suggested that a circulatory system be used in towns and cities to supply water and remove waste products, showing that the authorities would actually save money by building proper facilities. A water board expert for the Trent River Water Works showed that, whereas when water supplied at high pressure tended to burst the traditional bored elm trunks, it did no damage at all to iron pipes, while a surveyor to the Holborn Sewers Commission produced evidence showing that narrow-bore drains which had smooth inside walls, cleaned themselves when water closets were used. Agreeing that it would cost money to build pumps to supply fresh water to town dwellers and to provide sewer pipes of the type he recommended, Chadwick suggested that sewage could be processed and sold to farms as valuable fertiliser.

Chadwick's recommendations were incorporated into a Public Health Act in 1848 and, although not all his ideas were accepted (it was cheaper to import Chilean guano as a fertiliser than to treat human sewage for the purpose), he made a great contribution to the quality of life in Britain. Almost alone, Chadwick provided the initial impetus which eventually gave us clean streets, clean water supplies and sewage disposal facilities.

The proposals put forward in the 1848 Act were given additional impetus by the second major epidemic of cholera, which began that year and proved to be the most widespread of the four outbreaks of cholera to affect Britain. In London alone the 1848-9 outbreak was responsible for the deaths of nearly fifteen thousand people; slightly more than six out of every thousand people died from the disease.

It was in London during that epidemic that the relationship between cholera and water supplies was first proved, by a doctor called John Snow. Deciding that the only explanation for the way the disease seemed to spread was that it was carried in water supplies, Snow argued that the solution was to keep sewage away from drinking-water supplies. He considered that, because the commonest symptoms, diarrhoea and vomiting, both involved the alimentary tract, the disease must be transmitted by something ingested rather than something carried in the air. He argued that an airborne contaminant would enter the lungs rather than the alimentary tract.

In 1849, when the second cholera outbreak hit London, Snow gave up his general practice in order to investigate his theory. His first conclusive proof came from a survey of the district around Golden Square in the centre of London. At that time piped water was not supplied to all houses in the area, and the people took their water from pumps and wells. A pump in Broad Street supplied the majority of local inhabitants, and Snow's enquiries revealed that a cholera epidemic in the area was linked directly to the use of the Broad Street pump. A later investigation showed that the brick lining of a cesspool about three feet away from the well was cracked and decayed, and it seems likely that this was responsible for contaminating the previously drinkable water from the Broad Street pump. To prevent the further spread of cholera, Snow recommended that the pump's handle be removed so that water could no longer be drawn.

The evidence was complete when Snow began to compare the incidence of cholera in areas of London supplied by different water companies. He found, for example, that customers of the Southwark and Vauxhall Water Company, which supplied water from the polluted lower reaches of the River Thames, were far more likely to get cholera than customers of the Lambeth Water Company, which took its water from a pure source.

As a result of social pressures and the work of men like Chadwick and Snow, by the middle of the nineteenth century the taming had begun of these three major killers: smallpox, cholera and tuberculosis. Many more people would die before the diseases could be described as under control, but there is no doubt that the devastation they had wrought during the latter

135

part of the eighteenth century was being neutralised. Jenner's vaccination was conquering smallpox, while tuberculosis and cholera were soon to be brought under control by improvements in living conditions and standards of public hygiene.

Finally, there is one other 'disease' not usually included in books devoted to the history of medicine which should be mentioned here. When the Irish potato crop was destroyed by the blight in 1845 the resulting famine produced far-reaching international social, political and economic effects which equalled those produced by the infectious diseases directly affecting man.

Since it had been introduced into the European diet by Sir Walter Raleigh at the end of the sixteenth century, the potato had become a staple part of the daily diet in many countries. In Ireland in particular, where crops were not good and animal farming was not as widespread as elsewhere, the importance of the potato is difficult to overemphasise. The whole Irish economy depended on potatoes, which were eaten, used as pig food or sold, and the blight of 1845 was nothing less than a national disaster. Two or three million Irish people died from starvation as a result of the disease, and the final effects of that historic crop failure were still noticeable decades later, not just in Ireland but in other countries too.

The most obvious and immediate result of the Irish potato blight in England, for example, was the repeal of the Corn Laws. Passed in 1815 in an attempt to restore agricultural prosperity to a farming community threatened with ruin by the fall in prices at the end of the Napoleonic Wars, the Corn Laws had never been popular with town dwellers or the British poor in general. When the Irish potato crop failed, corn was in tremendous demand, and prices rose naturally, with the result that it was no longer necessary, or even practical, to maintain prices at an artificially high level. Other political and economic factors were involved in the decision to repeal the Corn Laws but the situation in Ireland was certainly of significance.

The extent of the famine in Ireland also resulted in the mass emigration of many Irish nationals. Some left to live in

England, while others travelled in the opposite direction to look for their fortunes in America. Many twentieth-century Irish-Americans are the descendants of those migrants who left Ireland to escape the famine and look for food, work and new homes.

As an influence on international social history, potato blight must take its place alongside smallpox, plague and cholera.

Chapter 33: The Hazards of Industry

Britain's industrial dominance built on the backs of little girls – The first investigation of health hazards resulting from the Industrial Revolution – The Factory Act

As the Industrial Revolution continued to change working conditions throughout the world, it became clear that employers would not be prepared to make improvements designed to protect their employees until forced to do so by government legislation.

By the end of the eighteenth century British factories were employing women on heavy, dirty work and using the services of young children. Children between the ages of five and twelve had been taken away from rural villages to work under foul conditions in the growing towns. William Cobbett, the social historian and author, claimed that England was building her industrial dominance on the backs of thirty thousand little girls.

Protesting loudly at these accusations, factory owners claimed that the nation's status depended on a large workforce, and profitability depended upon machinery being in use for as many hours as possible. The tools and equipment originally introduced to help men work more efficiently and effectively were rapidly becoming far more important than the human beings who operated them.

In Britain two Acts of Parliament (the Health and Morals of Apprentices Act of 1802 and the Factory Act of 1819) introduced some controls, ruling that children had to be at least nine years old before they could be employed, and later legislation reduced their maximum working day to ten hours, but the great advances in legislative control did not take place until after a British clinician had published his studies of some of the real problems then existing.

The first member of the medical profession to investigate the health hazards associated with industrial employment, Charles Turner Thackrah, worked in Leeds, a city where it was said there were more than 120 known trades and occupations.

Thackrah's book, entitled *The effects of the Principal Arts, Trades and Professions, and of Civic States and habits of Living, on Health and Longevity, with Suggestions for the Removal of many of the Agents which produce Disease and shorten the Duration of Life* and published in 1831, helped to encourage other members of the medical profession to take an interest in the enormous range of occupational diseases affecting the working population. In the book Thackrah describes how, despite the existing legislation, children aged seven had to start work at half past five in the morning and work through until seven in the evening with only a forty-minute break. It is not difficult to imagine the damage that such working conditions could do to growing children. In addition to the bald facts, however, Thackrah made numerous practical suggestions about ways in which workers could be protected from the disorders normally associated with their working conditions. He suggested, for example, that men whose work involved mining and grinding should be provided with masks in addition to proper ventilation, and pointed out that research had already been published showing that fork-grinders in Sheffield, who used a dry grindstone, usually died at the age of thirty, while knife-grinders, who worked on wet stones, usually lived to between forty and fifty years of age.

Thackrah died of tuberculosis at the age of thirty-seven, two years after his book was published, but in the same year as his death the Factory Act of 1833 was passed. This effective piece of legislation ruled that no one under eighteen years of age should work at night, nor for more than twelve hours a day or sixty-nine hours a week. The minimum age for young workers was set at nine years, and employers were required to see a certificate proving a child's age signed by a medical man, before they could employ children. To make sure that the Act was being properly applied, a system of factory inspections by government-employed officials was set up.

During the rest of the nineteenth century industrial medicine increased in importance, and new laws were passed in other countries to control conditions of employment. But that Act of 1833 was the first and most important breakthrough to be made in the fight to protect the health of industrial workers, and Charles Thackrah was the man who first succeeded in putting Ramazzini's theories into practice.

Chapter 34: Nursing Becomes a Profession

Hospital care before the nineteenth century – Fliedner's establishment leads the way – Elizabeth Fry and Theodor Fliedner – A birth in Florence

Advances in hospital organisation and nursing had been few and largely insignificant during the otherwise tempestuous first half of the nineteenth century. From the Renaissance until the end of the eighteenth century nursing had remained largely in the hands of the members of those religious orders who had dedicated themselves to the care of the sick. Although the ability of these nursing nuns to alleviate physical pain and suffering was unremarkable, they were undoubtedly able to contribute a great deal to the mental and spiritual welfare of their patients.

At the end of the eighteenth century the Church's role in caring for the sick had diminished dramatically. In France, for example, the Church-run hospitals had been taken over by the state in 1789, while reports on the horrors of institutional care produced by such men as Tenon and Howard had resulted in the rebuilding and reorganisation of some hospitals. Together these changes meant that nursing care was no longer the prerogative of the nuns, and there was now a growing demand for nursing assistants without ecclesiastical connections.

Yet, despite the political changes which had taken place at the end of the eighteenth century and the many scientific advances in medicine, hospitals were still stuffy, smelly and overcrowded and their nursing staff poorly paid and treated as domestic servants. A nurse might expect £5 a year for being in sole charge of seventeen beds for thirteen hours a day. There was no equipment, nor were many drugs widely available. Newly recruited nurses received no medical training and were expected merely to carry out fundamental household chores. There was no working relationship between nurses and midwives, nor between nurses and doctors.

Genuinely overworked and certainly underpaid, the professional nurse undoubtedly had a hard life. One woman in charge of a ward full of sick and dying patients would have found herself fully occupied in looking after the basic needs of those patients, with very little time left for more than cleaning and feeding them. Under these circumstances it is hardly surprising that the early nineteenth-century professional nurses acquired something of a reputation as heavy drinking whores. With alcohol and opium the only readily available drugs to have any definite sedative effect, there was probably no shortage of either in hospitals, and the overworked, unhappy nurses can hardly be blamed if from time to time they succumbed to the temptation to drown their miseries. Nor is it very surprising that some nurses took advantage of the ready availability of raunchy, lecherous medical students to earn a little extra money.

This enormous social, intellectual and economic chasm dividing nurses and doctors would undoubtedly have continued to exist but for the fact that during the nineteenth century several educated, intelligent and wealthy young ladies began to take an interest in the care of the sick and dying. Inspired by a desire to help others and fired by a mixture of religious zeal and subconscious guilt, these young ladies were not impressed with the idea of removing bundles of dirty straw or sweeping out fouled wards. They wanted more personal contact with their patients and obtained more satisfaction from sitting with, talking to and soothing the sick and troubled than from working alongside the professional nurses who were expected to work with broom and pail. It was from this class of amateur nurse that the revolutionaries in nursing care were to come.

The first major step towards the development of an organised, trained, properly administered nursing profession was taken in Germany, in a village called Kaiserwerth by Pastor Theodor Fliedner and his wife Friederike who, in 1833, opened a training school where, together, they intended to help discharged female prisoners become nurses. Fliedner and his wife recognised that nursing involves more than a series of basic domestic chores, acknowledged the need to provide potential nurses with some form of specific training and managed to organise a practical training programme.

Fliedner's establishment was the prototype for similar training schools later to be built in places as far apart as Scandinavia and the United States, but it was the visits made to his village by two British women which were to lead directly to the massive changes which produced the highly organised and well-established nursing profession we have today.

The first of these visitors was Elizabeth Fry, the daughter of a wealthy Quaker banker, who went to Germany in 1840 and was immensely impressed by what she saw. In fact, she had been instrumental in Fliedner's decision to start training nurses, since, when he had visited London in 1822, it was her work on prison reform which had most impressed him. Her recommendations on Newgate Prison had involved suggestions that prisoners be separated according to their sex and that they be given job training, so that on leaving prison they would be able to find some useful employment. In accordance with this suggestion, Fliedner's original plan had been to provide training for discharged female prisoners in the hope that they would be able to stay out of trouble.

The fact that he had chosen to train them as nurses was an additional bonus which so impressed Mrs Fry that, on her return to London, she opened Britain's first nursing school.

Like Fliedner, Elizabeth Fry based her training programme on religion, believing that nursing was and should be a Christian vocation. Her aim was to attract women willing to devote themselves 'to the glory of God and the mitigation of human suffering', and she never disguised the fact that, although the sick would undoubtedly benefit, the work would also be a type of religious martyrdom.

The efforts of both Fliedner and Mrs Fry were genuine and well intentioned but they lacked the fierce determination that was necessary to turn a vocation into a respected profession. They did not know that, at about the time of their first meeting in London, a Mr and Mrs Nightingale were staying at a villa in Florence where Mrs Nightingale was expecting her second child.

A few decades later, christened with the name of her birthplace, Miss Nightingale was to stamp her personality indelibly on the developing nursing profession.

Chapter 35: Florence Nightingale's Contribution

Florence Nightingale's decision – Florence studies hospital reports and meets Pastor Fliednor – The Crimean War – Florence is a heroine – New hospital designs

To judge from her own notes and private diaries, Florence Nightingale was a sensitive, imaginative, emotional and excitable child. Born in Italy and brought up by parents who considered European travel a normal part of everyday living, she had plenty of opportunity to see all aspects of human life. It was not long before she began to feel a desire to help the sick and the poor and to do something to relieve their pains and anxieties and as the years went by the more determined she became to ease the suffering of those less fortunate than herself.

In 1844 she decided to dedicate her whole life to the care of the sick. For a young woman from a prosperous background this was, to say the least, an unusual decision. Young women of good birth had spent time with the sick before, it is true, but their efforts had been strictly confined. Most had spent odd hours sitting with and talking to the sick, visiting them in their own homes and providing food and clothing. Professional nurses, however, had always been either dedicated members of a religious order or domestic servants who worked in hospitals because they could not obtain posts in private houses.

When Florence finally plucked up the courage to tell her parents her plans, they were horrified. Despite the work of Pastor Fliedner in Germany and Elizabeth Fry in Britain, hospitals were still invariably dirty, insanitary places largely staffed by dirty, insanitary women. The windows of most wards were boarded or bricked up to retain heat, and beds were crowded together. Patients came mostly from tenements or terraced houses, or from the streets. Bed linen was not usually changed between patients, and the nurses did not have the time to wash patients properly.

Despite her parents' reluctance, Florence remained determined and began to prepare herself by reading every hospital report she could lay her hands on and studying the public health reports that were beginning to appear in the late 1830s and early 1840s. Not satisfied with British reports, she succeeded in obtaining information about hospitals in Paris and Berlin. When she travelled abroad with her parents, she took every opportunity to visit hospitals of all kinds to study the facilities available. She was training herself to be the first practical hospital administrator.

In 1850, while in Germany, she managed to fit in a visit to Pastor Fliedner in Kaiserwerth. It was that visit which finally convinced Florence Nightingale that she had chosen the right profession and that, whatever her friends and family might say about it, her life was destined to be spent in caring for the sick. Full of enthusiasm, fired by the Kaiserwerth experiment and determined to ensure that some of what she had seen in Germany should be put into practice in Britain, she immediately wrote a pamphlet entitled *The Institution of Kaiserwerth on the Rhine for the Practical Training of Deaconesses, under the direction of the Rev. Pastor Fliedner, embracing the support and care of a Hospital, Infant & Industrial Schools, and a Female Penitentiary.* It was the first of a number of important publications devoted to the organisation and administration of hospitals to come from Florence Nightingale.

Three years later Miss Nightingale got her first chance to put into practice the information she had been so carefully collecting for the previous decade. The Institution for the Care of Sick Gentlewomen in Distressed Circumstances was about to undergo a reorganisation. Florence managed to obtain the post of Superintendent to organise the changes and to be in charge of the management of the Institution's new residential buildings.

The committee which governed the charity had taken on rather more than they had imagined. Miss Nightingale soon made it clear that she knew what was right and that everyone else should agree with her.

She arranged for call bells to be installed so that nurses could see instantly which patients required help. She insisted that the Institution should accept patients of all denominations. She made it clear that she considered clean beds and fresh linen essential. She signed tough contracts with wholesalers for supplies and refused to accept delivery if the goods were not up to standard. She was, in short, the very epitome of the classic senior hospital sister: brusque, determined and fearsome. Yet at the same time she cared deeply for the women in the Institution and they, recognising that her aggressive attitude was fired on their behalf, were more than fond of her.

To those who knew her, it must have been obvious that Florence Nightingale was not going to be satisfied running a small hospital in London for ever. She had greater things in mind.

While Miss Nightingale was running her small hospital in Harley Street, an enormous row was building up in Britain over the conditions said to be facing the British soldiers fighting the Crimean war. The controversy raged over the barracks at Scutari, which were said by *The Times* correspondent to be totally unsuitably prepared for the care of the sick and wounded, with too few surgeons, no nurses and no dressings.

Disturbed by the story, the Secretary of War, Sidney Herbert, wrote officially to Florence Nightingale asking her to go to Scutari and organise a proper hospital there. 'There is but one person in England that I know of', he wrote, 'who would be capable of organising and superintending such a scheme.' Mr Herbert need not have bothered. Florence Nightingale had the same idea and, as his letter to her was in the post, one from her to him was also on its way. Miss Nightingale told him that she had already organised a small group of nurses to travel to Scutari.

With government backing Miss Nightingale's small group grew to thirty-eight: some were professional nurses who had volunteered because the wages were good; others were nuns. Their nursing experience was as mixed as their religious backgrounds, but that small party changed many people's attitudes towards nursing and indeed proved to be a turning point in the history of hospital management as well as of general nursing care.

In the chaos that preceded her journey the death rate among the wounded at Scutari had been forty-two per cent. In the order that followed her arrival it fell to two per cent. There could have been no better proof of the efficacy of her methods.

When she returned from the Crimea, Florence Nightingale was a national heroine. Her uncompromising attitude towards the reactionary military authorities on behalf of the sick and wounded British soldiers had proved so popular that the staggering sum of £50,000 was raised on her behalf to found a school for nurses at St. Thomas's Hospital in London. The nurses who qualified there spread 'the Gospel according to Florence' to other major British hospitals, and within a few years every major hospital had its own training school. In a comparatively short time the nursing profession was established as a respectable, worthwhile part of the medical profession.

Florence Nightingale's influence was not confined solely to the organisation of nurses. In the years after the Crimean War she became known as an authority on the design and equipping of hospitals. She understood that fresh air, clean water and plenty of sunlight are essential to good health, and she always insisted that hospitals should be designed in such a way that the task of keeping them clean would not be too difficult. She recommended that hospitals be built in a 'pavilion' style with large wards and plenty of light and space, so that her nurses could move about easily and have a good view of their patients. She also believed in building hospitals with plenty of garden space so that patients could convalesce by walking among the lawns and flowers.

Nor was Florence Nightingale's influence limited to her home country. All over Europe and in America nursing schools were set up according to her design, and her publication *Notes on Nursing* was considered essential reading for all who intended to enter the nursing profession. Her impact also had a powerful effect on Jean Henri Dunant, the Swiss banker who founded the International Committee of the Red Cross and who was responsible for the Geneva Convention.

In 1872, when visiting London, Dunant read a paper in which he admitted that, 'Though I am known as the founder of the Red Cross and the originator of the Convention of Geneva, it is to an English-woman that all the honour of that Convention is due. What inspired me...was the work of Miss Florence Nightingale in the Crimea.'

Chapter 36: Proponents of Hygiene

The cause of infection is still a puzzle – Oliver Wendell Holmes has an idea – Dr Semmelweiss and puerperal fever

In the early sixteenth century Girolamo Fracastoro had suggested that infection might be caused by micro-organisms, and in the seventeenth century Leeuwenhoek had seen these minute organisms under one of his microscopes, but the fact that unhygienic habits might be related to the spread of micro-organisms and the consequent spread of disease seems to have escaped observers until well into the nineteenth century.

One disease that had always been closely associated with hospitals was puerperal fever, a disorder which affects women after childbirth and which Hippocrates had recognised as being both fatal and contagious. The first doctor to recognise that puerperal fever might be prevented by keeping the maternity ward as clean as possible was a Manchester surgeon called Charles White who practised in the late eighteenth century. Unfortunately for several million women, White's observations and recommendations attracted little attention, and lying-in wards remained dirty, dangerous places until well into the nineteenth century.

In 1843 the American poet, novelist, anatomist and lecturer Oliver Wendell Holmes read to the Boston Society for Medical Improvement a paper *On the Contagiousness of Puerperal Fever*, in which he explained his theory that the disease can be carried from patient to patient by doctors themselves. He recommended that pregnant women in labour should not be attended by doctors who had been in contact with possible sources of infection.

Holmes also suggested that surgeons should consider changing their clothes and washing their hands in calcium chloride after leaving a patient with puerperal fever. His controversial lecture, however, annoyed a large part of the medical establishment, and his advice was ignored completely.

A similar fate befell Ignaz Philipp Semmelweiss who, in 1846, at the age of twenty-eight, became an assistant in one of the obstetric wards at the Allgemeines Krankenhaus in Vienna. Semmelweiss noticed that the number of women dying in his ward was considerably higher than that in another obstetric ward at the hospital. Indeed, the difference was so noticeable that women frequently begged in tears not to be taken into Semmelweiss's ward.

Deciding that the difference in the number of deaths had to be due to something other than the quality of his own clinical skills, Semmelweiss looked for an explanation. It lay in the fact that the ward with the better survival rate was looked after by the hospital's midwives, while in his own ward medical students assisted the obstetricians with deliveries. Semmelweiss discovered that students came into the ward straight from the dissecting room and often performed intimate examinations with hands which only minutes before had been delving into corpses. The midwives, on the other hand, never went near the dissecting room and, on the contrary, had been taught that cleanliness is an important part of obstetric care.

Semmelweiss's theory that the women were contracting puerperal fever from the students was strengthened when he attended the post mortem on another doctor in the hospital. This unfortunate man, a Dr Kolletschka, had died from a wound he had received in the dissecting room, and when his body was opened, Semmelweiss noticed that the internal pathological signs were similar to those seen in women with puerperal fever.

Convinced that his theory about the spread of infection was correct, Semmelweiss insisted that students and doctors coming from the dissecting room should wash their hands in a solution of calcium chloride before examining female patients. The precautions he introduced produced a dramatic drop in the number of deaths on his ward, from one in ten to approximately one in a hundred within two years.

Like Oliver Wendell Holmes, Semmelweiss came under a tremendous amount of pressure from those colleagues at the hospital, and many other eminent obstetricians, who disagreed with his theory, despite its dramatic proof. Unable to cope with the opposition Semmelweiss left Vienna for Budapest, where he eventually became Professor of Obstetrics. Unfortunately, the pressure brought about by the controversy proved too much for this mild and thoughtful man and he died in a mental hospital a few years later. The history of medicine is full of men whose original work has been ignored or condemned by the establishment of the day. But no martyr in medicine suffered more, or contributed more, than Ignaz Semmelweiss, whose courage and persistence eventually led directly to changes in medical practice which resulted in massive improvements in the quality of obstetric care throughout the world.

Chapter 37: Women in Medicine

Charles Darwin and the concept of evolution – Medical education under discussion – The first woman doctor qualifies

While doctors, such as John Snow, continued to fight for the improvement of public health facilities and as the newly born pharmaceutical industry began to blossom into the beginnings of the massive international industry which exists today, scientists and clinicians in many parts of the world continued to add to the rapidly expanding library of information on human anatomy, physiology and pathology.

The nineteenth century witnessed the great contributions to science of such men as Charles Darwin who gathered information on the similarities and differences between hundreds of plants and animals, a meticulous and detailed study which finally provided him with the first solid evidence in support of the theory of evolution.

While scientific research and discovery advanced, members of the medical profession in many parts of the world were still looking for ways to organise and rationalise programmes of medical education and registration.

In the United Kingdom, for example, apothecaries, physicians and surgeons were still arguing and negotiating in the search for a satisfactory legislative compromise which would ensure that only qualified individuals were entitled to practise medicine. Although the Society of Apothecaries had control over apothecaries practising in England and Wales, there were still more than a score of different bodies with the right to permit students to practise medicine. Many of these were entitled only to allow their graduates to practise within strictly defined geographical areas. For example, while the Royal College of Surgeons in Edinburgh could allow its graduates to practise in the three Lothians, Fife, Roxburgh, Berwick, Selkirk and Peebles, the Faculty of Physicians and Surgeons of Glasgow was the exclusive licensing authority for Lanark, Renfrew, Ayre, Burgh and Dumbarton.

Several attempts were made to rationalise and reorganise these different licensing bodies and although, in 1844, the Home Secretary, James Graham, drafted a Bill designed to regulate the medical profession throughout the United Kingdom, it was not until 1858 that the Medical Act, which did succeed in regulating the medical profession as a whole, was eventually passed.

The aim of the Medical Act was to ensure that all medical graduates had the same basic qualification, so that citizens and local authorities throughout the United Kingdom would be able to recognise at once a fully qualified medical practitioner who had been deemed competent by the officially recognised authorities. Qualified practitioners were listed in a register set up by the newly formed General Medical Council (GMC). Anyone not registered with the GMC could still practise but could not claim to be qualified.

At first, any doctor with either a surgical or a medical qualification was entitled to be registered, and it was not until nearly thirty years later that all graduates had to be qualified in both medicine and surgery, as they do today.

An account of the scientific and political changes affecting the medical profession in these middle years of the nineteenth century would not be complete without a description of the impact made by a young American woman, Elizabeth Blackwell.

It is sometimes said that Dr Blackwell was the first woman doctor, but it is more accurate to say that she was the first female member of the newly organised profession. Although there

150

had been women surgeons and physicians in ancient Greece and Egypt, in post-Renaissance Britain women had been banished from the official medical establishment. They were, of course, allowed to continue to practise unofficially as midwives and as advisers in country areas, but they were denied the opportunity to acquire official status.

The changes which took place in medical education in the eighteenth and nineteenth centuries meant that, in many parts of the world, traditional women practitioners were being effectively forced out of business. The new laws introduced rules which meant that only the qualified could claim to practise medicine under official approval, and at the same time the new rules maintained the tradition that only men could qualify to practise medicine. Women, for so long the mainstays of the medical profession for the ordinary people, were being forced into a subordinate role and denied the opportunity to practise medicine at all.

Refused admission by the larger and better-established American medical schools, Elizabeth Blackwell managed to find a smaller medical school, Geneva Medical College, to allow her to enrol as a student. After completing her academic studies, Dr Blackwell travelled to Europe and worked in both Paris and London before finally settling down to practise in New York, where she and her newly qualified sister set up both an infirmary and a women's medical college.

In Britain the first woman to qualify was Elizabeth Garrett, who had met Dr Blackwell in London and subsequently decided on a career in medicine. For four years, from 1861 to 1865, the determined Miss Garrett seems to have applied to every college and hospital offering courses in medical education. Eventually, the Society of Apothecaries agreed to admit her as a medical practitioner if she could produce the necessary certificates showing that she had reached the required state of proficiency. It seems likely that the Society had considered it almost impossible for Miss Garrett to qualify under these restrictions.

To everyone's surprise, however Miss Garrett did obtain the certificates and passed the entrance examination. Within a few years Miss Garrett, and those who followed her, had succeeded in influencing public opinion so that more and more medical schools began to accept women as students. Similar changes occurred in other parts of Europe, and within a few years women were admitted to the medical registers in Switzerland, Germany and the Netherlands. By the end of the century women in medical schools around the world were qualifying as doctors.

Chapter 38: Solving Problems in Surgery

Surgery is still a primitive science – Two major problems remain: pain and infection – The first anaesthetics – Queen Victoria makes a point – Infection still kills in the operating theatres – Joseph Lister and his theory – The influence of Pasteur – Surgery catches up

By the middle of the nineteenth century, there had been developments in public health and community hygiene, improvements in working conditions and the organisation and administration of the medical profession. Pastor Fliedner, Elizabeth Fry and Florence Nightingale had taken the first steps towards establishing nursing as a respectable profession and physicians, such as René Laennec, had made positive contributions to the quality of practical clinical care. The American Oliver Wendell Holmes and the Austrian Semmelweiss had described the hazards associated with dirty hospital wards, and the Englishman Charles Darwin had made an enormous contribution to the understanding of the development of the human body.

But surgery was still a very primitive science, and few noticeable changes had taken place, either in the practice of the speciality or in the number of patients surviving. Surgeons had their own college and were accepted as academic and social equals by most other members of the medical profession, but their effectiveness was still very much in question.

When Paré and the other Renaissance surgeons had been in practice, four major problems made life difficult for the surgeon and dangerous for the patient – ignorance of human anatomy, a need to arrest the inevitable bleeding that occurs at operation, and an inability to control pain and infection.

By the middle of the nineteenth century most surgeons had a good grasp of human anatomy, thanks to the work of such men as Vesalius, and the fact that all students had the opportunity not only to watch their lecturers opening and carefully dissecting cadavers but also to dissect at least one dead human body for themselves. Improvements in surgical technique, introduced by Paré and others, meant that bleeding was no longer an insuperable problem for the skilled surgeon. However, the last two difficulties associated with surgery – pain and infection – unhappily remained unsolved, and both made surgery hazardous for the patient and unsatisfying for the surgeon.

Although adequate supplies of opium were available for the treatment of post-operative pain, even this powerful drug had its limitations, and patients frequently had to be held down by strong assistants while the surgeon operated.

Infection was still a major cause of operative failure. In 1850 nearly half of the amputations performed proved fatal because of gangrene, and one of the best surgeons in Berlin is reputed to have thrown down his scalpel and refused ever to operate again after ninety per cent of his patients had died from infection.

In an attempt to deal with these two remaining hazards, most nineteenth-century surgeons had developed the habit of working as fast they could. One surgeon is said to have taken off a patient's arm while a colleague turned round to take a pinch of snuff, while a gruesome entry in the *Guinness Book of Records* shows that a Scottish surgeon, Robert Liston, is said to hold the world record for the fastest amputation of a limb. He was timed at thirty-three seconds for an operation to remove a patient's leg at the thigh, but, unfortunately, he was so fast that his assistant could not get his fingers out of the way in time. In

addition to the patient's leg, three of the assistant's fingers succumbed to the saw and found their way into the waste bucket.

It was clear to anyone interested in medicine that the practice of surgery could not progress until these two major problems had been overcome. Someone, somewhere, would have to
come up with an effective way of numbing the patient, so that
operations could be carried out without the pain proving intol-
erable to both patient and surgeon. And it would also be necessary to find some way to prevent infection setting in during or
after an operation.

The first of these two problems, that of finding some way
to numb the patient during an operation so that he neither suffered nor made the surgeon's work impossible, was the first to
be solved.

Over the centuries many attempts had been made by surgeons and scientists to develop an effective form of anaesthesia,
and dozens of different techniques had been tried. Herodotus
described how hashish was used as an anaesthetic; Dioscorides
had described how a patient could be made drunk and insensible
by giving him an alcoholic extract of Mandragora; the Chinese
introduced opium; Paré had experimented with compression,
pressing firmly on a carotid artery in the neck to make the patient unconscious; John Hunter had used tourniquets and had
tried freezing the patient; and more modern surgeons had experimented with Mesmerism.

But all these methods had their drawbacks, the main one
being that, if the patient was anaesthetised sufficiently to avoid
pain, he could not always be aroused again afterwards.

The first genuinely effective and safe anaesthetic to be
developed was nitrous oxide. It was first used in 1799 by Sir
Humphry Davy, the inventor of the miner's lamp which bears
his name. Sir Humphry, in pain because of an erupting wisdom
tooth, experimented upon himself with the gas and found that it
provided considerable relief. He realised that nitrous oxide might
have a use in surgery, but his discovery seems to have gone
more or less unnoticed by the medical profession, who regarded

'laughing gas' as suitable for drawing-room games but not for the operating theatre. Michael Faraday, then a pupil of Sir Humphry's, described the anaesthetic qualities of ether, but his observations were also ignored by the medical establishment.

It was in America that these anaesthetic gases were first used in earnest, and it seems that a dentist called William Thomas Green Morton was the first man to anaesthetise a patient publicly in a hospital operating theatre. This operation, which took place at the Massachusetts General Hospital in 1846 and involved the removal of a tumour from the neck of a patient under an ether anaesthetic, alerted the surgical world to the possibilities and advantages offered by proper anaesthetics. Before the end of the year the technique was being used in Europe.

Interestingly, Robert Liston was the first European surgeon to operate on a patient who had been anaesthetised, but he does not seem to have been able to forget his habit of operating at speed. His first operation is said to have involved the amputation of a leg and to have been done in a time rivalling his own world record.

Technical advances in anaesthesia followed quickly but the major problem facing surgeons now was not a technical one but a social one. The difficulty was produced by the fact that several surgeons had begun using the anaesthetic gas chloroform on women for relief of pain in childbirth.

This horrified many male religious leaders who argued that it was unnatural for a woman to suffer no pain while giving birth. The anguished spokesmen quoted the Bible, and in particular the passage in which God says to Eve, 'In sorrow thou shalt bring forth children', as support for their opposition to anaesthesia. Dr James Simpson, who had introduced chloroform anaesthesia in midwifery, was not about to be out-manoeuvred, however, and he quickly quoted another passage from the Bible which states, 'And the Lord God caused a deep sleep to fall upon Adam and he slept; and He took one of his ribs and closed up the flesh instead thereof.'

Heaven only knows how long this theological gamesmanship would have continued if the anaesthetists had not been allowed to play a trump card and effectively put an end to all opposition. Their trump was no other than Queen Victoria, who, in 1853, gave birth to Prince Leopold while under the influence of chloroform administered by Dr John Snow; the same Dr Snow, incidentally, whose work on cholera and the Broad Street pump helped lead to the provision of cleaner water supplies in London.

With anaesthesia fashionable and given the royal approval, the religious arguments against it were quickly forgotten, and the opposition that had threatened to make any form of anaesthesia unacceptable, under any conditions whatsoever, melted away overnight. Over the next few years it became accepted that all operations would be conducted using anaesthesia.

The effect on surgeons and the practice of surgery was most remarkable. Whereas before they had had to concentrate on finishing an operation as quickly as possible, surgeons could now take their time and carefully plan their operations.

The conquest of pain by the introduction of anaesthesia marked the beginning of the modern era in surgery. However, post-operative infections were still killing many patients, and the full effects of the introduction of anaesthesia could not be appreciated until some means had been found to minimise the risk of a patient on the operating table contracting a fatal infection.

Dealing with the problem of infection as it affected surgical problems was still something of a nightmare for thinking surgeons. Earlier in the nineteenth century the American Wendell Holmes and the Austrian Semmelweiss had both realised that puerperal fever could be prevented by keeping doctors, patients and wards as clean as possible. But still no surgeon practised any sort of caution when operating. Indeed, on the contrary, many surgeons seemed to practise in such a way as to invite infection, wiping their instruments on their blood- and pus-stained coat tails, while their assistants carried needles threaded with silk for sutures in their coat lapels. One eminent New York surgeon is said to have whetted his scalpel on the sole of his shoe.

Dirty hands, clothes and instruments, and unwashed patients, must have made conditions perfect for bacteria. After the introduction of anaesthesia, operations were often successful, but patients still invariably died of infection. In Paris, a mortality rate of sixty per cent was recorded. In Edinburgh, a rate of forty-three per cent was noted. In America, one proud surgeon announced that he had cut his mortality rate to just under a quarter.

When, eventually, the first practical steps were taken to cut down the incidence of infection in the operating theatre and the recovery room, they were taken by a Scottish surgeon, Joseph Lister, who had read and studied the early work of a French chemist called Louis Pasteur.

Pasteur's impact on medicine in general and on surgical practices in particular was, therefore, dramatic, although Pasteur himself never qualified as a doctor or practised clinical medicine at all but had studied chemistry in Paris, where he had graduated in 1847.

Pasteur's early scientific work had included a study of the process of fermentation which had led him to the conclusion that under natural conditions fermentation is produced by small, unseen organisms which could themselves be disturbed or destroyed by rapid heating. (This, incidentally, is the process which now bears his name.)

Lister learned about Pasteur's work while working as a Professor of Surgery at the University of Glasgow in 1860. Dismayed and worried by the fearful mortality rate among surgical patients, he had been studying the problem for some time and accepted the idea, then prevalent among surgeons, that the majority of deaths were caused by some poison in the hospital atmosphere. Discussing this enormous problem with the Professor of Chemistry at the University, Lister was told about Pasteur's work and managed to get hold of some reports detailing the Frenchman's work. From the papers he studied, Lister then came to the conclusion that it was not the air that was the problem so much as the small organisms in the air. The solution, he decided, would be to find some way to keep the hospital atmosphere free of these small organisms. Pasteur had suggested that, in addition to using heat to destroy the organisms, fermentation could be controlled either by the use of antiseptics or by a process known as filtration.

It clearly was not practical to keep patients at a high enough temperature to destroy these small organisms, and nor was filtration practicable, and so Lister started experimenting with other ways to prevent the development of infection. After unsuccessfully trying out various chemicals, he hit upon carbolic acid, a substance which had already been used in the disinfection of sewage in Carlisle and which had, by coincidence, also been tried out by a French chemist called François Jules Lemaire a few years earlier. Lister's method was to use a piece of lint impregnated with carbolic acid to make an artificial scab. The first patient, who had suffered a compound fracture, did well, and after some more research and some experimentation, Lister published in the *Lancet* in 1867 a paper entitled *On the Antiseptic Principle in the Practice of Surgery*.

This paper was to provide the answer to the problem that had for centuries faced all surgeons, but it was not to be accepted by the medical establishment without some difficulty. The critics of Lister's theory ignored his evidence and attacked his recommendations with the tragic result that it was several decades before all surgeons were practising the sort of technique that had been advocated.

Convinced that he had hit upon the answer to the age-old problem of post-operative infection, Lister continued to experiment despite the criticism. Still believing that all pathological organisms were carried in the air, he next developed a steam-powered carbolic spray which would enable him to fill the operating theatre with a fine mist of carbolic acid. Since he operated in the centre of this mist and since the carbolic acid inevitably covered his hands, his instruments and the patient, Lister's new invention proved extremely successful, and the number of patients dying after operations was immediately reduced.

Lister's theory was, of course, that infection could be prevented by the use of antiseptic substances designed to kill or-

158

ganisms likely to cause trouble. In the years which followed his early experiments, other investigators showed that it was not necessary to smother the patient or the surgeon with antiseptics but that an equally good result could be obtained by thoroughly cleaning all instruments and by dressing surgeons and their assistants in clean gowns, caps and gloves.

But it was Lister's imagination and courage which first led to the conquering of that fourth major difficulty facing surgeons, and it was his pioneering work which led directly to the fact that, in the next few decades, surgeons around the world could begin to perform operations never dreamt of before. Within Lister's lifetime surgeons would be operating within the human chest and skull without fear of failure.

Surgery had, at long last, caught up with the other branches of medical science.

Chapter 39: Improvements in Public Health

Progress in public health and working conditions – A number of Acts are passed – Fall in death rates from infections

In the years since the passing of the first Public Health Act in 1848, the number of people dying from infectious diseases had continued to fall. Tuberculosis, for example, had become a far less significant cause of death. But even the most enthusiastic supporter of Chadwick's principles would have had to agree that the changes had not been brought about entirely by improvements in sanitary conditions.

The response to the proposals in that first Act had been mixed and, although Chadwick's recommendations were eventually to be accepted as vital to the health of every community, progress had been delayed by many who seemed to prefer the risk of disease to the restrictions and expenses proposed by Chadwick. In a leader approving of Chadwick's dismissal from the Board of Health in 1854, *The Times* said: 'We prefer to take our chance of cholera and the rest than to be bullied into health.'

The fall in the number of people suffering and dying from infections had been produced instead by improvements in general living standards which had resulted from the industrial, political and economic upheavals of the previous century. Better transport facilities which followed the growth of the network of railway lines throughout Britain in the first half of the century meant that food supplies could be carried at lower cost and with less wastage than before. As a result, food surpluses in one part of the country could be used to satisfy demands in other parts, while at the same time providing farmers and suppliers with additional profits. In addition, several improvements had been made to the ways in which food was produced. Although the Romans had recognised the importance of keeping soil fertile by rotating crops and using manures, little more had been done to improve the quality of crop production until the eighteenth and nineteenth centuries, when improvements in agricultural policies resulted in a greater output of food and consequently a higher nutritional standard for the general population. Well-fed people are better able to cope with and survive disease and infection.

Improvements in working conditions were also made during the nineteenth century. Factories were better ventilated and better lit, and working hours were restricted by law after the Factory Act of 1833. As a result men, women and children who had previously spent all their waking hours inside dark gloomy buildings could now begin to spend more time in the open air.

Better wages, which resulted from pressure produced by liberals in politics and exerted by the labour force themselves, also helped. All these improvements in living conditions helped to reduce dramatically the incidence and statistical importance of tuberculosis, an illness which, at the beginning of the century, had been a devastating endemic disease.

Although the sequence of change and improvement occurred first in Britain, where the Industrial Revolution had begun, a similar sequence occurred in other countries as they began to adapt to industrialisation.

Recognising that the effects of the 1848 Public Health Act had been far too haphazard, in 1860 the British Government instructed the Privy Council to review the state of public health in Britain. The team of experts brought together to pursue these studies found that, despite the improvements which had taken place, infant mortality still reached 250 per thousand births in some parts of the country, with an average for the whole country being something like 150 per thousand births. The number of adults falling ill and dying at an early age may have fallen but the number of infants surviving beyond the first year of life had still hardly changed. Today we use infant mortality rates to help us assess the health-care facilities, public health standards and general living standards in developing countries. The figures for Britain and most of Europe in the second half of the nineteenth century were as bad as any today in the most primitive developing countries.

The reports from the Privy Council led to a spate of Parliamentary Acts designed to interfere with community life in order to preserve public health. In 1866 the Sanitary Act was passed, followed in quick succession by the Factory Act and Workshop Act, the Artisans' and Labourers' Dwellings Act and a Vaccination Act. The culmination of the Privy Council's work was the Great Public Health Act of 1875 which at last put into action the majority of the suggestions made so much earlier by Chadwick and his colleagues. Hospitals were to be founded and inspected, food was to be sold without adulteration, sewage facilities were to be provided throughout the country, and much of British life was to be regulated by officials armed with legislative power.

These new controls were extraordinarily effective. For example, in 1869 there were 4,281 typhus deaths in England, with 716 people dying in London alone of this one disease. By 1885 there were 318 deaths from typhus in England and only twenty-eight in London. By the beginning of the twentieth century, before Charles Nicolle had discovered that typhus is spread by the body louse, there were no deaths at all from typhus in London. The disease had been more or less eliminated by simple environmental changes and improvements.

Other diseases were affected similarly, with smallpox, tuberculosis and cholera becoming relatively rare rather than endemic. The diseases still existed, of course, but they no longer caused the widespread slaughter that had epitomised the early part of the nineteenth century.

The changes and improvements which had taken place in Britain also occurred in other countries. In America, for example, New York appointed a Metropolitan Board of Health in 1866, and within the following half-century the infant mortality rate was cut by two-thirds. Sometimes the improvements which took place produced bizarre contrasts. In Germany, Hamburg had postponed improvements to its water supply whereas its neighbouring town, Altona, had installed a water-purification plant. During the epidemic which struck Hamburg in 1892, one street on the border between the two towns included houses on one side which were in Hamburg and houses on the other side of the road which were in Altona. The people living in houses supplied by the Hamburg water authority died of cholera. Their neighbours across the road survived.

The improvements in public health-care facilities and in general living conditions, themselves produced by political, social and economic pressures, in turn produced changes of their own.

In large towns and cities, for example, the number of people dying of infectious diseases had fallen dramatically by the end of the nineteenth century, with the result that the population in cities had begun to grow rapidly. The resultant overcrowding which put additional pressure on the improved facilities was exacerbated by the fall in the infant mortality rate. The improvements envisaged by Chadwick had, paradoxically, proved almost too effective.

Chapter 40: Unravelling the Microbe Mystery

Pasteur continues his work in France – Robert Koch in Germany – Anthrax and rabies – Public health gets a boost

While Lister was developing his antiseptic technique in Britain, Louis Pasteur was continuing his career as a chemist in France.

Pasteur had made his name by helping the wine industry deal with a particularly troublesome fermentation problem. The advice he had given about destroying the troublesome microbes by heating had proved so successful that, when the silkworm breeders of France found themselves facing ruin because of an infection which was killing their worms, they asked Pasteur for help.

It took five years, but eventually in 1870 Pasteur not only identified the diseases responsible for the destruction of a large part of the silkworm industry but also managed to make positive recommendations designed to enable the breeders to protect their worms and their livelihoods.

With that problem solved, Pasteur turned to help a third French industry – the beer producers – and again managed to give advice which proved to be of immense commercial value.

It was at this point that Pasteur became involved in the study of those organisms affecting human beings more directly; a study which was to involve him for the rest of his life.

Pasteur's interest in the diseases affecting human beings was aroused partly by the fact that Joseph Lister had written to tell him of the success that he had had with his carbolic spray and his general principle of antisepsis. Pasteur agreed with Lister that human diseases were caused by tiny organisms but disagreed with his theory that the organisms existed only in the air, claiming that heat treatment of the water, bandages and surgical equipment used in an operation would prove more effective than spraying everything with antiseptic.

Inspired, perhaps, by Lister and determined to produce more specific evidence linking micro-organisms with specific diseases, Pasteur began work on a disease called anthrax which at the time was killing large numbers of sheep and cattle.

Anthrax had already been the subject of work done by a German called Robert Koch who had qualified as a doctor in 1866 at Göttingen and who, while working as a country physician, had spent some time peering through a microscope.

Koch had discovered and described the entire life cycle of the organism responsible for anthrax and had written to a botanist called Ferdinand Cohn with details of his studies. Cohn was extremely enthusiastic and immediately published Koch's studies, which not only conclusively proved that the anthrax bacillus caused the disease but also showed that a culture of the organism grown in the laboratory could cause anthrax when injected into animals.

Pasteur continued to look for ways in which to provide animals with protection against anthrax. It obviously was not practicable to treat humans or animals with heat or to smother them with copious quantities of antiseptic. There had to be a better way. To Pasteur, that better way seemed to be vaccination. After all Jenner had succeeded in preparing a vaccine which would protect people against smallpox, so why shouldn't it be possible to prepare vaccines which would protect human beings and animals against other infectious diseases?

While Pasteur was working on his anthrax vaccine, Koch was continuing with his microscope studies and experimenting with ways of preparing bacteria for close examination. These purely technical advances had no specific bearing on health care, but they enabled Koch and his many successors to advance the science of bacteriology with greater ease and success. Of more immediate importance to the world of medicine was Koch's discovery in 1882 of the tubercle bacillus and his discovery in 1883 of the organism responsible for the killer disease cholera.

Then it was Pasteur's turn again. In the latter part of the 1880s, the Frenchman succeeded in developing a vaccine which could be used to protect the victims of rabies. As a boy, Pasteur had seen a mad wolf charging through his home town and had seen the agonies suffered by those unfortunate enough to be bitten by the creature. It was that memory which seems to have decided him to look for a vaccine against rabies.

Eventually he prepared a vaccine and with great trepidation tried it out on a young boy brought to him dying after a bite from a mad dog. The boy survived, and Pasteur had made a second vaccine with which human beings could be protected. It was almost a century since Jenner had first produced his smallpox vaccine.

In 1886 a fund was started to set up a special laboratory where Pasteur and his assistants could continue their work. Within a few months the sum of two and a half million francs had been collected, and in just over two years the Pasteur Institute had been built in Paris. Later on that small boy who had been the first to be saved by the anti-rabies vaccine became a gatekeeper at the Institute.

The work of Koch and Pasteur undoubtedly opened up a new world to scientists and doctors. Pasteur's research had inspired Lister and other doctors to study with scientific detachment the problems facing surgeons, and eventually to make surgery a relatively safe and effective procedure. Reducing the risk of post-operative infection meant that surgeons could begin to experiment with more daring surgery, without exposing their patients to unnecessary and unacceptable risks. The work of both men on the isolation of organisms that caused disease and the preparation of suitable vaccines eventually led to the development of campaigns which helped to eradicate such infections as tuberculosis and cholera from many parts of the world.

But perhaps the most important effect of their work was that it gave added strength to the campaign first started in London by Chadwick. The fact that it was now proven that infectious diseases could be spread by dirt and controlled by cleanliness, meant that those campaigning for clean water, better sanitation, better housing and cleaner streets had science on their side. Pasteur and Koch had between them founded the science of bacteriology, had provided medical men with solid evidence explain-

ing the existence and spread of infectious diseases of all kinds
and had proved not only that specific infections were caused by
specific organisms but that those organisms could be controlled.

Chapter 41: Sigmund Freud's Obsession

Sigmund Freud and Charcot in Paris – Freud's theory
about sex – The impact of Freud on medicine – The impact
of Freud on life

Sigmund Freud was born in 1856 in Freiburg (part of what
was, until 1993, known as Czechoslovakia) and qualified
as a doctor in 1881. He specialised in neurology, the practical branch of medicine which deals with physical disorders of
the nervous system, and after working for a time in Vienna he
obtained a post at the Salpêtrière hospital in Paris where Jean-
Martin Charcot worked as a physician. Charcot had acquired a
tremendous reputation not only as a general physician but also
as a specialist in nervous disorders, and his work involved a
study of the value of hypnosis. While working with Charcot the
young Freud soon forgot his enthusiasm for pure neurological
research, which he recognised as being unlikely to provide him
with much of a living, and instead developed an interest in a
range of disorders usually grouped together as neuroses. From
being a student of anatomy and neurology, Freud had become a
student of psychiatry.

At the age of thirty Freud set up as a private specialist in
Vienna, the city where he was to work for most of his life and
where during the next few decades he was to found a medical
philosophy which, within his lifetime, would have a worldwide
effect on the attitudes of doctors and patients towards mental
illnesses of all kinds.

He began by experimenting with hypnosis, putting patients
into a trance and then suggesting to them that their symptoms
would disappear as soon as they came out of the trance state.

He soon discovered, however, that to achieve results hypnosis was unnecessary; instead, by persuading his patients to relax and learn to trust him, he could successfully tap their unconscious memories in an attempt to search for clues which might explain their subsequent fears and behaviour patterns. Freud was learning how to take his patients back down memory lane.

From his research on patients relaxed in his consulting room, Freud formed his theory about the importance of sexual influences on the subconscious mind. He claimed that many repressions were sexually based and that secret, unrecognised sexual impulses explained all deeds and thoughts whether good or bad. Dreams, he argued, provided additional clues to the activities within the unconscious mind and again indicated the basic sexual needs and desires of the individual patient. Freud was obsessed with sex: when he noticed that the physical symptoms which accompany an anxiety state were similar to those experienced by someone who has just practised coitus interruptus, he came to the conclusion that all anxiety and neurotic behaviour must be produced by some sort of sexual pressure. On another occasion, when a young girl opened the door to his consulting room by accident, Freud is said to have pardoned her by explaining that her action simply denoted her curiosity about the sexual behaviour of her parents.

His theories about the importance of unrecognised sexual desires inevitably caused considerable controversy and a great deal of publicity. Freud dealt with the controversy by claiming that those who disbelieved his theories or opposed his arguments were themselves repressed and fired by hidden desires which they were not prepared to accept; he dealt with the publicity by putting up his consulting fees.

Although Freud influenced many contemporary neurologists and psychologists, founded the school of psychoanalysis and provided students of medicine with a wider understanding of mental illness, it gradually became clear that the value of psychoanalysis was severely limited. The speciality could only be practised effectively if doctor and patient could spend long periods of time together and, even then, relatively few patients benefited from this expensive treatment.

Consequently, the effect that Freud had on clinical medical practice and the health of people in general was limited by the fact that, while a very large number of qualified medical practitioners devoted their working lives to the practice of this specialised and relatively unproductive aspect of psychiatric care, only a small number of patients could be treated. Psychoanalysts tended to congregate in areas where the general standard of living was high and the quality of medical care good, and their fashionable status in society eventually matched in many ways the status and position of astronomers such as Nostradamus.

More important than his specific clinical role was the effect that Freud had on general attitudes both within the medical profession and in society in general. His influence within the establishments providing medical education resulted in the fact that many graduates had a wider understanding of the basis of mental illness, although a number were probably limited by his obsession with the importance of repressed human sexual urges. His effect on social attitudes was probably more important, since it seems likely that the increased readiness of people to discuss sexual problems resulted in part from his work, and it may also be true that the wider availability of contraceptive advice, which was to have such an important effect on all aspects of human life in the twentieth century, was in part a consequence of his making more people aware of their sexual feelings and needs.

Chapter 42: Surgery Knows No Bounds

Surgery progresses by leaps and bounds – The first heart surgery – Putting surgery in its place

In the few years following the introduction of anaesthetics and the practice of asepsis, surgeons made quite phenomenal progress. Whereas a few years earlier they had been limited to working as quickly as possible to remove damaged, gangrenous or otherwise functionless limbs, they could now develop proper surgical techniques, designed not just to destroy or remove unwanted tissues but to repair and restore function to almost any organ. The progress a surgeon could make was limited only by his own imagination and his dexterity, and while older, more established surgeons sometimes mocked and jeered, braver and wiser surgeons explored previously uncharted territory with astonishing success.

Before the introduction of aseptic techniques, for example, abdominal surgery was dangerous and almost unthinkable. In the 1880s, however, a number of surgeons performed operations that are now still considered standard and classical procedures. An Italian, Pietro Loreta, performed the first pyloroplasty in 1882 and an Austrian, Christian Albert Theodor Billroth, performed the operation which bears his name, in the previous year. Both these operative procedures are still used by surgeons operating on patients with peptic ulceration. The first colostomy was performed in 1888 by a German called Karl Maydl, and the first gall bladder was removed by another German, Carl Langenbuch, in 1882, although an American called John Stough Hobbs had actually opened the gall bladder and removed stones in 1868.

The prospect of opening a patient's chest and performing intra-thoracic surgery of any kind would have certainly appalled any surgeon who could not rely on anaesthesia to keep his patient quiet and an aseptic technique to give him a reasonable chance of keeping the patient alive. In the 1890s, however, a number of surgeons took the plunge and performed surgery within the chest cavity. One of the most remarkable pioneering operations was performed by Professor Dr Ludwig Rehn of Frankfurt who, in 1896, successfully repaired a right ventricular stab wound despite the fact that Billroth, an internationally respected abdominal surgeon, had announced that, 'A surgeon who would attempt such an operation should lose the respect of his colleagues.'

In the paper announcing the success of his operative procedure, Rehn explains that he was forced to operate by the fact that his patient was bleeding to death. Stabbed with a kitchen knife through the fourth intercostal space, the unnamed, and now forgotten, patient enabled Rehn to begin a surgical fashion that was to escalate rapidly within the next few years. A mere two years later surgeons were proposing to operate on the mitral valve in order to restore cardiac function.

Brain surgery was developed too in those remarkable early years of the surgical renaissance, and it seems now that the braver, more imaginative surgeons considered no operation impossible and nothing impractical.

The main difference between the type of surgery being practised at the end of the nineteenth century and the type of surgery practised in the middle of the nineteenth century was that anaesthesia and asepsis had made elective surgery a real practical possibility. When mortality rates for surgical patients were as high as fifty per cent, few surgeons and fewer patients were prepared to risk any surgical procedure unless the alternative was certain death. So the mid-century surgeons had had to confine themselves to amputating dangerously infected limbs or clearly defined tumours.

Once surgery had become a comparatively safe and painless alternative, the number of operations available obviously increased dramatically, as did the number of patients prepared to offer themselves for surgery.

Although these changes obviously led to longer and better lives for many people, the truth is that the emphasis on curative surgery as a solution to people's individual problems attracted far too much enthusiastic support from both the public and the medical profession. The new type of surgery being practised at the end of the nineteenth century was a glamorous and attractive speciality. Its practitioners could, and often did, perform what seemed, to the ordinary individual, to be miracles.

But surgical operations employed large numbers of skilled doctors and nurses and required a great deal of money if they were to be done successfully.

In the shadow of these surgical advances the importance of preventive medical techniques and their effectiveness in saving and improving lives was often forgotten.

Chapter 43: The Control of Exotic Disease

The effect of malaria – Ronald Ross makes some inquiries – Yellow fever is a threat – Cuba plays a part – Walter Reed and his colleagues – Yellow fever defeated – The Panama Canal is cut.

While the incidence of tuberculosis, smallpox and cholera was on the decline in Europe, there were two diseases which were still endemic in many parts of the world and which were, together, responsible for much illness and many deaths. Neither of these diseases, malaria and yellow fever, had attracted much interest from theoretical research workers or clinical investigators, perhaps because neither disorder was still common in the European countries where most medical research work was being done.

Malaria had not always been confined to those parts of the world commonly described as the tropics. It had, for many centuries, been the scourge of Europe, and there is good evidence that malaria was one of the major reasons for the collapse of the Roman Empire. Known as the ague, it affected soldiers in all parts of the widespread Roman Empire and caused many deaths as well as a considerable amount of incapacitating illness.

In the years following the collapse of Roman authority, malaria had continued to have a powerful influence on European life. At a seventeenth-century papal conference in Rome, for example, eight cardinals and thirty secretaries are reported to have died of malaria. Oliver Cromwell, the English Parliamentarian of the seventeenth century, is believed to have suffered from malaria for most of his life, while there is evidence that malaria existed in America well before Columbus crossed the Atlantic for the first time.

From the days when it was first recognised as a specific disease, malaria had been the subject of a number of investigations. The Indian physician Susruta, who lived about 500 BC, suspected that malaria was transmitted by insects and specifically attributed it to the bite of the mosquito. The Romans also suspected the involvement of mosquitoes and there is written evidence that they believed that marshlands were breeding grounds which made the spread of the infection more likely.

Although these suspicions were not proven and the full life history of the malaria parasite was not investigated until much later, an effective treatment for malaria was discovered and widely used as far back as the seventeenth century. According to legend, the idea of using Peruvian bark in the treatment of the infection happened by accident when a Peruvian Indian suffering from malaria and its accompanying fever drank copiously from a pool near to some trees. The water was bitter but, to his surprise, it seemed to cure his fever. When he told his friends they went and drank from the pool and discovered that their symptoms disappeared. After some study the Peruvians found that the water was given its unusual taste and 'magic' qualities by the fact that it was full of small pieces of bark from one of the nearby trees. The bark had fallen into the water and produced what was effectively an infusion. The tree was the cinchona, and the drug was the one known to us now as quinine.

Eventually, the value of cinchona bark became known in Europe and when used by the English physician Sydenham in the seventeenth century quinine was the first and, at the time, only drug available which had a specific, recognised purpose.

It was not until the end of the nineteenth century that the relationship between malaria and the mosquito was properly established. The first step was taken by a French army surgeon working in Algeria, Alphonse Laveran, who, in 1880, published a paper in which he announced that he had found minute amoeba-like organisms in the blood of patients suffering from malaria.

The discovery of these organisms made it possible for physicians to diagnose malaria accurately, but it did not help in either the treatment of the infection or its prevention. Laveran had shown that patients suffering from malaria had tiny parasites in their blood which grew and changed shape as the days went by and that the breeding of the parasites was associated with bouts of ague fever. But he had not found out how the parasites got into the blood in the first place.

It was left to a British officer in the Indian Medical Service, Ronald Ross, to find and publish the evidence which eventually led to a direct understanding of the mechanism of malaria and, consequently, to an all-out international campaign to eradicate the disease. Ross first became interested in mosquitoes when he found himself living in a bungalow where there was a tub of water outside the bedroom window. He found that he could rid himself of mosquitoes simply by emptying the tub of water, and he suggested that the whole army mess could be freed of the insects by emptying all other water containers. To his astonishment, the local adjutant rejected his suggestion, arguing that to do so would be to upset the order of nature. That bizarre objection seems to have fired Ross to take an even greater interest in the subject, and whereas previously he had spent his leisure time studying literature and mathematics, he subsequently began a study of malaria, a disease which he recognised as being the cause of millions of deaths and which he knew was little understood.

Ross obtained some of the papers and books written by Alphonse Laveran and began to study both the parasites and the mosquitoes which he felt certain were implicated. His first research work was done with a microscope which had a cracked eye-piece and screws rusted with his own sweat. Slowly he made progress, and when he returned to London in 1894, Ross met Dr Patrick Manson, a graduate of Aberdeen University, who had worked with the Chinese Imperial Maritime Customs Service and who had studied in fine detail a great many tropical diseases, including malaria. The two men discussed the possible relationship between the malaria parasites described by Laveran and the mosquitoes, and when Ross returned to India in 1895, he re-started his personal investigations, writing each week to Manson to describe his progress and ask for advice.

In his book *Studies in Malaria*, Ross describes how his colleagues in India laughed at him while he was doing his work; none of them seems to have understood the potential importance of his work. Even those senior officers responsible for him failed to comprehend the value of his researches, and on at least one occasion he was posted to another part of India just as his work was nearing a conclusion. Ross plaintively points out that, although one third of all the hospital admissions in India at the time were caused by malaria, hardly any of the one thousand British Government doctors working in the country had investigated the problem.

Finally, after working on malaria for nearly a decade, Ross found the evidence he had been looking for, and he published papers describing the close association between the malaria parasite and the anopheles mosquito just before the end of the nineteenth century. He showed that it is through the bite of this mosquito that malaria is transmitted from an infected individual to a healthy person and that the malaria parasite matures and reproduces inside the mosquito.

The other disease, endemic in many tropical countries, which had resisted all attempts at control, was yellow fever, an often fatal infection which had been recognised for several centuries as posing a tremendous threat to all travellers, adventurers and armies. Local inhabitants in countries where yellow fever was common invariably inherited some slight resistance to the disease, a single attack of which will produce complete immunity for life. For those people, living in a country where yellow fever was present, the infection was, therefore, not too dangerous. They suffered a fairly mild attack, got better and suffered no more. For travellers and visitors, however, the disease was far more serious, since that one attack often proved fatal to the individual with no inherited resistance at all. In 1800, for example, Napoleon Bonaparte sent an army of 30,000 to Haiti, but yellow fever killed 23,000, enabling the local army to resist the colonists.

It seems likely that yellow fever began its devastating career in Africa and was spread to America and southern Europe by explorers and slave traders in much the same way as syphilis travelled in the other direction. Known as 'yellow jack' to sailors, the infection is thought to explain the fate of the legendary Flying Dutchman, a sailing ship which was condemned to sail for ever around the seas off the Cape of Good Hope because no port would admit the ship, on board which yellow fever raged. If each infected man had been thrown overboard by his remaining shipmates, the only real mystery is what happened to the last man on board.

The idea that the mosquito might carry yellow fever from one individual to another had been put forward several times in the nineteenth century by doctors who had been puzzled by the fact that the infection can disappear for weeks at a time and can be carried across whole oceans without any of the sailors on board ship seeming to be infected. In 1881, for example, a Dr Carlos Finlay of Havana had suggested that the mosquito carried the fever, and according to his argument the infection could be carried on board ship if a water barrel contained a fever-carrying insect.

Two things finally led to the conclusive discovery that yellow fever really is carried by a mosquito. One fact was Ronald Ross's research, which had shown that malaria is carried in this way. Once the path had been established by one brave researcher, it was far easier for others to travel in the same direction without drowning in the scorn poured on their heads by professional sceptics. The other factor was the more practical need discovered by the Americans to find some way to deal with yellow fever, which was killing large numbers of the American marines stationed in Cuba, which was at the beginning of this century occupied by the United States.

Major Walter Reed was put in charge of a special commission given instructions to investigate the causes of the infection and to find some way to control its spread. In 1900, with three other investigators, Reed travelled to Cuba. One of the men with him, Aristide Agramonte, was a pathologist, one James Carroll, a bacteriologist, and the other, Jesse Lazear, an expert on insects. They began their studies at Pinar del Rio where there were thirty-five cases of yellow fever in the barracks. The first thing they discovered was that none of the doctors or nurses involved with these patients had contracted yellow fever. This simple fact alone seemed to rule out any possibility that the infection could be transmitted directly from one victim to another.

While pondering on this fact, Reed and his colleagues met the previously disregarded Dr Finlay, who had for many years been arguing that mosquitoes carried yellow fever. The team decided that the only way to investigate the truth of Finlay's theory was to try to produce yellow fever in volunteers from mosquito bites. Since each member of the team knew that yellow fever could kill, this was an extraordinarily brave thing even to contemplate.

Because of the risks, the commission decided that they could not call for volunteers without being prepared to experiment on themselves. The first man to face the risk was Lazear, the insect specialist, who began by allowing a mosquito to bite the arm of a yellow fever sufferer and then to bite his own arm. Nothing happened as a result of that experiment, since, although Lazear and the others did not realise it, yellow fever takes a while to develop inside the body of the mosquito, and the insect which had bitten the known victim would not be carrying the infection when it was put onto Lazear's arm.

The experiments continued and eventually both Carroll and Lazear contracted yellow fever. With extraordinary professional determination, Lazear wrote notes about his own condition and the course of the disease, and when he died, the other three members of the commission were well on the way to establishing the natural history of yellow fever. Carroll, the first of the two to succumb, survived.

The work of Ross and Manson on malaria and Reed and

his colleagues on yellow fever established that mosquitoes were responsible for the spread of both diseases and made it practicable for public health officials around the world to begin the slow fight to eradicate both diseases. It quickly became clear that, by draining the swamps, marshes and expanses of free-standing water which were used by mosquitoes as breeding grounds, the life cycle of the infections could be broken. Without the mosquito, the two diseases would be paralysed, unable to move from victim to victim.

One project which benefited almost immediately from the work on malaria and yellow fever was the cutting of the Panama Canal, which was designed to connect the Atlantic and Pacific oceans by providing a waterway through the Panama isthmus.

Back in the sixteenth century, the Spanish had had the idea of digging a canal across this narrow stretch of land but the size of the project had proved too daunting. Then, in 1846, the Americans had signed a treaty with the country, then known as New Granada and now known as Colombia, which had control over Panama. The Americans, having thereby obtained effective control over this valuable stretch of land, built a railway which stretched from one ocean to the other. The idea of building a canal had not been forgotten, however and in 1880 the French Panama Canal Company, under the leadership of the engineer who had built the Suez Canal, Ferdninand de Lesseps, began work.

The project begun by de Lesseps inevitably faced delays and financial difficulties, but the major problem was that the workers were dying off rapidly of yellow fever and malaria. By the time the attempt was abandoned in 1889, the death rate had reached frightening proportions.

The discoveries made by Reed and Ross encouraged the Americans to try again, and in the first decade of the twentieth century the project was reopened.

This time the man in charge, Colonel Gorgas, took great precautions to preserve the lives of his engineers and labourers. He drained pools that could be drained and used netting to protect the men in their rooms and built what were effectively mosquito-proof rooms for sleeping and eating.

The precautions had a dramatic effect on the success of the project, and by 1914, when the canal was finished, the mortality rate was about three per cent of what it had been when de Lesseps had tried.

It seems unlikely that the Panama Canal could ever have been built without the work of men like Reed and Ross. During the rest of the twentieth century the preventive techniques employed by Colonel Gorgas in Panama were introduced in many countries around the world.

But the story of these two diseases is not one of total success. For one thing: the cost of introducing campaigns designed to eradicate malaria from a country can be considerable and, even by the early 1980s, only a quarter of the countries which had originally been classified as malaria-infested had been freed of the infection. In another quarter of the 146 countries involved, no organised action at all had been started. The unwillingness of some governments to introduce anti-malaria campaigns inevitably means that those countries which do eradicate the disease cannot afford to relax, since neither the mosquitoes nor the parasites involved recognise international boundaries. In Turkey, for example, there were only 1,263 cases of malaria in 1970 but in 1975 the number of people suffering from the disease had risen to 9,829. The country's guard stayed down, and in 1976 there were 37,320 cases, while in 1977 the number infected had risen to 115,350.

Chapter 44: Röntgen's Discovery

The importance of good luck – The role of the non-professional – Professor Röntgen's contribution – The speed of communication makes his discovery known within weeks

During the centuries many of the most important inventions and discoveries within the world of medicine and healing have been made by a mixture of good fortune

178

and good luck. If Laennec had not seen those two boys playing in the Bois de Boulogne, would he have invented the stethoscope? If Auenbrugger had not been brought up among barrels of wine and seen his father tapping the wine casks, would percussion have occurred to him as a useful means of judging the fluid content within a chest cavity? If Florence Nightingale had not visited Pastor Fliedner, would she have had the fire and courage to make such a mark on the medical world? If William Brockeden had not been fed up with pencils full of grit, would he have built that first tablet-making machine?

The list of discoveries made as a result of a single lucky incident is enormously long. It is quite true, of course, that luck alone does not produce anything tangible and that, in every one of the cases I have mentioned, the individual responsible for each discovery or innovation was alert enough to take advantage of the circumstances, but the point is an important one, for today many researchers seem to believe that money and logic must inevitably produce solutions to any questions posed. The truth is that the good researcher needs to be alert and observant at all times, since there is never any way of knowing which piece of information will prove to be the most important one.

Another important point about the major innovations and discoveries which have had an effect on healing and the healers is that a great many of them have been made by individuals who had neither any medical training nor any particular interest in medicine. Louis Pasteur, for example, was a chemist. Edwin Chadwick was a solicitor and a journalist, Benjamin Franklin was a trained printer, Charles Darwin was a natural historian, Leonardo da Vinci was an artist. Medicine has always been a subject which has attracted the interest of intelligent men and women from all professions.

I make these two points here because they serve as an admirable introduction to the fact that in 1895 a fifty-year-old Professor of Physics at Würzburg in Germany made an accidental discovery which was to have as great an effect on the practice of clinical medicine and practical surgery as any other single

179

technological step forward in the history of healing.

Professor Wilhelm Konrad von Röntgen was an experimental physicist, and in 1895 he was investigating the effects of cathode rays (which consist of nothing more mysterious than electrons freed from the negative electrode, or cathode, of a gas-filled tube through which an electrical discharge has passed). Cathode rays had been studied many times before, but what caught Röntgen's attention was the fact that, although the tube he was working with was covered with black cardboard, a greenish glow seemed to come from a piece of paper coated with a substance called barium platinocyanide which happened to be lying on a nearby bench. Many researchers would just have moved the piece of paper, but Röntgen realised that the paper must have been made luminous by some unknown rays – something other than the cathode rays he had started off intending to investigate.

Fortunately for the medical profession and millions of patients throughout the world, Röntgen decided to investigate further. He put a thousand-page textbook between the tube and his piece of coated paper and found that the paper still became luminous. Next he placed his own hand between the tube and the piece of paper, and discovered X-rays.

The bones of his hand appeared on the luminous paper as dark shadows since they were obviously dense enough to prevent the flow of these unseen rays.

Röntgen then did two more things. First he experimented with photographic plates and showed that the invisible rays he had discovered could produce a permanent effect on the plates. And then he published a report describing the effect that he had noticed.

In an earlier, or later, decade his work might have taken months or even years to travel around the world, but in the 1890s the efficiency of the printing industry and the postal services of the world were at their peak. Röntgen himself published his paper describing his research work in the *Würzburgh Physico-Medical Society Proceedings* on 28 December 1895, and a month later the *Lancet* in London published an X-ray photograph of a human hand taken by Campbell Swinton in a laboratory in London. At the end of February 1896, just under two months after Röntgen's original experiment, the *Lancet* published a report from Liverpool which described how a surgeon had used X-rays to help him localise an air-gun pellet before arranging for its removal. Similar reports quickly appeared in other medical journals around the world.

Within a remarkably short time, specialist radiologists had appeared in hospitals in many parts of the world and, since the risks subsequently associated with radiation therapy were not recognised until much later, many of these early specialists suffered and died as a result of their endeavours. With the help of these specialists, however, surgeons found that they could use the new X-rays to help them diagnose and locate fractures, dislocations and foreign bodies such as bullets. In 1898 W.B. Cannon, later to become an eminent American physiologist, found the movements of the stomach and the intestines could be studied by watching the progress of bismuth paste within the body, and in 1906 this procedure was used by surgeons to help them plan operative work.

Meanwhile other research workers had discovered that radioactive materials could be used to burn and destroy pieces of unwanted tissue, such as those involving cancerous growths. Pierre and Marie Curie were just two of the researches who investigated the possibility of using radium as a therapeutic material in the early years of the twentieth century.

But it was as a diagnostic aid that X-rays proved most useful. By enabling surgeons and physicians to see inside the living human body, they made it possible for far more accurate diagnoses to be made, often at a much earlier stage than ever before. Many of the therapeutic advances made in the twentieth century would have been impossible to prepare or use had Röntgen not taken note of that bizarre incident in his laboratory at Würzburgh. There have been a number of minor technical developments in the field of radiology in the years since then, but none of these have had the impact or value of Röntgen's original discovery.

Chapter 45: The Shrinking World

Transport progress – motor cars and aeroplanes – The social and economic effects – The effects on health are widespread and important – The world gets smaller

Throughout the nineteenth century, inventors in Europe had been experimenting with transport machines which would run along roads rather than on rails. The first vehicles were steam-powered, and at the beginning of the century steam buses ran in Paris and steam-driven vehicles were seen on the streets of Philadelphia. In 1831 a regular steam coach service carrying paying passengers ran between Gloucester and Cheltenham, some time before the railways were built.

However, steam-driven vehicles were never popular on the roads, and towards the end of the nineteenth century several inventors began work on automobiles powered by gasoline. A French engineer, Alphonse Beau de Rochas, and an Austrian, Siegfried Marcus, both built engines which ran on gasoline but it was two Germans, Carl Benz and Gottlieb Daimler, who first turned amusing inventions into effective forms of popular transport by manufacturing automobiles for public sale.

Before the end of the nineteenth century motor cars were being built in factories all over Europe and America. Peugeot, Renault and Fiat were all in business before 1900, and in America, just after the turn of the century, the young Henry Ford started a motor car manufacturing company which was to produce seventeen hundred cars in its first full year of business. While a group of engineers and inventors had been designing automobiles, another group of inventors and would-be aviators had been toying with the possibility of building flying machines. Gliders and hot-air balloons had enabled men to drift in the sky but, without some means of controlling their activities, these inventions had remained toys rather than commercial propositions.

In 1900 Ferdinand Graf von Zeppelin became the first man to build a rigid dirigible balloon. Then, in 1903, Wilbur and Orville Wright succeeded in producing a flying machine capable of making a sustained, controlled and powered flight. Zeppelin and the Wright brothers had produced machines which were to revolutionise life in the twentieth century. International travel, which had previously taken weeks or days, could now be completed in hours.

Within the space of a very few years, travel had become simple, quick and relatively cheap. At the beginning of the twentieth century few citizens would have travelled more than a thousand miles in a year; within a few decades many people would be travelling ten times that distance and thinking nothing of it.

The social, economic, cultural and medical effects of such easier travel were enormous. The railway engine had enabled people to journey between large cities at little cost and in some comfort, and it had allowed businessmen to sell their goods in markets which they would otherwise never have explored. The changes produced by road and air travel were even more extensive. The internal combustion engine enabled families to travel the countryside unhindered by any lack of public transport facilities. The flying machine made deserts, mountains and even oceans as insignificant as ruts in the road and allowed travellers to cross international boundaries with speed and without inconvenience.

Communities which had been isolated and introspective for years became cosmopolitan within a very short space of time. People could travel around the country, and even around the world, and see how others lived and coped with their problems. Military authorities saw enormous possibilities for the transportation of weapons and men, and quickly realised that air travel had added a new dimension to espionage.

These changes inevitably had a number of effects on the mental and physical health of the individuals concerned. The social and economic advantages offered by these two new forms of transport were undoubtedly vast, but the effects on the general good health of the public are more difficult to assess. It is certainly true that the general living standard rose quickly in those countries where air and road transport were developed most speedily. The advantages to industry were so enormous that the wealthy industrial nations began to grow richer and more prosperous at an almost indecent rate. Wholesale prices of all kinds of goods fell quite dramatically in America, Britain and Germany at the end of the nineteenth century and the beginning of the twentieth century.

But it is also true that the incidence of many physical and mental disorders also increased during this period and in the years that followed. Dietary changes, which accompanied the improvement in living standards, did not always add to physical health. For example, the greater consumption of meat and animal fats is likely to have been an important factor in the development of heart disease and cancer later in the century, while the increased consumption of refined foods is now thought to have led to an increase in the incidence of serious bowel disorders.

And in addition to these effects, people also faced more immediate hazards. The motor car was soon capable of travelling at much greater speeds than a horse-drawn vehicle, and as a result accidents, when they occurred, tended to be more serious. The pollutants added to the atmosphere by motor-car engines in large cities did nothing but harm to the lungs of pedestrians exposed to them each day. Finally, because more people could now travel long distances, there was a much greater mixing of infectious diseases. Air travel, in particular, meant that individuals from one part of the world could within hours be exposed to bacteria and viruses normally endemic in another part of the world.

When the only way to travel around the globe had been by ship, foot or horse, international travel had been so slow that someone leaving one part of the world with an infection would have either acquired obvious symptoms, died or recovered com-

184

pletely by the time he reached his destination. With the introduction of air travel, however, it became possible for a traveller
to contract a disease on one side of the world and to be walking
about on the other side before he became aware of being ill.
This made quarantine regulations impractical and was to make
the work of public health workers in later years far more difficult than it had ever been.

Chapter 46: The Rise of the Specialist

*Specialisation becomes a necessity – Harley Street
becomes popular – Sigmund Freud's effect*

Medical science had developed so rapidly during the nineteenth century that by 1900 it was no longer possible
for one man to be familiar with all the theoretical
information and practical skills available to the practising clinician. In a way this was ironic because, after centuries of wran-
gling, the profession had just begun to act as a united force.

During the years which followed the Renaissance, medicine and surgery had developed along separate lines largely because the physicians, whose training included academic study at
one of the major universities, considered the surgeons, whose
training consisted largely of the acquisition of simple practical
skills picked up during a rather haphazard apprenticeship, to be
socially and professionally beneath them. The midwives and
apothecaries, whose education also consisted of an informal type
of apprenticeship, were also considered rather inferior by the
haughty physicians, and so they too continued to work within
their own rather specialised fields.

Then, in Britain, at the beginning of the nineteenth century, Acts of Parliament were passed which brought the apothecaries, surgeons and physicians together for the first time. (In
other countries, the apothecaries remained outside the strict
confines of the medical profession, but the surgeons and physi-

185

cians recognised each others' qualifications and complementary values.) Long-established jealousies and professional suspicions seemed to have been buried for the first time, and the profession developed a united front with which to overpower the ever-growing threat posed by the mass of unqualified practitioners.

Then the information explosion, which began to produce shock waves in every institution in the Western World during the nineteenth century, forced practitioners to specialise not just in medicine or surgery but in the diagnosis and treatment of disorders confined to one particular system or organ of the body. Although many doctors before this time had chosen to special-ise in one type of operation or form of treatment, they had cho-sen to work within a specific medical area, either because they found that area of particular interest or because they found it exceptionally profitable; until the nineteenth century it was not vital for a physician or surgeon to specialise just because the amount of available information made any other course impractical.

The increased specialisation meant that, for the first time in history, doctors began to call in colleagues for consultations. The very fact that it was now acceptable for a man to specialise also made it possible for any physician or surgeon to admit openly, without losing face, that a particular problem was outside his range of knowledge. At the same time, a growing number of practitioners, instead of taking full and exclusive responsibility for their own group of patients, began to rely on the 'referral system', whereby a general practitioner or doctor with a wide range of patients to look after would call on a specialist for advice. This produced changes in the way in which doctors or-ganised their practices. Instead of each doctor having a house in the area where he worked and seeing his patients in a few rooms specially set aside for the purpose, consultant specialists began to take rooms in central positions where they would be conven-ient for both patients and general physicians visiting for advice.

London was an obvious centre for specialists in Britain, since it not only had a large population of its own but was also within fairly easy reach of most outlying country districts. Road and rail travel was becoming much more comfortable and less expensive, and specialists who set up consulting rooms in London could not only expect a steady trickle of patients from villages, towns and even cities where there was no resident specialist but, for an appropriate fee, also be persuaded to venture out of town themselves to visit patients in their own homes.

Many of the London specialists chose to open their consulting rooms in Harley Street, an area in the north of London which had been previously known as a rather smart residential area. It had the twin advantages of being extremely close to two main-line railway stations – Euston and Paddington – and of being in the centre of one of London's most fashionable and exclusive developments.

In 1873 there were thirty-six qualified medical men in Harley Street, and by the end of the century 157 specialists were practising there. Since almost the whole street had been taken over by members of the medical profession it acquired the nickname 'The Valley of the Shadow of Death'. This area was so popular with doctors that the houses in the surrounding streets of Wimpole Street, Welbeck Street, Devonshire Place and Portland Place began to shine with brass plates on display. One of the first doctors to put up a plate in Wimpole Street was Dr Conan Doyle (the creator of Sherlock Holmes) who had been a general practitioner in Southsea and had studied eyes in Paris and Vienna. He intended to become an eye specialist but within three months had abandoned medical practice to become a full-time author. Even in those early years, when most doctors owned their own houses and only a few shared premises, some specialists were more popular than others. It is reported, for example, that dermatologists were unpopular because their patients tended to frighten away other patients, while paediatricians were unpopular because their young patients had a habit of being sick on the waiting-room carpet.

In other European countries the rise in the number of specialists grew at very much the same rate, but in America the process assumed extraordinary proportions. It seemed that every young qualifying doctor wanted to specialise, and by the 1890s in large cities there were relatively few doctors in general practice. As a result, when an individual fell ill, he had to decide for himself which specialist to call on. This arrangement was far from satisfactory, since not only was it often difficult for an unqualified person to decide which type of specialist he required but also many specialists were available for consultation only during office hours. If someone fell ill at night, he often had considerable difficulty finding and persuading a doctor of any kind to call on him at home.

This situation was also open to corruption, because there was little control over the number of times that a patient could be referred between specialists. Specialists frequently referred patients to other specialists, and rumours were rife of groups of practitioners referring patients for unnecessary consultations and then splitting the fees between them.

Anaesthetics had been one of the first branches of medical practice to acquire its own group of specialists, and after Dr John Snow successfully administered chloroform to Queen Victoria, many other physicians chose to specialise in the administration of anaesthetics. Other specialities developed as technical skills and knowledge became too complex for the general practitioner to master, and before the end of the nineteenth century there were specialists dealing with the skin, the throat, the bladder, the nervous system, infectious diseases, rheumatism, gout, cancer, the heart, the lungs, the mouth, the eye, the liver and just about every other part of the body. There were specialists dealing with single diseases, groups of diseases, single organs, groups of organs, patients requiring specific types of investigation and patients requiring specific forms of treatment. When the principle of asepsis was accepted by surgeons and the number of operations which could possibly be performed successfully expanded, surgical specialists began to develop too. Then the discovery of X-rays not only led to the introduction of a new speciality, radiology, but, by opening up whole areas of the body which had hitherto remained mysterious and impregnable, led directly to even more specialities developing.

There was one other important area which was by now acquiring specialists of its own. Mental illnesses had for several centuries been considered something clearly distinct from other forms of illness, but it was only now, at the end of the nineteenth century, that psychiatric problems really began to merit the development of an independent speciality. This upsurge in interest in mental problems had been brought about largely through the efforts of Sigmund Freud.

Chapter 47: Blood Transfusion Becomes a Reality

Karl Landsteiner's discovery – Man's experiments with blood transfusion – Surgeons able to do much more intricate operations – The rise of the casualty surgeon

For many centuries doctors had unsuccessfully tried to transfuse dying men with fresh supplies of blood. Even before Harvey described how blood circulates around the human body, physicians had played with the idea of supplementing a sick person's blood with blood from a healthy individual or even a healthy animal.

The first successful transfusion was probably made by the French doctor Jean Baptiste Denys, who was Professor of Philosophy at Montpellier and court physician to Louis XIV. Denys is said to have given a young boy eight ounces of blood from a lamb in 1667. His success with that patient encouraged him to try with another the following year, but the unfortunate death of the recipient of that transfusion resulted in a lawsuit against Denys and, after his arrest, the procedure of transfusing blood from animals into man was prohibited by an Act of the Chamber of Deputies in 1668.

In Italy a physician in Florence called Francesco Folli published a book in 1680 in which he described similar experiments that he had conducted, while in England both Christopher Wren, the architect, and Robert Boyle, the scientist, wrote papers on the subject. The diarist Samuel Pepys included an account of a transfusion done by Richard Lower, who, like Denys, put lamb's blood into a man, and reports that the subject had aroused much interest including the comment that it might be entertaining to let the blood of a Quaker into an archbishop.

An early example of medical litigation, occurring when a suit was brought against Dr Denys by the widow of the man who had died after an attempted transfusion, effectively put a stop to all further transfusions for some time, and it was not until 1818 that a London doctor, Dr Blundell, and a surgeon, Mr Cline, performed the next transfusion on a dying man, obtaining blood from several volunteers and transferring it to the recipient with the aid of syringes. Subsequently, in the Lancet in 1829, Dr Blundell reported how a female patient who had bled heavily after childbirth had received blood from his own assistant and had subsequently done well.

Many of the early transfusion attempts were foiled, however, when the blood intended for the transfusion clotted in the syringe and could not be used. In view of what we now know about blood groups and the dangers of transfusing mismatched blood, this problem may have saved many lives.

The major breakthrough came when the biologist Landsteiner discovered that different human beings have different types of blood. By a series of tests he showed that, whereas there are some individuals whose blood can be given to any recipient, there are also individuals whose blood will not mix safely. Once this technique of identifying individual blood groups had been perfected, it became feasible for doctors and surgeons to transfer blood from one individual to another compatible individual. When, a little later, it was discovered that a substance called sodium citrate can be used safely to prevent the clotting of blood intended for transfusion, the final major problem had been removed.

This newly developed ability to transfuse blood from one person to another had two important practical effects.

First, it meant that surgeons were now able to perform even longer and more intricate operations without having to worry unduly about their patients losing too much blood on the operating table. The ability to transfuse blood, the availability of X-rays, the introduction of the principle of asepsis and the development of effective forms of anaesthesia all revolutionised surgical techniques, and no single later development matched these for importance.

Second, it also meant that surgeons working in casualty stations and accident departments could, for the first time in history, hope to save those individuals who had been badly wounded and whose injuries had been accompanied by a severe loss of blood. Advances in radiology, anaesthesia and asepsis had meant that surgeons could hope to save the lives of badly injured patients, and the fact that blood could be safely transfused into those patients meant that life could be prolonged and maintained while these surgical repairs continued.

Ironically, of course, the advance in surgical techniques which inevitably resulted from the work of Landsteiner did not lead to a dramatic decrease in the number of people dying from accidental injuries. The reason for this paradox was simple: the wider availability of the motor car, the aeroplane and other pieces of machinery meant that the total number of accident victims was increasing annually.

Chapter 48: Disease and War

The Russo-Japanese War – The importance of infection to generals – The Boer War and typhoid – The example is followed around the world.

The Russo-Japanese war of 1904-6 was a landmark in military and civil health care. It was the first major military encounter in which the number of casualties produced by infection and disease did not exceed the number of men wounded by enemy action.

Before the Russo-Japanese War military campaigns were always bedevilled by infectious diseases, and generals had become accustomed to losing large numbers of men to unseen opponents. The conditions under which battles were fought were ideal for the development of infections: the soldiers were invariably tired and weak after marching hundreds of miles, their food supplies were rarely adequate or properly balanced, their drinking water was often polluted and the sewage facilities in their camps were crude. Additionally, soldiers in a new country were often exposed to types of infection against which they had no acquired immunity. As a result, many campaigns were won or lost because of the presence or absence of small organisms rather than through the skills and experience of their military leaders.

In the spring of 1812, for example, Napoleon had reached the peak of his power. His new French Empire spread from Russian and Austrian frontiers in the east to the sea on the north, south and west. His two brothers and his son sat on thrones, and everyone except the British had succumbed to his power.

But not even Napoleon had been able to defeat typhus, a disease which thrives in dirty conditions and which was endemic in hospitals, prisons and all the other places where overcrowding was common during the seventeenth, eighteenth and nineteenth centuries. Army camps were perfect breeding grounds for the louse which carries the disease, since it was almost impossible for the soldiers to wash or change their clothing. Napoleon's army had been fighting and travelling for so long that most had probably not seen themselves naked for years. To Napoleon typhus was probably a greater threat than Wellington.

The disease was still a major problem for the British in the Crimean War nearly half a century later. Together with cholera and smallpox, typhus killed ten times as many British soldiers as were killed in action by the enemy. Typhus alone was responsible for the deaths of nearly a million soldiers.

Even during the Boer War at the end of the nineteenth century and the beginning of the twentieth century, five times as many British soldiers died of disease as of bullets.

By that time it had been recognised that dirty conditions encourage disease, and the town and city dwellers in most European countries had been effectively protected by public health regulations. Inexplicably, however, military authorities still seemed to consider soldiers expendable and did nothing to protect them against infection. Anti-typhoid injections were available before the Boer War but they were not used; if they had been, many of the eleven thousand men who died from the disease could have been saved.

It was not until the Russo-Japanese War that the generals first began to consider infection and disease a serious threat to be combated. Both Japanese and Russians took two important steps towards protecting their soldiers. First, they made a positive effort to improve the living conditions of their armies and to ensure that clean water supplies were made available; second, they introduced vaccination on a wide scale. The effect of their policy was dramatic. The Japanese lost nearly sixty thousand men to the enemy, but only a third of that number to disease, while the Russians claim that only one in a hundred of their soldiers died from infections.

Following this example, military authorities around the world slowly began to introduce similar forms of protection for their men.

Chapter 49: The First Organised Health Services

Improvements in medical education begin in America – The library with no books – Hospitals poorly staffed despite Florence Nightingale's example – The general availability of medical care – The early health services

More changes had taken place in the quality and availability of medical care during the nineteenth century than in any other single century. And yet, despite the advances which had taken place in medical science and which had resulted in theoretical improvements in the quality of surgical care and the quality of nursing care and in practical improvements in the standard of living conditions in most major towns and cities, there were still many problems to be overcome.

For example, although the medical profession had succeeded in establishing the principle that only those surgeons and physicians who were officially registered and recognised as such could practice medicine freely, there had been relatively few improvements in the quality of medical education available.

In America in 1910, when Abraham Flexner published a comprehensive study of the quantity and quality of medical education available in his country, he found that there were an extraordinary number of independent schools offering many standards of education. He found, for example, thirty-nine medical schools in Illinois, fourteen in Chicago, forty-two in Missouri, forty-three in Pennsylvania, eighteen in Tennessee, twenty in Cincinnati and eleven in Louisville. Inevitably there were many medical graduates, and whereas at the time there was one doctor for every two or three thousand people in Germany, France and Austria, there was one doctor for every seven hundred people in America, with the ratio reaching one for every four hundred and sixty people in New York.

Visiting medical schools all over America quite unannounced, Flexner found an enormous variety in the quality of medical teaching. In Los Angeles he opened the door to the library at the College of Physicians and Surgeons and found that it contained no books. In Kansas he opened the dissecting room door at a local medical school and peeped inside to find a chicken yard covered with straw. The laboratory at the Maryland Medical College was said to consist of a few dirty test tubes kept in cigar boxes.

Of the one hundred and fifty medical schools which he managed to visit, Flexner found that eighty had no educational requirements at all, while many more were far more interested in the student's ability to pay his fees than in his academic prow-

194

ess. Very few of the medical schools had any arrangements with local hospitals for practical tuition, and it seemed that, in many cases, all a student had to do to qualify was to pay his fees regularly.

Flexner's conclusion was that quantity was not everything, and in his report to the Carnegie Foundation for the Advancement of Teaching he recommended that the schools which should be supported were the ones which were using modern teaching methods and approaches. As a result of his report many medical schools failed to survive, while those that did live on often received donations from charitable organisations in order to make them independent of their students.

Another problem which had to be faced at the beginning of the twentieth century was the fact that many hospitals were still poorly staffed, poorly equipped and not administered properly. Florence Nightingale's enthusiasm for hospitals built in the pavilion style had resulted in the development of a number of admirable buildings, such as the Johns Hopkins Hospital in America and the Rudolf Virchow Hospital in Berlin, Germany, but lack of money meant that in many areas the only hospital buildings existing were old fashioned, poorly ventilated, badly lit and cramped. These inadequate working conditions inevitably made administration difficult, and whereas 'show' hospitals built in the largest cities and attached to the leading medical schools may have had excellent facilities, people living in small towns and cities had too often to put up with hospitals which were far inferior in almost every respect.

The vast variety in the quality of hospital buildings around the world resulted from the fact that the buildings in use had been erected by many different organisations, some voluntary, some statutory, some public, some private, and their original designers had been commissioned to satisfy the specific requirements of the potential owners.

In Britain, for example, there were hospital buildings which had been built for religious organisations and others which had been built by local authorities having to comply with the Poor

Law Act of 1835, which had required the building of institutions and asylums for the poor and sick, the mentally ill and those patients suffering from contagious diseases. Many of these hospitals had been over-crowded since the days of their opening, and as voluntary hospitals found it harder and harder to collect funds from citizens who knew well that there were public facilities and public funds available, the overcrowding problem became more acute.

The type of staff and facilities available in the better hospitals differed a great deal from the staff and facilities available in the older buildings. In the more well-equipped and well-endowed hospitals, for example, doctors and nurses found that not only did they have better equipment but that they were assisted by other specialists. Röntgen's X-ray equipment, for example, made the employment of special technicians inevitable, while, at the Massachusetts General Hospital in America, Dr Richard Cabot hired the first medical social worker to work with him in his out-patient department in 1905. But, at the same time, in the Poor Law hospitals and in other similar institutions around the world, nursing care was often as bad as it had been before Florence Nightingale's days.

There was one other factor which was just as important as the quality of medical education and the quality of hospital services, and that was the general availability of medical care.

During the nineteenth century and the early part of the twentieth century laws had been passed in most parts of the world which made it difficult for anyone not possessing an officially recognised qualification to practise medicine. Theoretically, these laws were designed to protect patients from quacks and charlatans, but in practice there was a problem in that a very large number of people had traditionally relied upon these very people, now outlawed, for their medical care.

In part, the problem had been solved by the increase in the number of medical graduates, which made it possible for most people to find and afford a registered practitioner. In America, the number of graduates had grown to extraordinary proportions as a result of the fact that medical schools could be turned into profitable institutions by charging healthy fees. In Britain, the Society of Apothecaries had deliberately increased the number of qualified doctors in order to provide a practical answer to those who argued that the quacks were providing a necessary and worthwhile service. (Many of those qualified and registered were probably less able than some of the unqualified and unregistered practitioners, but as educational standards improved, so this problem subsided in importance.)

In addition, however, there was one other important development which improved the availability of medical care and helped to accustom those individuals used to obtaining help from midwives, quacks and other unqualified advisers to the idea of seeking help from properly qualified and registered practitioners. The development which enabled people to make this transition involved the introduction of the first types of organised health service.

The idea of individuals being able to take advantage of some form of organised health care programme, which provided care free of charge or which required small regular payments rather than large irregular sums, was not a new one. At the end of the eighteenth century there had been a number of clubs and societies in existence around Europe which collected small payments from their members and in return provided medical services and sick pay. Many of these organisations had been run by trades and guilds and had existed for the protection of their own members.

In addition, in England, the local Boards of Guardians, appointed under the Poor Law Act of 1835, had been required to appoint district medical officers who were obliged to provide medical care for anyone needing it.

Then, in 1862, the Russians had introduced what they had hoped would be a comprehensive health service. However, although the service was free, it was also rather inadequate since, to begin with at least, there were not enough trained workers to cover the whole country. More effective than this was the scheme organised by the German government in 1880, which was based partly on a form of health insurance. The Swedish government introduced a similar scheme at the beginning of the twentieth century, and its National Board of Health appointed doctors to act as both public health officers and general practitioners. It was the German scheme which inspired the British Prime Minister, Lloyd George, to organise a National Health Insurance Act in 1911. Under this legislation wage-earners were entitled to sickness benefit and a free general practitioner service as long as they made the necessary contributions.

By 1914 health care schemes were in action in several European countries, while in many parts of the world the first steps had been taken to base the education of medical practitioners on a sounder footing and to make their skills and services available to as large a number of people as possible.

The cost of building properly designed, well-equipped hospitals was still prohibitive, however, and few of the establishments in use would have satisfied the strict requirements of Florence Nightingale.

Chapter 50: The Birth-control Protagonists

The population explosion – The history of contraceptives – A practical necessity – The Malthusian League – Margaret Sanger leads the way – The importance of contraception – Religious opposition

Since man first walked upon the earth, the human population had grown slowly and steadily, suffering intermittent and local setbacks due to plagues and epidemics and taking thousands of years to edge towards a total of 1,000 million people. Then, during the nineteenth century, the rise in the population – particularly in the Western world – began to accelerate rapidly, taking another one hundred years to reach 2,000 million and only another thirty to reach 3,000 million.

Many explanations have been offered for this rapid increase in the world's population. It has been said that improved medical facilities, techniques and knowledge helped to reduce death rates and, to a small extent, this is probably true. It has also been said that, on purely statistical grounds, when a population reaches a certain size it will begin to grow at a far more rapid rate. That, too, is certainly true. It is also argued that, with time, even the most threatening infectious disorders lose some of their potency as people acquire immunity. There is undoubtedly evidence to support that hypothesis.

But there were other important factors which were probably just as responsible for the fact that the population of the world first began to rise rapidly towards the end of the nineteenth century. There were far better food supplies and better public health facilities; clean water was widely available, and many countries had introduced sewage disposal schemes; the Industrial Revolution had produced enormous changes in general living standards, and the introduction of the railways and the motor car had meant that supplies of all kinds could be distributed far more equitably.

The influence of all these factors on the incidence of important infectious diseases, which had a century or two before proved to be such an enormous threat, was dramatic. Better fed, fitter people, living in cleaner houses and drinking cleaner water, are far more likely to be able to resist infection than poorly fed individuals living in damp, cold homes. In particular, babies and young children became far better able to survive attacks of gastro-enteritis and the many other infections which cause some havoc among the young.

Whatever the cause may have been, and it is likely that it was a combination of these explanations, the fact is that the population of the world began to rise most rapidly at the end of the nineteenth century, with the population of the developed Western world rising far more dramatically than the population of the rest of the world.

The effect on individual families at this time was undoubtedly a powerful one. A few decades previously a woman could expect to lose at least half her children in their first year of life. By the end of the nineteenth century that had changed and she could now expect most of them to survive.

Whereas the increase in the total population of the world had produced only a slight effect on individual families, the decrease in the infant mortality rate obviously produced an important and dramatic effect on individual family life. If the population of a country increases by a third, the impact on a working man and woman will not be noticeable. If the population of a family increases by a third, however, the impact will be very noticeable.

It was, therefore, through sheer necessity that many people began to demand contraceptive advice and practical help. Those politicians and satisticians who claim that the size of the current world population is a threat might, perhaps, be comforted by the knowledge that, if the birth rate in England and Wales had stayed at the level that it had reached in 1870, the population of England and Wales today would have been something in the region of 150 million. That such a disastrous rise was prevented is due almost entirely to the good sense of those individuals who first recognised that contraception is a social weapon without which we could not survive.

Contraceptives have been used since men and women first recognised the consequences of making love. Coitus interruptus, needing no special skills or equipment, is probably the oldest form of birth control, and the Hebrews, in particular, practised it. Recognising the aesthetic disadvantages of this method, however, many women have, over the years, experimented with different forms of chemical contraception. Four thousand years ago Egyptian women were mixing and moulding honey and crocodile dung into contraceptive pessaries. Arabian women were said to have made contraceptives from pomegranate pulps treated with alum and rocksalt, and Aristotle described a chemical concoction consisting of cedar oil, frankincense and olive oil, which was said to prevent conception. It is quite possible that all these preparations might have had contraceptive value, since they would have affected the acidity of the internal environment of the vagina, and sperm are very sensitive to changes of this nature.

The sheath is also a fairly well-established device, although its use does not seem to go back beyond the sixteenth century. At that time venereal disease was common, and the sheath was used more as a protection against infection than as a contraceptive. Japanese men are said to have worn sheaths made of tortoiseshell, horn or leather, but Europeans usually followed the example of the Italian Gabriele Fallopio who recommended a moistened linen sheath.

Diaphragms and caps have been used for many years, and Chinese and Japanese women are said to have covered their cervices with discs of oiled tissue paper. Anal intercourse was favoured by some, and there is evidence that the Greeks at the time of Hippocrates used intra-uterine devices.

Dioscorides suggested that after intercourse women who did not want to get pregnant should get up, sneeze, douche and then drink something cold, before making violent bodily contortions designed to displace the sperm, and an ancient Persian writer suggested that in order to dislodge sperm any women reluctant to become a mother should take nine backward jumps before sitting on her toes stroking her naval with her thumb. He does not seem to have specified which thumb. Those who failed with their precautions to prevent pregnancy often tried to remedy the situation later, and both abortion and infanticide were used to limit the size of individual families. Indeed, although we may equate infanticide with primitive cultures, it was practised in Europe until the nineteenth century.

But none of these contraceptive techniques had any great popular support at the end of the nineteenth century, and the average man and woman were obviously expecting something more effective and more acceptable than crocodile dung or coitus interruptus. In the second half of the nineteenth century considerable progress was made in the development of new forms

201

of contraception. An English pharmacist, Walter Rendell, began to sell moderately effective pessaries containing quinine sulphate in 1885. After it became possible to manufacture rubber, contraceptives made of the material began to replace the older variety prepared from animal skins or linen. In 1882 a German, Dr Hasse, invented the type of diaphragm that many women still use today, and in 1883 a Dutch physician, Aletta Jacobs, built and described the first Dutch Cap – a special device intended to cover the entrance to the cervix itself. The *Lancet* of 1868 contained illustrations of small devices made of gold, silver, wood and ivory which were recommended for various complaints affecting the womb, and ten years later it was recognised that these devices were both used and useful in the prevention of conception.

But these technical advances in the development of effective contraceptives were not all that was needed. Even by the end of the nineteenth century there was still a considerable amount of ignorance about the mechanics of reproduction and about the various ways in which conception could be prevented. And, even more important, there were enormous social, political and religious barriers to be overcome. Progress in the availability of contraceptives and the effect that they could have on both the population growth and the size of individual families did not come until some of the opposition to the introduction of contraception had been brought out into the open.

The idea of controlling the size of the population by some form of birth-control, as opposed simply to preventing an individual conception, had been first suggested by a clergyman, Thomas Malthus, at the end of the eighteenth century. Malthus had suggested that sexual abstinence was a good way to cut down the birth rate and had also advocated later marriages. Then in 1832 Charles Knowlton published, in America, a book entitled *The Fruits of Philosophy: or, the Private Companion of Young Married People*, which contained an account of the various forms of contraception available at the time. Knowlton was fined and sent to prison for his impertinence.

In the 1860s George Dysdale started the Malthusian League, which tried again to propagate the idea of birth control. Dysdale was joined by one of the first female reformers, Annie Besant, but they made little progress at first because of the opposition to birth control which came from both the Church and the medical profession. An Act of 1857 had made it illegal to sell books describing contraceptive techniques, simply by categorising them as obscene, and Annie Besant managed to obtain a considerable amount of useful publicity and support for the Malthusian League by deliberately republishing Knowlton's book and attracting prosecution.

The eventual success of the Malthusian League in Britain was followed by the formation of similar groups in the Netherlands, France and Germany. A small number of clinics were opened in the Netherlands in the final decade of the nineteenth century under the leadership of Aletta Jacobs, and slowly the supporters of the various leagues began to make progress in their fight to make contraceptive advice freely available.

The greatest impact in the field of birth control was made by two women. In America, the fight to provide contraceptive advice was led by Margaret Sanger. In Europe one of the most important campaigners was Marie Stopes. These two women, both determined feminists, were together responsible for the introduction and organisation of birth control clinics and for the dissemination of advice and equipment.

Margaret Sanger, herself the sixth of eleven children, began her career as a nurse in New York City, where she saw at first hand the close links between poverty, large families and disease. There were at that time, in America, laws forbidding the promotion of any information about contraception, and so when, in 1914, Mrs Sanger published a magazine and a pamphlet including details about contraception, she was arrested. That case was dismissed, but when, in 1916, she opened the first birth-control clinic, she was charged with maintaining a public nuisance and sent to the workhouse for thirty days. (Mrs Sanger invented the phrase birth-control'.) The publicity aroused by the case and the furore that followed other similar battles eventually led to a relaxation of the law. The 1873 Comstock Act, under which contraceptive devices and literature describing them had been classified as obscene, was, in 1936, interpreted as allowing doctors to prescribe contraceptives if they were essential to the health of their patients.

Marie Stopes, born three years earlier than Margaret Sanger, in 1880, qualified as a botanist in Munich and taught her subject at Manchester University, until the failure of her marriage led her to a study of the problems of matrimony. Her research in this area led her to believe that birth control could help to save some marriages, and in 1921 she founded Britain's first birth-control clinic.

The opposition which Sanger and Stopes faced came mainly from the Church, and in particular from the Roman Catholic Church, which considered contraception of any kind to be a sin. Most members of the medical profession were fairly easily convinced that contraception was essential for women, families and society in general.

The moral and religious arguments put forward in opposition to the campaign, led first by Margaret Sanger, are complex and probably of genuine interest only to those who follow the religions concerned. What is far more important on purely social and medical grounds is the influence that those views had on the success of Mrs Sanger and her followers.

In general, it seems that the influence of those who oppose the free availability of contraception has been greatest in those undeveloped countries which are most in need of some form of population control but which, because of their low economic status and political instability, are most vulnerable to pressure. In the developed Western countries many thousands of individuals may have been prevented from using contraceptive techniques by the stated preferences of their religious leaders or by feelings of guilt and shame engendered by religious teachings, but religious leaders have found it impossible to stem the force of Mrs Sanger's arguments, and even in those countries which are predominantly Catholic, such as Spain and Italy, birth control is not unknown.

Unfortunately, and paradoxically, the availability of contraceptives and contraceptive advice in the developing countries, where population growth frequently exceeds food supplies and prevents further development, has been prevented not by inherent national fears or superstitions but by the prejudices of a powerful minority group in the West which, by applying political and economic pressure to those most vulnerable, has succeeded in delaying the ready availability of birth control.

Technically, Margaret Sanger and Marie Stopes had only the simplest forms of contraceptives to offer; intra-uterine devices were available only to a very small number of women, oral contraceptives did not come onto the market until the 1950s, and sterilisation did not become popular until surgical techniques had made it a simple and relatively painless operation. But socially and politically modern attitudes towards birth control were formed in those early years of the twentieth century when the establishment was confronted by that small but determined group of women.

Chapter 51: Magic Bullets

Limitations facing the general practitioner – The bottle of medicine – Ehrlich's magic bullet – Fleming and penicillin – Domagk and the first synthetic anti-bacterial drug – Penicillin production stepped up for the Second World War – Other pharmacological developments in the twentieth century

The wider availability of professional medical care may have had several theoretical advantages but in practice there was not a lot that an ordinary general practitioner could do to treat his patients. He could help protect them from infections by vaccination and he could, either by himself or with the aid of a local surgeon, deal effectively with their accidental injuries. But the variety of drugs that he could prescribe was small, and most were ineffective. The four most important products available were quinine, opium (or morphine), digitalis and aspirin. The first three had been readily available for several centuries and the fourth, available since 1899, could be obtained without a doctor's prescription.

Most of the bottles made up by general practitioners contained relatively ineffective and generally harmless mixtures of herbal extracts. The best medicines were expected to taste unpleasant, to be prepared in such a way that they needed shaking in order to disturb some sort of sediment, to have an offensive smell which would impress anyone within range and to need taking at least three times a day, preferably before or after meals. Arsenic, strychnine and sarsaparilla were just three of the popular ingredients employed by many doctors at the end of the nineteenth century.

The revolution within the world of pharmacology began in Germany, where Paul Ehrlich, a chemist, began the search for what he called the 'magic bullet', a drug that would have a specific action against a particular disease. Undoubtedly inspired to some extent by the success that Lister had enjoyed with antiseptics, Ehrlich's aim was to find a type of antiseptic which could be used inside the body. He believed that, if ordinary antiseptics could kill bacteria outside the body, antiseptics designed to be taken internally might attack bacteria within the body.

With great patience and determination Ehrlich experimented with compound after compound in an attempt to find a product which would do as he wanted. Finally, in 1910, after no fewer that 605 failures, he produced a substance called Salvarsan, which included some arsenic but which seemed both safe and effective when used against the organism responsible for syphilis. To prove the effectiveness of the product, Ehrlich and the company which had worked with him on the project, Farbwerke Hoechst, gave 65,000 units of Salvarsan free to doctors around the world. As a result of this massive clinical trial, the compound was proved both safe and effective.

Remarkably, Salvarsan was only the second drug to be identified as having a specific action against a particular disease. The first, quinine, had been used in the treatment of malaria since its discovery in Peru many centuries before. It is perhaps hardly surprising that it has been said that it was not until 1910 that a patient stood a better than fifty per cent chance of benefiting from an encounter with a physician.

Ehrlich's research had been specifically directed towards the discovery of an anti-infective substance, but the next major step in this direction – Alexander Fleming's discovery of penicillin in 1928 – was as much the result of good fortune as of careful planning.

According to the now well-established legend, Fleming had been working in his laboratory at St. Mary's Hospital in London on a study of the staphylococcus bacteria when he noticed that a culture dish containing the bacteria appeared to have been contaminated. The contaminant had in some way stopped the growth of the bacteria. In retrospect it seems that someone had left a laboratory window open through which spores of a common fungus had blown. (Historians have in fact argued about this, and while some agree with the window theory, others say that the spores entered through a door, while a third group claim that the spores reached the culture dish through a ventilation shaft.)

Contamination is a common problem in laboratories, and normally such cultures are simply thrown away. Fleming, however, like Röntgen and so many others, was too good a scientist just to toss away the contents of the dish and forget about the incident. He made careful notes on the culture and the following year published a paper in the *British Journal of Experimental Pathology* describing the way in which the growing spores (which he had identified as being those of penicillium notarum) had contaminated the culture dish and prevented the growth of the bacteria. Tests showed that the penicillin mould was safe for human use, and Fleming realised that one day it would prove useful as a drug, but he found that it was too unstable to be manufactured in any quantity.

Fleming's work on penicillin was to lie untouched for a decade. During that period, however, research for effective anti-infective agents made progress in Germany. In 1932 Gerhard Domagk, a director at the Bayer Laboratory for Experimental Pathology and Bacteriology in Wuppertal-Elberfeld, who had been experimenting on new dyes and drugs, decided to investigate a new wool dye, prontosil red, to evaluate its use as a drug.

The story goes that Domagk's daughter, Hildegarde, had pricked her finger with a knitting needle and had developed blood poisoning at just about the time that the therapeutic effect of prontosil was discovered, and that in an attempt to save her Domagk decided to try the new drug. The drug worked, and realising the commercial value of a synthetic product which could be used to combat infection, many of the world's major drug companies began work in attempts to develop similar products. (One of the products which resulted from this international search was M & B 693, an anti-bacterial developed by a company called May & Baker which was used to treat a patient called Winston Churchill when he developed pneumonia during the Second World War.)

The success of prontosil encouraged other scientists to begin work again on penicillin. The next vital step took place in Oxford, where a team of scientists led by Professor Howard Florey and Dr Ernst Chain solved the problem of how to manufacture penicillin in a stable form. Their research coincided with the outbreak of the Second World War, and when it was realised that the new drug would be an important asset to any army, many scientists and drug companies on both sides of the Atlantic began to study ways of manufacturing penicillin in large quantities. By the end of the war, thanks to the combined efforts of British and American manufacturers, penicillin was being produced with comparative ease. (Undoubtedly the drug's military significance resulted in its large-scale production being achieved at an earlier date than would otherwise have been the case.)

During the years following Ehrlich's first discovery, many drugs were produced, and in recent years the production of new compounds has reached almost epidemic proportions. But no other drugs have had such an important effect on the community as the anti-infective products – the antibiotics. In the 1930s, before antibiotics were widely available, the number of people dying from pneumonia in the United States sometimes exceeded fifty per cent of those who had contracted the infection. After the introduction of antibiotics, the death rate fell to about one in twenty. Similar improvements were noticed with other infectious disorders. Once general practitioners were able to provide prescriptions for antibiotics, the number of people needing prolonged bed rest or nursing care for the duration of an infective illness also fell.

Antibiotic drugs were the most important weapons to be added to the doctor's armoury in the twentieth century, but the ever-expanding pharmaceutical industry, which had begun with William Brockeden's first tablet-making machine back in the first half of the nineteenth century, prepared and marketed a great many drugs besides antibiotics. Some of these were of enormous clinical importance to individual patients, but others were of dubious value to anyone except those involved in their manufacture and distribution.

In the field of chemotherapeutics, one of the most profitable areas turned out to be the development of drugs for the treatment of mental disorders, and the absence of any single product with clear advantages over all other products meant that there were soon many alternatives on the market. Barbiturates were among the earliest drugs in this field, and they were soon followed by many other sedatives and tranquillisers.

Just after the conclusion of the Second World War, doctors at the Mayo Clinic in Minnesota isolated a substance called cortisone, a vitally important hormone which proved invaluable in the treatment of diseases as superficially different as rheumatoid arthritis and asthma.

Perhaps even more important than cortisone, in terms of problems facing the world, was the manufacture of synthetic sex hormones, with which researchers in the 1950s succeeded in preparing the first contraceptive pills.

The twentieth century also saw the introduction of new vaccines against tetanus, diphtheria, tuberculosis and poliomyelitis, while nutritional scientists managed for the first time to identify and establish the importance of the individual vitamins, with the result that those suffering from vitamin shortages could also be identified and treated appropriately.

Together, these individual advances helped to give the medical profession a restricted but useful armoury of weapons against a relatively small but important group of diseases. To a certain extent, however, the success in these few areas was misleading. Undoubtedly encouraged by the medical profession and the pharmaceutical industry, the public began to believe that scientists had solved most of the existing problems facing the world and that doctors had cures for all ailments. Although considerable progress had been made in combating disease by drugs, there were still far more disorders that doctors could not treat than could be treated.

This false faith was to lead to much public frustration, dissatisfaction and even anger, most of which was directed against the medical profession and which manifested itself in complaints, litigation and a popular search for support and advice from the alternative practitioners who, ironically, had been more or less outlawed a century before by members of the orthodox medical profession.

Chapter 52: International Control of Disease

Infectious diseases know no barriers – The need for international control – The World Health Organisation – The fight against smallpox – Other contributions made by the WHO

The struggle to deal with the major communicable diseases had been an almost continuous process for many centuries. There had been quiescent periods, when it must have seemed as though no progress would ever be made, and there had been moments when it must have appeared as though man's susceptibility and vincibility to infection must have been almost at an end. Jenner's first trials with the smallpox vaccine, Chadwick's first successes in persuading the mid-nineteenth-century politicians in London to spend money on improving the public health facilities in London, Pasteur's idea about the vulnerability of infections to antiseptics, Ross's discovery of the link between malaria and the mosquito, and Ehrlich's first magic bullet – all these breakthroughs must have promised an end to the tyranny of infection.

But the truth was that each one of these innovations depended not just upon the individual man nor upon the effectiveness of his proposal but also upon the willingness of the world's leaders to act upon the advice given and to put into practice the suggestions made. A vaccination programme will not work unless there are political leaders prepared to allocate the necessary funds; a campaign for clean water and clean streets does no good if the appropriate legislation is not passed; the effectiveness of antiseptics goes unnoticed if the principle behind their use is not accepted by the establishment; the knowledge about the links between specific parasites and insects is valueless if funds and campaigns are not available to use that information; the availability of a magic bullet does no good if there is no one to pay for the gun or to hire a man to fire it.

Gradually during the nineteenth century, as more and more effective ideas became available, they were put into practice in most of the developed countries. The Industrial Revolution had produced social changes which had made it politically desirable for politicians to take advantage of these developments as quickly as possible, and the economic growth which had accompanied the Industrial Revolution had made it possible for them to do so. Working men and women were demanding cleaner homes, cleaner streets and better air to breathe, and their employers were anxious to keep morbidity and mortality rates as low as possible in order to keep their factories running smoothly.

But while there were immense social and political pressures in northern Europe and in North America which ensured that every new advance in the fight against such diseases as smallpox, cholera and malaria was eventually greeted, if not with enthusiasm, at least with some sense of resigned acceptance, the same was not true of the under-developed countries of eastern Europe, Africa, Asia and South America. In those countries there was little if any enthusiasm for the fight against infection, and there was no money to pay for the fight even if there had been any enthusiasm for it.

This state of affairs might have continued but for the fact that it slowly became clear that the organisms responsible for the infectious diseases concerned do not respect any of the international boundaries which exist between developed countries (those making every effort to defeat infection), and the under-developed countries (which were making either a minimal effort or no effort at all).

It quickly became apparent, therefore, that there was very little point in struggling to eradicate smallpox, cholera or whatever from one country if the causative organisms were breeding unchecked a few miles away. Indeed, there were positive dangers in such an approach since, with the improvement in forms of personal communication which had followed the building of the first steam train and which later followed the building of the first motor car and the first aeroplane, the eradication of a disease in one country would eventually make the citizens of that country exceptionally vulnerable to that very same disease were they to be exposed to it elsewhere.

Consequently, the enthusiasm of the developed countries for some way of controlling infectious diseases internationally, and for some way of dealing with infection within the national borders of the undeveloped countries, was not entirely altruistic.

The first active sign of any co-operation between different countries in the fight against infection involved the holding of an International Sanitary Conference in Paris in 1851. The aim of this meeting was simply to try to produce a single quarantine regulation which could be imposed in all European countries and, in particular, in all their Mediterranean ports. The meeting, and the four others which followed in the subsequent thirty-four years, failed mainly because no one had any real idea about what caused plague, cholera or yellow fever, and those attending the conferences could not agree on the best way to avoid any one of these three diseases.

Eventually, at the seventh International Sanitary Conference, held in Venice in 1892, an agreement was reached with regard to cholera. That was the first step in the development of international co-operation in the fight against disease, and it was followed in 1907 by the establishment in Paris of an Office International d'Hygiène Publique which included America as well as most European countries.

A number of meetings followed, but not a lot happened until after the First World War, when the League of Nations was created and formed its own organisation known as the Health Organisation of the League of Nations. Exhausted by this effort, the nations of the world did little more until the outbreak of the Second World War, when international health work naturally came to an entire standstill.

It was only after the Second World War, when the World Health Organisation (WHO) was founded in 1946, that progress really began and an international campaign was started in an attempt to control and eradicate the major infectious diseases.

The new organisation was instructed to keep records of the statistics and patterns of disease, to stimulate the eradication of epidemic and endemic diseases and to assist in the development and improvement of national health services around the world. It also had other objectives, such as the improvement of working conditions, the promotion of co-operation between health professionals in different parts of the world, the promotion of health education and the development of international standards for all areas of health; but its single most important task was the eradication of infectious disorders.

The WHO's success in this endeavour has, perhaps inevitably, been mixed. One of the major problems facing the Organisation was its Charter, which gives it authority to assist in any particular country only when that country has requested advice or practical help. This has meant that attempts to eradicate infectious diseases have often been hampered by a country's refusal, on either political or military grounds, to invite observers in.

However, the Organisation has made a particular effort to eradicate two diseases.

In 1955 the WHO declared that an all-out campaign should be waged against malaria, a disorder which was by then virtually unknown in most of the developed countries but which was still responsible for many thousands of deaths each year in other countries. The most important weapons in this battle were considered to be the insecticides, such as DDT, which kill the mosquitoes which transmit the disease, and although a great many insects have acquired immunity to these chemicals, it was believed that the number of mosquitoes could be reduced to a point where the disease could be threatened with extinction. The theory was that, if the total number of mosquitoes is cut, the number of malaria-carrying mosquitoes must also be cut. This reduction will then inevitably mean that the number of people contracting the disease after a mosquito bite will fall, and that, in turn, would mean that the number of mosquitoes picking up the parasite by biting infected sufferers would fall as well. Eventually, the argument was, the life cycle of the parasite would be broken and the disease would be made extinct.

Unfortunately, the Organisation's programme did not go entirely according to plan, since not all countries were prepared to operate in the necessarily expensive campaign to destroy the mosquito. This inevitably meant that successful campaigns within one country's borders were negated by token or absent campaigns in neighbouring countries. The Organisation's plan was defeated by the very problem which had inspired its own development in the first place.

The campaign to get rid of smallpox, which began in 1966,

has been much more successful, and within fifteen years of the beginnings of the campaign the World Health Organisation was able proudly to boast that smallpox had been eradicated from the earth. This had been done despite the fact that even today no treatment against smallpox is available. The WHO had relied on vaccination, which was first organised in the late eighteenth century by Dr Jenner and which is a recognised and effective way of preventing the disease. It was simply by vaccinating whole populations that the WHO succeeded in dealing with smallpox and fulfilling the prophecy made by President Jefferson, who nearly two centuries before had forecast that with the aid of Jenner's vaccine the world would eventually be rid of smallpox.

The contributions made by the World Health Organisation to the living standards and good health of the people of the world have been many. There have been numerous campaigns designed to make people more aware of the hazards of smoking, of the needs of pregnant women and young children and of the dangers associated with specific occupations. There have been a great many successful educational programmes organised in attempts to improve the quality of health care in underdeveloped countries. There have been many important research programmes produced in an attempt to improve the extent and availability of medical knowledge. And there have been many instances where the Organisation has undoubtedly been able to offer individual governments important advice on the administration of health services and on the practical problems likely to be met during the development of any one of a wide range of health-care plans.

But the Organisation's most important role has undoubtedly been to co-ordinate efforts designed to attack and defeat the major communicable diseases. To the citizens of developing countries these infections can be as crippling and as damaging in commercial and social terms as they were in Europe and North America more than a century ago. Until they are finally eradicated, they remain a threat to everyone.

Chapter 53: Modern Health Care

Better national health schemes are suggested – Mr Bevan takes on the doctors and wins – The balance of power moves towards the bureaucrats – The effects of this change on health – Judging the quality of a country's health services

In 1948, the year in which the World Health Organisation first became fully operational, health care was the subject of much discussion and many arguments in individual countries around the world. The insurance schemes founded at the beginning of the century were no longer considered adequate, and many brave new proposals had been put forward.

In Britain, for example, where for decades the government and the medical profession had played with the idea of founding an organised health service, the world's first fully comprehensive national health service actually came into being in 1948.

Until Labour politician Aneurin Bevan became Minister of Health in 1945, politicians and doctors had repeatedly failed to agree on the best ways in which to administer such a scheme. Bevan, however, was a determined, thoughtful and immensely skilful politician who was determined to put theory into practice. He succeeded by deliberately driving a wedge between the hospital consultants and the general practitioners, so that he would not have to negotiate with a united and strong profession. Later, after the ink had dried on the agreements, he confessed that he had silenced the protests of the hospital doctors by 'stuffing their mouths with gold'. Once the consultants had been won over, he succeeded in forcing the general practitioners to accept his proposals and his conditions of employment.

Before the National Health Service came into being, general practice in Britain had been run by a large number of individualists, operating very much on their own. Most general practitioners worked without partners or ancillary workers of any kind and provided their own comprehensive service for patients under their care. While some patients had paid private fees for consultations and prescriptions, many paid for their care through the insurance scheme that had been introduced in 1911. When a general practitioner wanted to retire, he would sell his list of patients to his successor.

Before 1948, Britain's hospital service consisted of an incredible assortment of mixed hospitals and institutions which varied enormously in quality and size. Some of the hospitals and been organised in response to the Poor Law Act of 1835, but many were run on an entirely voluntary basis. All these hospitals were brought into the health service, as were the doctors employed within them as specialists.

The third type of medical care which had existed prior to the formation of the National Health Service involved the Medical Officers of Health and their nurses, midwives and health visitors.

Bevan brought these three groups together under one administration so that, although the same general practitioners, the same hospitals, the same Medical Officers of Health and the same district nurses still provided exactly the same sort of service, there was no longer any question of individual patients having to pay for any services. Private practice was allowed to persist but the National Health Service ensured that anyone who wanted free treatment could get it. For the first time in modern history the doctor was employed not by the patient himself but by a third party.

Incidentally, it is no coincidence that the birth of the world's first comprehensive health service followed the end of the Second World War. The war had led to the introduction of many emergency services and had given many hundreds of thousands of soldiers and civilians the chance to see the advantages of a well-organised free health service. The proposal for a similar service in peace time was therefore welcomed.

Following the formation of the British National Health Service, many other countries introduced similar schemes. In some places, notably the United States, the emphasis remained on the provision of private medical care, and the majority of potential patients enrolled with private insurance companies. Several countries, however, introduced state-run schemes, and these, like the British system, also introduced schemes whereby the sick, elderly, disabled and otherwise unfortunate could obtain state support. The provision of such payments did a great deal to eradicate poverty and to minimise the social and economic pains traditionally associated with illness.

The introduction of state-controlled health care and state-run benefit schemes marked the beginning of a new era for many developed countries. During the Industrial Revolution, dominated by capitalism, most of the developed countries had supported the concept of survival for the fittest. During the 1950s and the 1960s, however, those countries which had introduced public control over the provision of health care, disability benefits, sickness insurance and old-age pensions began to show signs of social and economic changes which were to alter dramatically the balance of control and authority, giving more of both to the bureaucracies which had evolved during that period and which, by the end of the 1960s, were expanding in size and influence without opposition from politicians, electors or consumers.

There are many examples of the ways in which bureaucratic control has affected health care but many critics looking for specific targets would probably choose the hospital services. In several countries, such as Britain, the percentage of hospital employees directly involved in the care of patients has fallen since the inception of the Health Service, while the number of hospital employees not directly involved in the care of patients had risen dramatically. This change in emphasis, from medical care to general administration, has not only produced a change in the quality of care provided but also changed the ways in which the hospitals themselves are organised. As a result, many new hospitals now being planned and built are designed according to the requirements of the administrators rather than to the needs of the patients. It is, for example, better for administrators if a hospital is built as a multi-storey building. It is far easier to manage such a unit than a sprawling hospital which follows the designs recommended by Florence Nightingale. On the other hand, all the modern evidence suggests that her favoured pavilion type of hospital is much better for patients than the multistorey building. It is remarkable, but true, that, whereas in a twelfth-century monastery hospital the patients' ward was the most important part of the hospital, in a modern centre of medical excellence, wards for the patients may take up only about one-fifth of the available space.

Another problem often associated with the increase in the number of administration-heavy, high-technology hospitals has been the deterioration in the quality of the doctor-patient relationship. Florence Nightingale described with remarkable accuracy the damage that apprehension, uncertainty, waiting and fear can do to patients. It is daunting to contemplate what she might have had to say about the fact that some hospitals, for administrative convenience, do not have casualty departments and must turn away unexpected patients. In the whole history of medicine, I doubt if there has ever been a time before when a patient would be turned away from a hospital.

Chapter 54: The End of an Era?

Medicine has lost its impetus – The medical profession is devoted to a search for cures – Iatrogenic diseases – Problems in the developing countries – Threats for the future – The end of an era?

Medicine has lost much of the impetus which took it through the nineteenth century and brought it into the twentieth. In some of the developed countries, life expectation is actually less today than it was several decades ago, while in the developing countries there is evidence that the fight against disease is making little, if any, progress.

In the developed countries, both those which have favoured

state control and those in which private medical schemes predominate, the medical profession has acquired almost total control over the provision of health-care facilities. Alternative medical groups may be attracting an increasing amount of support, but it is the orthodox and registered medical practitioners who control both the quantity and variety of medical services generally available.

Unhappily, the medical profession has always been organised in such a way that it operates most effectively in a society which expects doctors to provide treatments for existing disorders and which offers rewards accordingly. This 'interventionist' philosophy was developed many centuries ago when the cause of most disorders was unrecognised and when doctors could do little more than offer hypotheses and theories.

Today we know a great deal more about the background to many disorders. In particular, we know that most of the major diseases are preventable. Logically, medical care should be organised with the greatest emphasis on prevention. But that logical interpretation of our present needs does not suit a medical profession dedicated to the provision of cures. So much of the effort in today's developed countries is devoted to the accumulation of information designed to satisfy this particular ambition either by assisting in the diagnosis of specific disorders or by providing new therapies, regardless of the fact that improvements in the quantity of knowledge and the quality of technology available are not always accompanied by improvements in either the quality or quantity of medical care for the individual patient. Put simply, this means that late twentieth-century medicine is often practised to satisfy the needs and ambitions of the doctors rather than the patients.

Indeed, the type of medicine practised today in the developed countries seems to some observers to be a considerable threat to the patients, and today, if a patient is suffering from two diseases, the second disease was probably caused by the treatment for the first disease.

In the developing countries the major tragedy has been

the comparative failure of groups such as the World Health Organisation to convince local health administrators and medical professionals that improvements in the quality of care can best be provided by the provision of clean water supplies, sanitation facilities, good food and a basic foundation of public services, rather than by modern, high-technology hospitals.

Leaders in many developing countries have tried to leap straight from conditions comparable to those in Stone Age or medieval Europe to conditions similar to those in twentieth-century Europe, with the result that, while citizens in the major cities have access to modern scanners, heart transplant surgery and other wonders of medicine, the majority of citizens outside those cities are still exposed to threats of infection. Approximately half of the world's population is still without clean water or sanitation facilities. Since it is now recognised that something like eighty per cent of all common disorders in developing countries are associated with polluted water supplies, this is no simple political misjudgement but a catastrophe of astronomical proportions. The number of infants dying each year from diarrhoeal diseases caught through drinking dirty water is in the region of five million.

The leap from a Stone Age civilisation to an Atomic civilisation has produced, and will continue to produce, other problems in the developing countries. For example, in regions where the number of people dying from infectious diseases has fallen but agricultural developments have failed to produce an equivalent improvement in food supplies, the number of people dying from starvation has naturally risen. The size of this problem has been increased by the fact that the provision of birth-control facilities has often been denied or delayed by health organisations under pressure from religious groups.

The almost universal failure to recognise the major areas requiring medical attention and to acknowledge the outstanding importance of preventive medicine as opposed to curative medicine (in both the developed and the developing countries) means that there is a real risk that infectious disorders now considered rare in the developed world may become common again in the future. Experts believe, for example, not only that there is a risk of diseases such as plague or cholera recurring on a worldwide basis but that viral diseases may wreak havoc if the emphasis on high-technology curative medicine is allowed to persist (very few drugs are effective against viruses). The impact made by the two major influenza epidemics to hit the world in the twentieth century showed our vulnerability to virus infection. In the 1918 epidemic about half the world's population is believed to have contracted the virus, and at least twenty million died. In the more recent 1957 epidemic, only about half as many people caught the bug and fewer died, but the social and economic impact was still considerable.

Not that the threat comes only from infectious disorders. Although the factors responsible for eighty per cent of all cancers have been identified, very little effort is made to reduce human exposure to these substances (such as meat and tobacco).

Similarly, other industrial hazards are recognised as common causes of disease but, although the diseases themselves may be subjected to close study, the causes are rarely considered. The same is true for the factors recognised as responsible for the high death rate due to heart disease and other degenerative disorders.

The conclusion has to be that, unless a medical paradigm, which was formulated centuries ago and which is demonstrably unsuitable for today's conditions, can be overthrown and replaced by one more in keeping with our understanding of history, the extent of our knowledge today and the peculiar requirements of a world united by progress but divided by unequal technological advances, the second half of the twentieth century will be seen by future historians as having marked the end of a remarkable era, during which the availability and quality of public and personal medical care improved far more rapidly than at any previous time in the history of the world.

Dramatis Personae

I have included dates and biographical details in the text only where they seem relevant. Brief notes on the individuals who appear in this book are included in the following alphabetically arranged list.

ACHILLES: Brave, handsome, powerful but mythical Greek said to have been dipped in River Styx by Thetis and thereby to have gained invulnerability.

ADDISON, Thomas: (1793–1860) British physician after whom a disease is named. He claimed that Laennec contributed more towards the advancement of medical art than any other single individual of ancient or modern times.

AESCULAPIUS: Otherwise known as Asklepios and Asclepius. Greek god of medicine. Reputed to have lived about 1250 BC.

ALEXANDER THE GREAT: (356–323 BC) King of Macedonia and one of the world's greatest generals. Taught by Aristotle. Said to have died after eating and drinking too much.

ALEXIS: (1904–18) Otherwise known as Alexei Nikolayevich. Son and heir of Nicholas II of Russia. A haemophiliac. Alexis was the boy Rasputin looked after so well.

AMHERST, Jeffery: (1717–97) Created a baron 1776. Englishman who fought in America and captured Canada.

ANSON, George: (1697–1762) British Admiral who spent four years sailing round the world and unhappily lost half his crew, most of them dying from scurvy.

APOLLO: Most influential Greek god. Primarily concerned with healing and prophecy.

ARISTOPHANES: (446–380 BC) Greek playwright who described doctors as lazy, long-haired, foppish individuals and who produced the lines: 'My wind exploded like a thunder clap,...Iaso blushed a rosy red, And Panacea turned away her head, Holding her nose: my wind's not frankincense.' This is believed to be the first medical reference to flatulence.

ARISTOTLE: (384-322 BC) Greek philosopher and scientist. Author of many important books. Said to have written that, 'It is easy to fly into a passion – anybody can do that – but to be angry with the right person and to the right extent and at the right time and with the right objects and in the right way – that is not easy and it is not everyone who can do it.'

ARKWRIGHT, Richard: (1732–92) British businessman and inventor at the forefront of the Industrial Revolution. Knighted in 1786.

AUENBRUGGER, Leopold: (1722–1809) Austrian physician who discovered that by tapping the human chest it is possible to diagnose the condition of the organs within. Composed an opera entitled The *Chimney-sweep* at the request of the Empress Maria Theresa. The importance of his discovery was not recognised until after his death.

BACON, Roger (1214–94) Born in England but worked for many years in Paris. A Franciscan monk, he has been described as a mathematician, physicist, chemist, physician, astronomer, geographer, philosopher, comparative philologist; he was known as 'Doctor Mirabilis'. Bacon is sometimes credited with the invention of the telescope, the microscope, the diving bell, spectacles, gunpowder, locomotives and flying machines and is said to have moaned that, 'Medical men don't know the drugs they use, nor their prices.'

BAGLIVI, Giorgio: (1668–1706) Described by anglophiles as 'the Italian Sydenham'. A physician and professor of Anatomy in Rome. Early experimental physiologist but believed in the value of astrology. Follower of Hippocrates.

BAUER, George: (1494–1555) Also known as Georgius Agricola. Studied in Leipzig, Bologna, Padua and Venice. Expert on mines and mining.

BEAUMONT, William: (1785–1853) Surgeon in the US Army and famed for his early studies of digestion. Wrote in his notebook that, 'Of all the lessons which a young man entering upon the profession of medicine needs to learn, this is perhaps the first – that he should resist the fascination of doctrines and hypotheses till he has won the privilege of such studies by honest labour and faithful pursuit of real and useful knowledge.'

BECKET, Thomas: (1118–70) Also known as Thomas à Becket.

Archbishop of Canterbury killed by four knights in Canterbury Cathedral because he persistently argued with King Henry II.

BESANT, Annie: (1847–1933) Born in Britain, died in India. Socialist, social reformer, women's liberation leader and general rebel. Married an Anglican clergyman but became good friends with an atheist. Became a strong advocate of birth control.

BICHAT, Marie-François-Xavier: (1771–1802) French anatomist and surgeon who influenced many students of his time. An early histologist, Bichat studied and described human tissues.

BILLROTH, Theodor: (1829–94) German surgeon who pioneered intestinal surgery. Remembered today by an operation which bears his name.

BLACKWELL, Elizabeth: (1821–1910) Born in Britain, emigrated to the USA with her family in 1832 and established a school for girls in 1838. Began her medical education informally and after repeated applications was accepted for full-time study in 1847. Later became Professor of Gynaecology in London.

BLANE, Gilbert: (1749–1834) Powerful naval physician who introduced lime juice to the British navy and subsequently saw a dramatic decline in the incidence of scurvy. Blane was by no means the first man to see the value of lime or lemon juice but he was the first with sufficient influence to use the information effectively. British sailors are known as 'limeys' around the world because of their use of lime juice. It is perhaps fortunate that Blane did not choose to favour lemons. Created Baronet in 1812.

BOERHAAVE, Herman: (1668–1738) Professor of Chemistry at Leyden University, who influenced medical education and medical thinking throughout the world in the eighteenth century. Said to have had the largest practice in Europe. First man to establish real bedside teaching methods. In addition to teaching clinical medicine, he also taught chemistry, physics and botany. It is said that a letter addressed to 'The Greatest Physician in the World' reached him safely. His reputation even reached China.

BORELLI, Giovanni: (1608–79) Italian physiologist who tried to explain the movement of animals on mechanical grounds.

BOUQUET, Henry: (1719–65) Born in Switzerland, fought with the

British army and ended up in command of all the troops in the southern colonies of British North America.

BOYLE, Robert: (1627–91) Distinguished English chemist. Remembered today by schoolboys who must learn his law.

BRIGHT, Richard: (1789–1858) British-born physician who studied in Berlin and Vienna and worked in London. His work on kidney disorders earned him immortality. In an address given at the beginning of a course of lectures he told students that, 'Acute disease must be seen at least once a day by those who wish to learn; in many cases twice a day will not be too often.'

BROCKEDEN, William: (1787–1854) Watchmaker's son who invented the compressed tablet and inadvertently founded the modern pharmaceutical industry.

BURKE, William: (1792–1829) Friend of Hare. Enterprising but over-enthusiastic supplier of cadavers to the medical profession.

CABOT, Richard: (1868–1939) Innovative American physician who, among other things, introduced social workers to medical care.

CAESAR, Julius: (110–44 BC) Great Roman general who had enormous influence on the development of the Roman Empire and on later European history.

CALVIN, John: (1509–64) French Protestant Reformer who settled in Switzerland. Not above indulging in a bit of persecution.

CARNEGIE, Andrew: (1835–1919) Born in Scotland, died in America. He stated that, 'A rich man should, after acquiring his wealth, distribute the surplus for the general welfare' and followed his own philosophy. His generosity helped the development of many American medical schools and hospitals.

CARROLL, James: (1854–1907) British-born physician who worked in America and was a member of Walter Reed's team of researchers who invested yellow fever in Cuba.

CARTIER, Jacques: (1491–1557) French mariner, born and died in St. Malo. Cartier's explorations of the North American coast enabled the French to claim Canada.

CATHERINE II: (1729–96) Also known as Catherine 'the Great' of Russia. Ambitious, astute, German-born Empress. Did much to stimulate interest in medicine. Said to have suffered from insomnia and to have had a hearty sexual appetite. She advocated intercourse six times a day, had twenty-one official lovers and employed a procurer and physician to test and examine all new applicants.

CELSUS, Aulus: (Lived during first century AD) Roman medical writer who produced a massive, encyclopaedic work which remained popular until the Renaissance. This is still a vital source of information for historians.

CESALPINO, Andrea: (1519–1603) Also known as Caesalpinus-Andreas. Italian physiologist.

CHADWICK, Edwin: (1800–1890) Civil servant, lawyer, journalist and reformer who probably did more than anyone to help 'keep Britain tidy'. His influence spread around the world and led to sanitary reforms in many other countries.

CHAIN, Ernst: (1906–79) The biochemist who, working with Florey, turned Fleming's theoretical discovery of penicillin into a useful practical drug.

CHAMBERLEN, Peter: (1560–1631) A French surgeon and male midwife said to have invented the obstetric forceps for the delivery of babies. Peter died in London, where his heirs also practised. The forceps remained a secret of the Chamberlen family for well over a century, which must give them a head start in any race to find the least public-spirited family in history.

CHARCOT, Jean-Marie: (1825–93) French physician who worked at the Salpêtrière hospital. His neurology clinics attracted students from all over the world. Sigmund Freud was one of his students.

CHAUCER, Geoffrey: (c.1342–1400) English poet and author of *Canterbury Tales*.

CHESTERFIELD, Philip: (1694–1773) English statesman and author. He became an earl in 1726. Was a friend of Pope, Swift and Voltaire. Famed for his *Letters to His Son*.

CLOVIS: (c.446–511) Known as Clovis the Frank (not because of his reputation for straight talking but because he was found of the Frankish kingdom which made up a large part of Western Europe in the Middle Ages).

COBBETT, William: (1763–1835) Journalist who fought to protect rural England from the ravages of the Industrial Revolution. Shortly before his death he was elected to Parliament.

COHN, Ferdinand: (1828–98) Bacteriologist born in Poland.

COLBERT, Jean-Baptiste: (1619–83) Finance minister to Louis XIV with considerable power.

COLUMBUS, Christopher: (1451–1506) Born in Italy, died in Spain. His voyages had tremendous effects on all aspects of life. Financed by the King and Queen of Spain but did not always do what they wanted.

COOK, James: (1728–79) Explorer and navigator who was not, in fact, promoted to Captain until after his most famous voyage to Australia and New Zealand. Cook managed to keep his crews free from scurvy.

COPERNICUS, Nicolaus (1473–1543) Polish astronomer.

CORTEZ, Hernan: (1485–1547) Also Cortes. Spanish lawyer, farmer and traveller who conquered Mexico.

CROMWELL, Oliver: (1599–1658) Major English soldier and statesman who led the Parliamentary forces in the English Civil War. He seems to have been badly plagued by warts.

CUGNOT, Nicolas-Joseph: (1725–1804) Frenchman who designed, built and presumably drove the world's first automobile. His vehicle was powered by steam.

CURIE, Marie: (1867–1934) First woman professor at the Sorbonne University in Paris. Born in Poland. Discovered radium and worked on the use of radioactivity in medicine. Attractive figure for historians but her contribution to practical medical care was much less than that of Röntgen, who is usually ignored.

CURIE, Pierre: (1859–1906) French Professor of Physics at the Sorbonne, who worked with his wife on radioactivity.

DARWIN, Charles: (1809–82) British naturalist best known for his book *On the Origin of Species*. Provocative and influential among scientist and religious students. He wrote that 'Natural selection ... implies that the individuals which are best fitted for the complex, and in the course of ages changing conditions to which they are exposed, generally survive and procreate their kind.'

DAVY, Humphry: (1778–1829) British chemist remembered for his Davy Lamp and his work with Michael Faraday. He experimented with laughing gas and gave many popular lectures in London. In 1813 Napoleon granted him safe conduct across Europe to study volcanoes.

DEFOE, Daniel: (1660–1731) Sometimes described as the first English novelist. He was interested in trade and politics but is best remembered for having written *Robinson Crusoe* and *Moll Flanders*. He also wrote *A Journal of the Plague Year*.

DESCARTES, René: (1596–1650) French philosopher and physiologist who lived for most of his life in the Netherlands and died in Sweden. He wrote that, 'The mind is so intimately dependent upon the condition and relation of the organs of the body, that if any means can ever be found to render men wiser and more ingenious than hitherto, I believe that it is in medicine they must be sought for.'

DEVENTER, Hendrik van: (1651–1724) Dutch goldsmith who has been called the father of modern midwifery. He was the first to describe the pelvis and its importance in labour.

DIOSCORIDES, Pedanius: (AD 40–90) Greek pharmacist and physician who wrote *In Re Materia Medica*. He travelled to Italy, France, Spain and Germany, usually as a surgeon with Nero's army, and described the distribution and medicinal properties of many plants and minerals. His book remained a popular best seller for sixteen hundred years.

DOMAGK, Gerhard: (1895–1964) Born in Poland. Discovered the first sulphonamide drug (prontosil). He was unable to receive his Nobel award in 1939 because of Nazi policy.

DOYLE, Conan: (1859–1930) Usually known as Sir Arthur Conan Doyle. Scottish writer who created the character Sherlock Holmes, based on a teacher in Edinburgh whose diagnostic skills were founded on an ability to observe and assess small titbits of information. Conan Doyle was knighted in 1902 for his work in the Boer War.

DUNANT, Henri: (1828–1910) Swiss founder of the Red Cross and a joint winner of the first Nobel Prize for Peace in 1901. Dunant neglected his business work and went bankrupt.

DÜRER, Albrecht: (1471–1528) German Renaissance artist.

EDWARD the CONFESSOR: (1003–66) Weak but pious King of England.

EHRLICH, Paul: (1854–1915) Born in Poland. Described his work as 'Much testing: accuracy and precision in experiment; no guess-work or self deception'. Pioneer in work on chemotherapy.

ERASISTRATUS: (Lived around 250 BC) Anatomist and physician and early student of physiology.

ERASMUS, Desiderius: (c.1466–1536) Born in the Low Countries, died in Switzerland. Great scholar, who wrote that, 'No reward could be found worthy enough for a learned and faithful doctor.' He also asked: 'Who is so persistent a preacher of abstinence, sobriety, re-straining anger, fleeing care, avoiding gluttony, rejecting love, moderating sex, as the doctor?'

EURIPIDES: (c.484–406 BC) Gloomy Greek scholar and poet.

FARADAY, Michael: (1791–1867) British physicist and chemist.

FÉLIX, Charles-François: Royal seventeenth-century French surgeon who operated on a fistula which had troubled King Louis XIV. For his fee Félix received a farm, a lot of money and a title.

FINLAY, Carlos: (1833–1915) Cuban physician who first guessed that yellow fever might be transmitted from human to human by the mosquito. He did some important experimental work to prove his theory but was ignored until Walter Reed and his party reached Cuba.

FLEMING, Alexander: (1881–1955) British bacteriologist who received the Nobel prize and knighthood for his early work on penicillin. When asked for his advice about treatment for colds, he said, 'A good gulp of hot whisky at bedtime – it's not very scientific, but it helps.'

FLEXNER, Abraham: (1860–1959) American remembered for his study of medical education. He wrote that, 'From the earliest time, medicine has been a curious blend of superstition, empiricism and that kind of sagacious observation which is the stuff out of which ultimately science is made.'

FLIEDNER, Theodor: (1800–1864) A German Protestant minister perhaps most remembered for the fact that he inspired Florence Nightingale.

FLOREY, Howard: (1898–1968) Born in Austria, died in Britain. Worked with Ernst Chain on penicillin and shared a Nobel prize. He was made a life peer in 1965.

FORD, Henry: (1863–1947) The industrialist who introduced assembly-line methods into car manufacture. Increasing the number of cars being produced enabled him to reduce the price.

FRACASTORO, Girolamo: (1478–1553) Also known as Hieronymous Fracastorius. Italian astronomer and physician who put forward a theory explaining diseases by the existence of germs some three hundred years ahead of Louis Pasteur.

FRANKLIN, Benjamin (1706–90) American author of an apparently endless series of aphorisms and epigrams. Franklin was an eighteenth-century Renaissance man. For years afterwards every other American mother seems to have christened her boys after him. He wrote that, 'Quacks are the greatest liars in the world except their patients.'

FREUD, Sigmund: (1856–1939) Born in what was until 1993 Czechoslovakia, died in London.

FRY, Elizabeth: (1780–1845) Independent British reformer who studied prisons and hospitals and had considerable influence. Her maiden name was Gurney.

GALEN: (129–99 AD) Greek physician who worked with the gladiators for a while, but later in his career became immensely powerful. His theories and writings influenced medical practice fore more than a thousand years. He was a clever physician and imaginative writer, and it is not his fault that his work was treated so seriously by later members of the medical profession that progress was effectively stifled.

GALILEO: (1564–1642) Italian mathematician, astrologer and scientist who also studied medicine. He supported Copernicus, who had claimed that the planets revolve around the sun, and this got him into trouble with the all-powerful Church.

GAMA, Vasco da: (c.1460–1524) Portuguese navigator and explorer who opened up a trade route to the East round the Cape of Good Hope.

GARRISON, Fielding: (1870–1935) American medical historian whose book *History of Medicine* (published by W.B. Saunders of Philadelphia) is a vital reference source for any historian.

GIBBON, Edward: (1737–94) British historian who wrote *The History of the Decline and Fall of the Roman Empire.*

GOETHE, Johann Wolfgang von: (1749–1832) German Renaissance man who acquired a reputation as a novelist, playwright, poet, scientist, philosopher, critic, journalist, painter, statesman, administrator and educationalist. There is no record of his having been a successful sportsman.

GORGAS, William: (1854–1920) American surgeon-general whose war against the mosquito ensured that the Panama Canal could be built.

GUILLOTIN, Joseph-Ignace: (1738–1814) The instrument known as the 'guillotine' was introduced into popular usage by a bill passed through the efforts of the Frenchman Dr Guillotin. His aim was to make execution as painless as possible.

GUTENBERG, Johann: (c.1398–c.1468) Also known as Johann Gensfleisch zur Laden. Successful German inventor of improved printing techniques but not a successful businessman.

HAMILTON, Emma: (1765–1815) Also known as Amy Lyon and as Lady Hamilton. British mistress of Admiral Horatio Nelson. Her unusual life style ended when she died in impecunious exile.

HAMMURABI: (Lived about 2000 BC) The King of Babylon who produced the famous Code of Laws which bears his name. Part of the Code which relates to medical practice translates as follows: 'If a doctor has treated a gentleman for a severe wound with a bronze lancet and has cured the man, or has opened an abscess of the eye for a gentleman with a bronze lancet and has cured the eye of the gentleman, he shall take ten shekels of silver. If he (the patient) be the son of a poor man, he shall take five shekels of silver.... 'if he be a gentleman's servant, the master of the servant shall give two shekels of silver to the doctor.... 'If a doctor has cured the shattered limb of a gentleman or has cured the diseased bowel, the patient shall give five shekels of silver to the doctor.... 'If he be the son of a poor man, he shall give three shekels of silver.... 'If a gentleman's servant, the master of the slave shall give two shekels of silver to the doctor.'

HARE, William: Partner of William Burke.

HARGREAVES, James: (?–1778) The British inventor of the spinning-jenny had a young daughter called Jenny who one day knocked over a spinning wheel...

HARVEY, William: (1578–1657) English anatomist and physician whose book describing the circulation of the blood (*Exercitatio anatomica de motu cordis et sanguinis*) was dedicated to Charles I.

HASTINGS, Charles: (1794–1866) Physician at the Worcester Infirmary and founder of the British Medical Association in 1832.

HEBERDEN, William: (1710–1801) British scholar and physician who refused to have anything to do with some of the more curious medical superstitions.

HERBERT, Sidney: (1810–1861) Also known as first Baron Herbert of Lea. Secretary of War from 1859 to 1861 but is now remembered largely for his association with Florence Nightingale.

HERODOTUS: (Lived about 450 BC) Greek author and historian.

HEROPHILUS: (Lived about 300 BC) Early anatomist who lived in Alexandria and took advantage of a lifting on the ban on human dissection to study human anatomy.

HIPPOCRATES: (Lived about 400 BC) Believed to have lived on the island of Cos. Widely described as 'the Father of Medicine'. An original thinker, observer, wise teacher, thoughtful physician and prolific author. The true practice of medicine began with Hippocrates, and his theories have been revived time and again throughout the centuries. Historians argue about whether or not Hippocrates was one man or a whole medical school. The Hippocratic Oath is still used by many medical schools today as a basic principle for medical ethics. It is: "I swear by Apollo the physician, and Aesculapius, and

Health and Allheal [these two are sometimes known as Hygeia and Panacea], and all the gods and goddesses, that according to my ability and judgement, I will keep this Oath and this stipulation – to reckon him who taught me this Art equally dear to me as my parents, to share my substance with him, and relieve his necessities if required; to look upon his offspring in the same footing as my own brothers and to teach them this Art, if they shall wish to learn it, without fee or stipulation; and that by precept, lecture and every other mode of instruction, I will impart a knowledge of the Art to my own sons, and those of my teachers, and to disciples, bound by a stipulation and oath according to the law of medicine, but to none others. I will follow that system of regimen which, according to my ability and judgement, I consider for the benefit of my patients, and abstain from whatever is deleterious and mischievous. I will give no deadly medicine to anyone if asked, nor suggest any such counsel; and in like manner I will not give to a woman a pessary to produce abortion. With purity and holiness I will pass my life and practise my Art. I will not cut persons labouring under the stone, but will leave this to be done by men who are practitioners of this work. Into whatever houses I enter, I will go into them for the benefit of the sick and will abstain from every voluntary act of mischief and corruption and, further, from the seduction of females or males, of freemen and slaves. Whatever, in connection with my medical practice, or not in connection with it, I see or hear, in the life of men, which ought not to be spoken of abroad, I will not divulge, as reckoning that all such should be kept secret. While I continue to keep this Oath unviolated, may it be granted to me to enjoy life and the practice of the Art, respected by all men, in all times! But should I trespass and violate this Oath, may the reverse be my lot!". This version taken from *Familiar Medical Quotations* edited by Maurice B. Strauss, MD (Little Brown and Co. 1968)

HODGKIN, Thomas: (1798–1866) British-born anatomist who in 1832 described the condition which still bears his name.

HOLMES, Oliver Wendell: (1809–94) Physician, anatomist and author of several books, including *The Autocrat of the Breakfast Table*, *The Professor of the Breakfast Table*, *The Poet of the Breakfast Table* and *Over the Teacups*. His son, Oliver Wendell Holmes, became a justice of the United States Supreme Court. Famous for having said, 'I firmly believe that if the whole materia medica, as now used, could be sunk to the bottom of the sea, it would be all the better for mankind – and all the worse for the fishes.' His formula for longevity was, 'Have a chronic disease and take care of it.'

HOOKE, Robert: (1635–1703) English microscopist.

HOPKINS, Matthew: (?–1647) Professional English witch-hunter.

HOWARD, John: There was an eighteenth-century surgeon called Dr John Howard who wrote that, 'Every childbearing woman may be satisfied that it is impossible for women to generate and bring forth rabbits, as it is impossible for rabbits to bring forth women', but the John Howard who made the most significant contribution to medical progress was a British philanthropist who also lived in the eighteenth century (1726-90) but who spent his life investigating conditions in prisons and hospitals.

HUNTER, John: (1728–93) A surgeon and anatomist and an exceedingly brave man. In an attempt to study syphilis and gonorrhoea, he infected himself with both diseases. He once stated that he was at the mercy of any man who made him angry. He died of a heart attack at a hospital board meeting. His brother William was also an eminent surgeon and anatomist. John Hunter was a friend of Edward Jenner.

IVAN IV: (1530–84) Also known as Ivan 'the Terrible'. First Tsar of Russia.

JACOBS, Aletta: First woman in the Netherlands to study medicine. She qualified in 1878 and took a keen interest in birth control.

JEFFERSON, Thomas: (1743–1826) Third President of the United States of America. Principal author of the Declaration of Independence.

JENNER, Edward: (1749–1823) Born, worked and died in Berkeley, Gloucestershire, where his father was vicar. He studied under John Hunter, used to vaccinate the poor in an arbour in his garden and was also a keen naturalist. He wrote that, 'The deviation of man from the state in which he was originally placed by nature seems to have proved to him a prolific source of diseases' and reflected that, The scepticism that appeared, even among the most enlightened of medical men when my sentiments on the important subject of the cowpox were first promulgated was highly laudable. To have admitted the truth of a doctrine at once so novel and so unlike any thing that ever had appeared in the annals of medicine without the test of the most rigid scrutiny, would have bordered upon temerity.'

JOHN OF GADDESDEN: (c.1280–1361) English physician and author, said to have cured the son of Edward I of smallpox by draping him in scarlet. Thought to be the model for Chaucer's Doctor of Physic, 'that verrey parfit practisour'.

JOHNSON, Samuel: (1709–84) Englishman usually known as Dr Johnson. Famous for his Dictionary, Johnson earned his living as a critic and journalist. A notoriously good talker, much of his wit was recorded by his biographer James Boswell.

KIRCHER, Athanasius: (1602–80) German Jesuit priest who was a mathematician, physicist, optician and microscopist. Probably the first man to use the microscope in attempts to investigate the causes of disease. In 1658 he described how he had seen 'worms' in the blood of plague patients.

KNOWLTON, Charles: (1800–1850) American physician with a special interest in birth control. In 1832 he published anonymously a book called *The Fruits of Philosophy: or, the Private Companion of Young Married People*.

KNOX, Robert: (1791–1862) British anatomist who worked as a surgeon at Waterloo and whose career was effectively ruined by the Burke and Hare scandal.

KOCH, Robert: (1843–1910) German physician and bacteriologist. Won a Nobel prize in 1905.

LAENNEC, René: (1781–1826) Full name René Théophile Hyacynthe Laennec. French physician who invented the stethoscope but was prouder of his proficiency on horseback. Lacnnec wrote: 'Do not fear to repeat what has already been said. Men need the truth dinned into their ears many times and from all sides. The first rumour makes them prick up their ears, the second registers and the third enters.'

LANDSTEINER, Karl: (1868–1943) Austrian immunologist and pathologist who discovered the major blood groups and received a Nobel prize in 1930.

LARREY, Jean: (1766–1842) Also known as Baron Dominique-Jean

Larrey. Served with Napoleon throughout all his great wars. Is reputed to have performed two hundred amputations in one day and to have been the first man to amputate at the hip joint.

LAVERAN, Alphonse: (1845–1922) French physician, pathologist and parasitologist who discovered the parasite that causes malaria. His work provided the background information necessary for Ross to study the practical problems associated with malaria. Laveran also studied many other tropical disorders.

LAVOISIER, Antoine-Laurent: (1743–94) French scientist and chemist. He was a member of the commission which led to the adoption of the metric system, and was executed during the French Revolution.

LAZEAR, Jesse: (1866–1900) Died as a result of a mosquito bite intended to prove how yellow fever was transmitted. He was a surgeon with Walter Reed.

LEEUWENHOEK, Antonj van: (1632–1723) Former draper's apprentice and prolific paper-writer and lens-grinder.

LESSEPS, Ferdinand de: (1805–94) French diplomat who built the Suez Canal and tried to build the Panama Canal. After his failure, the French Government sentenced him to five years imprisonment but this decision was reversed on appeal.

LETTSOM, John: (1744–1815) Born in the Virgin Islands, studied in Edinburgh, Paris and Leyden and practised in London. He was called 'the Friend of Humanity', 'the Patron of Science'. Supported Jenner and vaccination and helped found the Royal Sea Bathing Hospital in Margate.

LINACRE, Thomas: (c.1460–1524) English scholar and physician.

LIND, James: (1716–94) Born and educated in Edinburgh. Remembered for his publication *A Treatise on the Scurvy* published in 1753 and based on his naval experience. He wrote that: 'Armies have been supposed to lose more of their men by sickness, than by the sword. But this observation has been much more verified in our fleets and squadrons; where the scurvy alone, during the last war, proved a more destructive enemy, and cut off more valuable lives, than the united efforts of the French and Spanish arms.'

LISTER, Joseph: (1827–1912) Later Lord Lister (1897). Met Pasteur at the Sorbonne in 1892, and it is said that there was not a dry eye in the lecture hall. His wife, Agnes Syme, is said to have been the woman behind the great British man.

LISTON, Robert: (1794–1847) Scottish surgeon who was swift in the operating theatre, kind to the poor, abrupt in public and gentle in the sick-room.

LOCKE, John: (1632–1704) English philosopher and scientist. Worked variously as a diplomat and physician. He wrote: 'And thus I have done with what concerns the body and health, which reduces itself to these few and easily observable rules. Plenty of open air, exercise and sleep; plain diet, no wine or strong drink, and very little or no physick; not too warm and straight clothing, especially the head and feet kept cold, and the feet often used to cold water, and exposed to wet.'

LOWER, Robert: (1631–91) English anatomist and physician.

MAGELLAN, Ferdinand: Early sixteenth-century explorer and traveller. First to cross the Pacific Ocean from east to west and, although he died before the voyage was over, he led the first expedition to circumnavigate the earth.

MAGENDIE, François: (1783–1855) French physiologist.

MALPIGHI, Marcello: (1628-94) Italian physician, anatomist, microscopist and biologist. Served as chief physician to Pope Innocent XII in Rome.

MALTHUS, Thomas: (1766–1834) British economist who believed that the size of the population will always exceed the available food supply.

MANSON, Patrick: (1844–1922) British physician who did much work on tropical diseases and spent twenty-four years in China. Knighted in 1903.

MAURICEAU, François: (1637–1709) French obstetrician and author of *Traité des maladies des femmes grosses*.

MESMER, Franz: (1734–1815) German physician who qualified in Vienna and had much influence on Charcot and Freud.

MICHELANGELO: (1475–1564) Also known as Michelangelo di Lodovico Buonarroti Simoni. Italian painter, sculptor, architect and poet. A leading figure in the Renaissance, he designed the dome of St. Peter's in Rome, painted in the Sistine Chapel and sculpted the Pietà inside St. Peter's.

MOLIÈRE: (1622–73) The pen-name of Jean-Baptiste Poquelin, French dramatist, satirist and actor. He died after collapsing on the stage during an early performance of his play *Le Malade Imaginaire*. He said a lot of rude things about medicine and about doctors, including: 'I find medicine one of the greatest follies of mankind; and if I look at it from a philosophical point of view, I've never seen a sillier lot of humbuggery. I don't think there is anything more ridiculous than that one man should undertake to cure another....'

MONRO, Alexander: (1773–1859) Like his father and his grandfather, Alexander Monro was Professor of Anatomy at Edinburgh University. The three members of this Scottish family were known as Monro primus, secondus and tertius. It is said to be largely due to these three men that Edinburgh became a major teaching centre. Monro tertius was professor during the unhappy Knox, Burke and Hare affair, but he managed to keep the university out of trouble.

MONTAGU, Mary: (1689–1762) Also Lady Mary Wortley Montagu. British writer, traveller, feminist and distinguished supporter of the use of smallpox inoculation. She had been scarred by an attack as a young girl.

MORGAGNI, Giovanni: (1682–1771) The first man to correlate pathology findings with clinical records.

MORGAN, John: (1735–89) American physician who served as a surgeon in the French wars, graduated in Edinburgh and wrote *Discourse upon the Institution of Medical Schools in America*. He was co-founder of the medical department of the University of Pennsylvania and was appointed Director General and Physician in Chief of the American Army in 1775. Unfortunately, he made several enemies and died rather poor in health and wealth.

MORTON, William Thomas Green: (1819–68) An American dentist who practised in Boston and was awarded an honorary MD in 1852 by the College of Physicians and Surgeons in Baltimore. The story of who was actually the first to use anaesthesia is confused and full of controversy, but Morton was undoubtedly important in introducing anaesthesia to the practice of medicine.

NAPOLEON: (1769–1821) Full name Napoleon Bonaparte. A Corsican who temporarily extended the French territories to cover most of Europe. He was a Brigadier General at the age of twenty-four and crowned himself Emperor in 1804. In 1814, when France was defeated, Napoleon was exiled to Elba. He made a historic and heroic comeback for the Hundred Days but was defeated at Waterloo by the British and the Prussians. He was then exiled again, this time further away, on St. Helena in the South Atlantic, where he died.

NELSON, Horatio: (1758–1805) Also known as Admiral Nelson and as Lord Nelson. He had a scandalous affair with Lady Hamilton and died at the Battle of Trafalgar which was, ironically, a great victory for the British navy.

NESTORIUS: (Lived around AD 400) Early Bishop of Constantinople. He started a theological debate, which still continues, by claiming that Mary should not be called the Mother of God, his argument being that a God does not have a mother.

NEWTON, Isaac: (1643–1727) English physicist and mathematician who developed the law of gravity. A leading figure in the seventeenth-century scientific revolution and, indeed, one of the most important scientists of all time.

NICOLLE, Charles-Jules-Henri: (1866–1936) French bacteriologist who established the link between the disease typhus and the louse.

NIGHTINGALE, Florence: (1820–1910) British lady who revolutionised nursing. She is said to have enjoyed poor health.

NOSTRADAMUS: (1503–66) Also known as Michel de Notredame. French astrologer and physician. Published rhymed quatrians which are said to forecast the future, but cynics claim that the forecasts are vague and open to many interpretations.

PARACELSUS: (1493–1541) Also known as Aureolus Philippus Theophrastus Bombastus von Hohenheim. Born in Switzerland, travelled over most of Europe (very well travelled even by the standards of today's jet-set) but made enemies by lecturing in German rather than in Latin. He was undoubtedly something of a showman but also a vital figure in the re-emergence of medicine as a science.

PARÉ, Ambroise: (1510–90) A French barber-surgeon who served with the French army and later became surgeon to royalty. He devised many instruments and techniques but is best remembered for his approach and philosophy. He was the first great surgeon of modern times, and wrote, 'Always give the patient hope, even when death seems at hand'; 'Better a tried remedy than a new one', and 'I dressed him and God healed him.'

PARKINSON, James: (1755–1824) One of John Hunter's pupils, he is today remembered by the disease which bears his name. In addition to being a physician, Parkinson was a radical and a reformer, who seems often to have been in trouble with the government.

PASTEUR, Louis: (1822–95) French chemist who founded the science of bacteriology. An Institute in Paris still bears his name, and many milk-users remember him eponymously. He wrote, 'To him who devotes his life to science, nothing can give more happiness than increasing the number of discoveries, but his cup of joy is full when the results of his studies immediately find practical applications.' His cup was often full.

PEPYS, Samuel: (1633–1703) English diarist and also a naval administrator but best remembered for his diary. Sometimes saucy and full of gossip, it provides an excellent picture of seventeenth-century London.

PERICLES: (Lived about 450 BC) Greek statesman who aimed to make Athens the political and cultural centre of Greece. The Acropolis was built on his instructions.

PETTY, William: (1623–87) English economist and statistician. Studied medicine at Leyden, Paris and Oxford and worked as a Professor of Music, Professor of Anatomy and Member of Parliament. He argued that sanitary reform and health care could be cost-effective.

PEYRONIE, François de la: (1678–1747) Eminent surgeon from Montpellier who, with Georges Maréschal (1658-1736) founded the French Academy of Surgery.

PINEL, Phillipe: (1745–1826) French physician and the first practical, humane psychiatrist. He regarded mental illness as being linked to stress, physiological damage and heredity rather than demoniacal possession. Despite much opposition he led the way for a more humane approach to the treatment of the mentally ill.

PLATO: (Lived about 400 BC) Greek philosopher who, together with

Aristotle and Socrates, provided much of the framework for our culture. He wrote: 'Medicine is an art, and attends to the nature and constitution of the patient, and has principles of action and reason in each case.'

POLO, Marco: (1254–1324) An Italian merchant and adventurer who was born and died in Venice but who spent many of the intervening years away from home. His book *Travels with Marco Polo* is considered a classic, and thousands of schoolchildren around the world have plotted his route with crayon. He lived in China for nearly twenty years. His father, Niccolo Polo, was also a traveller and explorer.

POPE, Alexander: (1688–1744) British writer, poet and satirist.

POTT, Percival: (1714–88) A British surgeon who worked at St. Bartholomew's in London. He had a large and successful private practice and wrote on many subjects. A particular type of fracture of the leg still bears his name – he sustained the fracture himself from a fall in the street.

QUINCEY, Thomas de: (1785–1859) British author of *The Confessions of an English Opium Eater*. He wrote: 'A due balance and equilibrium of the mind is best preserved by a large and multiform knowledge; but knowledge itself is best served by an exclusive (or at least paramount) dedication of one mind to one science.' He is said to have taken opium for the first time when aged nineteen, at Oxford University. He spent much of his life under the influence of the drug but wrote a great deal and lived to the age of seventy-four years.

RALEIGH, Walter: (1554–1618) English adventurer, importer and favourite of Queen Elizabeth I. Knighted in 1585.

RAMAZZINI, Bernardino: (1633–1714) Italian Professor of Medicine and founder of industrial medicine. He is thought to have been the first doctor regularly to ask his patients: 'What is your occupation?'

RAMSES V: King of Egypt perhaps best remembered for the fact that he died of smallpox.

RAPHAEL; (1483–1520) Also known as Raffaello Sanzio. Italian painter and architect.

RASPUTIN, Grigory: (c.1872–1916) Russian peasant and monk who obtained great power over the Russian imperial family by his apparent ability to improve the medical condition of Alexis Nikolayevitch, the Empress's son, who had haemophilia. He was grubby, satyric, mysterious and brilliant. His behaviour started rumours of an affair with the Empress, and eventually a group of ousted aristocrats decided to assassinate him. They gave him poisoned cakes but he did not die (it is thought that his high intake of alcohol had given him certain immunity) so they shot him. When he still refused to die, they tied him up and threw him through a hole in the ice into the nearest river. He then died.

REED, Walter: (1851–1902) American army surgeon remembered for the fact that he led the Commission to investigate the cause and mode of transmission of yellow fever. The Walter Reed Hospital in Washington is named after him.

REHN, Ludwig: (1849–1930) German surgeon who pioneered work on the human heart.

RHAZES: (c.850–932) Also known as Abu Baker Muhammad ibn Zakariyya. Persian physician, sometimes referred to as 'the Arabian Hippocrates'. He was also a mathematician, philosopher, astronomer, chemist and musician. He wrote several books on medicine but died in poverty. He wrote: 'When the disease is stronger than the patient, the physician will not be able to help him at all, and if the strength of the patient is greater than the strength of the disease, he does not need a physician at all. But when both are equal, then one needs a physician who will support the patient's strength and help him against the disease.'

RÖNTGEN, Wilhelm: (1845–1923) German physicist who, while Professor at the University of Würzburg, discovered X-rays. He received the Nobel prize for physics in 1901. He wrote: 'For brevity's sake I shall use the expression "rays" and to distinguish them from others of this name I shall call them "X-rays".'

ROONHUYZE, Hendrik van: Seventeenth-century Dutch male midwife who performed several Caesarian sections. His son, Rogier, is said to have bought the secret of obstetric forceps from Hugh Chamberlen in about 1693.

ROSS, Ronald: (1857–1932) British zoologist and bacteriologist who worked in the Indian Medical Service for eighteen years and studied the relationship between malaria and mosquitoes. He was awarded a Nobel prize in 1902 and knighted in 1911. He wrote: 'I was tired and what was the use? I must have examined the stomachs of a thousand mosquitoes by this time. But the Angel of Fate fortunately laid his hand on my head.'

RUSH, Benjamin: (1745–1813) American physician, signatory of the Declaration of Independence and friend of Benjamin Franklin. He was Treasurer of the US Mint from 1797 to 1813.

SANCTORIUS: (1516–1636) Also known as Santorio Santorio. Italian physician, physicist and physiologist. He devised a watch, a thermometer and a weighing machine and was the first person to employ precision instruments in medicine, adapting several of Galileo's inventions to medical practice. For one experiment he weighed himself before, during and after meals to estimate the weight of invisible perspiration.

SANGER, Margaret: (1883–1966) Born Margaret Higgins. An American who had ten brothers and sisters and two husbands. Having first taught and nursed, she then devoted herself to the promotion of birth control and founded the American Birth-Control League in 1921. She became the first President of the International Planned Parenthood Federation which was founded in 1953.

SEMMELWEISS, Ignaz: (1815–65) Obstetrician whose views on puerperal fever brought him ridicule. He was depressed by the opposition from the medical establishment and became insane. He died, ironically, from a septic wound. Semmelweiss worked most of his life in Vienna but was born in Budapest, Hungary.

SERVETUS, Michael: (c.1511–53) Spanish physician who, with his heretical beliefs, annoyed both the Protestants and the Catholics and was eventually executed by Calvinists. Calvin himself played a major part in the trial. Servetus's major contribution to medical thinking was his discovery of the circulation of blood to and from the lungs.

SHIPPEN, William: (1736–1808) American teacher of medicine and supporter of male midwifery.

SIMPSON, James: (1811–70) British obstetrician, gynaecologist and archaeologist who introduced chloroform anaesthesia in midwifery.

He was a professor at Edinburgh and knighted in 1866.

SMITH, Adam: (1723–90) Scottish economist who wrote *An Inquiry into the nature and causes of the Wealth of Nations*. He had tremendous influence on many politicians, and his theories about free trade, individual self-interest and competition are followed by many modern economists.

SNOW, John: (1813–58) British physician who proved the relationship between cholera and contaminated water supplies. He was also one of the first anaesthetists.

SOCRATES: (c.470–399 BC) Born and died in Athens. Philosopher who said 'Know thyself' and spent much time talking and teaching in public places. With Plato and Aristotle, Socrates was one of the 'big three' Greek philosophers. He was sentenced to death for neglect of the gods and corruption of the young, and committed suicide by drinking hemlock. He said: 'Base men live to eat and drink, and good men eat and drink to live.'

SOPHOCLES: (c.500–406 BC) Classic, tragic Greek playwright, who wrote 123 plays, including *Oedipus Rex*. He was also a statesman and an army general.

STERNE, Laurence: (1713–68) British novelist who wrote *Tristram Shandy*. He suffered from tuberculosis.

STOPES, Marie: (1880–1958) British advocate of birth control. She influenced the Church of England but made little headway with the Roman Catholic Church.

SUSRUTA: (Lived about the fourth century AD) Indian medical writer.

SYLVIUS, Franciscus: (1614–72) Also known as Franz de le Boe, François du Bois and by other combinations of those names. German physician, physiologist, anatomist and chemist who believed that disorders are caused by chemical actions and can therefore be diagnosed and treated logically. Professor of Medicine at Leyden University, where he acquired a considerable reputation as a teacher.

TENON, Jacobus René: Eighteenth-century French writer who, in 1788, published *Memoires sur les hôpitaux de Paris*.

THACKRAH, Charles: (1795–1833) British physician who specialised in industrial medicine.

THUCYDIDES: (Lived about 450 BC) Greek politician.

TULL, Jethro: (1674–1741) English inventor who, in 1701, invented a seed drill which sowed in neat rows. The improvement in farming techniques that followed his inventions had a tremendous effect on agricultural productivity.

VESALIUS, Andreas: (1514–64) Belgian physician whose de scriptions of human anatomy made an important contribution to the Renaissance in medicine.

VINCI, Leonardo da: (1452–1519) Italian artist and scientist, generally regarded as the real Renaissance man. In addition to his many drawings and paintings, he left a vast number of sketches and notes describing the structure of the human body.

VIRCHOW, Rudolf: (1821–1902) Born in Poland. Pathologist, statesman and advocate of public health.

WARREN, John: (1778–1856) American surgeon who gave the first public demonstration of ether anaesthesia. (Cf.Morton).

WATERHOUSE, Benjamin: (1745–1846) American physician who pioneered smallpox vaccination.

WATT, James: (1736–1819) British inventor whose steam-engine helped to get the Industrial Revolution under way.

WITHERING, William: (1741–99) British physician who introduced digitalis into clinical practice. He wrote: 'It is much easier to write upon a disease than upon a remedy. The former is in the hands of nature and a faithful observer with an eye of tolerable judgment cannot fail to delineate a likeness. The latter will ever be subject to the whim, the inaccuracies and the blunders of mankind.'

WRIGHT, Orville: (1871–1948) American joint inventor of the first aeroplane. Brother of Wilbur.

WRIGHT, Wilbur: (1867–1912) American joint inventor of the first aeroplane. Brother of Orville.

ZEPPELIN, Ferdinand: (1838–1917) German army officer who rose to the rank of Lieutenant General before concentrating on developing the rigid airship which bears his name.

Turning Points

A summary of some of the major influences on the social history of medicine.

1. Hippocrates: About 400 BC

Medicine really began in Greece in the time of Hippocrates. The Greek scholars brought together information from many sources. Hippocrates taught a logical approach to clinical medicine.

2. Rome: Approximately 100 BC to AD 200

The Romans were not great scholars but they were great engineers. They built roads, baths and aqueducts, and public health in their cities was generally good. Galen was to have influence on medical thinking for many centuries.

3. The Renaissance: About 1400 to 1600

Medical care regressed during the Middle Ages. There were many advances during the Renaissance. Anatomy studies began again, and men like Vesalius helped to spread basic information. Paracelsus was one of the most spectacular leaders during this period. Travellers such as Columbus helped to break down geographical barriers, and the development of printing improved communications. Paré began to make surgery respectable once again.

4. The Scientific Revolution Continues: 1600 to 1700

Galileo and Sanctorius introduced medical instruments, and Harvey introduced logic to experimental science.

5. A Century of Social Change: 1700 to 1800

The Industrial Revolution begins in Britain, and America declares her independence. In France the Revolution starts.

6. The Control of Infection: 1800 to 1850

Jenner introduces vaccination and smallpox declines around the world. Chadwick and others press for reforms designed to improve public health facilities. Agricultural advances, industrial improvements, economic growth and political changes all improve living standards. Cholera and tuberculosis also decline in importance.

7.   *Improvements in Practical Medical Care: 1850 to 1900*

This half-century saw many changes. Florence Nightingale revolutionised nursing. Pasteur and Lister introduced the principles of asepsis and antisepsis. Anaesthesia was introduced. Röntgen introduced X-rays. Ross recognised and proved the relationship between mosquitoes and malaria. Ehrlich began the search for a 'magic bullet'. The aims of the medical profession came closer to meeting the needs of the population, and the advances of the twentieth century resulted largely from work begun in this period.

Further Reading

I consulted hundreds of books and journals while writing *The Story of Medicine*. I particularly recommend the following:

An Introduction to the History of Medicine, Fielding H. Garrison, (W.B. Saunders Co. Philadelphia and London 1929)

An Introduction to Social Medicine, Thomas McKeown and C.R. Lowe, (Blackwell Scientific Publications, Oxford, 1966)

A Social History of Medicine, F.F. Cartwright, (Longman, London and New York, 1977)

Familiar Medical Quotations, M.B. Strauss, (Little Brown & Co, Boston, 1968)

Doctors by Themselves, Edward F. Griffith, (Cassell, London, 1951)

Florence Nightingale, Cecil Woodham-Smith, (Fontana, London, 1964)

Medical History and Medical Care, A Symposium of Perspec-

tives, (Oxford University Press, London, New York and To-
ronto, 1971)

Magic, Myth and Medicine, John Camp, (Priory Press, London)

Witches, Midwives and Nurses, Barbara Ehrenreich and Deirdre
English, (Feminist Press, New York, 1974)

Call the Doctor, E.S. Turner, (Michael Joseph, London, 1958)

INDEX

Cartier, Jacques, 99, 226
Catherine II, 103, 226
Celsus, 32, 227
Celestial bed, 110
Cesalpino, Andrea, 72, 227
Chadwick, Edwin, 133-134, 227
Chain, Ernst, 208, 227
Chamberlen, Peter, 82, 227
Charcot, Jean-Martin, 166, 227
Charles IV of Spain, 107
Chaucer, 45, 109, 227
Chesterfield, Philip, 108, 227
China, 23-24
Cholera, 132-133
Chosroes, 39
Christianity, 35-39
Cinchona, 58, 89, 172
Clovis the Frank, 38, 227
Cobbett, William, 137, 228
Code of Hammurabi, 22, 232
Cohn, Ferdinand, 164, 228
Colbert, 79, 228
College of Physicians, 68
Columbo, Matteo, 72
Columbus, Christopher, 54, 55, 228
Constantinople, 39
Contraceptives, 200-204, 210
Cook, Captain, 100, 228
Copernicus, Nicholas, 64-65, 228
Corinth, 31
Corn Laws, 136
Cortez, Hernan, 57, 101, 228
Cowpox, 105
Crimean War, 144–146, 192
Cromwell, Oliver, 228
Crusaders, 41, 45-46
Cugnot, Nicholas-Joseph, 228
Curie, Marie and Pierre, 181, 228

da Gama, Vasco, 54, 99, 232
da Vinci, Leonardo, 61
Dancing Mania, 49

Darwin, Charles, 149, 228
Davy, Humphry, 154, 229
De Contagione, 77
de la Peyronie, Francois, 119
de Lesseps, Ferdinand, 177, 237
De Humanis Corporis Fabrica, 61
De Motu Cordis, 72
De Re Medica, 32
De Re Metallica, 96
De Sedibus et Causis Morborum, 123
Defoe, Daniel, 114, 229
Dennis, Alice, 74
Denys, Jean Baptiste, 189
Descartes, René, 71, 229
Deventer, Hendrik van, 76, 229
Digitalis, 90
Dimsdale, Thomas, 103
Dioscorides, 32, 229
Domagk, Gerhard, 208, 229
Doyle, Conan, 187, 229
Dr Bateman's Pectoral Drops, 88
Duffy's Elixir, 88
Dunant, Jean Henri, 146, 229
Dürer, Albrecht, 61, 230
Durnton, Jacob, 118
Dysdale, George, 203

Edinburgh University, 86, 126
Edward the Confessor, 38, 230
Ehrlich, Paul, 206, 230
Elements, theory of, 33
Erasistratus, 30, 230
Erasmus, Desiderius, 56, 230
Essay on Mithridanum and Theriacs, 90

Factory Act, 137
Famine, 136
Faraday, Michael, 155, 230
Félix, Charles François, 119, 230
Finlay, Carlos, 175, 230
Flagellation, 49

Knowlton, Charles, 202, 236
Knox, Robert, 125-126, 236
Koch, Robert, 164, 236

Laennec, Rene, 122, 236
Landry, Bishop, 37
Landsteiner, Karl, 189-191, 236
Larrey, Dominique-Jean, 120-121, 236
Laudanum, 89
Laveran, Alphonse, 172-174, 237
Lazear, Jesse, 176-177, 237
League of Nations, 213
Leeches, 125
Leeuwenhoek, Antonj van, 71, 78, 83, 237
Leprosy, 12, 37, 80
Lesseps, Ferdinand de, 177, 237
Lettsom, John Coakley, 106, 132, 237
Leyden, University of, 84, 86
Linacre, Thomas, 67, 237
Lind, James, 100, 237
Lister, Joseph, 157-159, 237
Liston, Robert, 153, 155, 238
Locke, John, 65, 83, 238
London Pharmacopoeia, 88
Louis XV, 119
Louis XIV, 119
Lower, Robert, 190, 238

Magellan, Ferdinand, 54, 238
Malaria, 34-35, 171-174, 177-178, 214
Malpighi, Marcello, 71, 238
Mareschal, Georges, 119
Malthus, Thomas, 202, 238
Malthusian League, 203
Manson, Patrick, 173, 238
Mapp, Sally, 109
Maréschal, Georges, 119
Massachusetts General Hospital, 155

Medical Act, 150
Medical Schools, 41-46, 84, 194-195
Mercer, Margaret, 73
Mesmer, Franz, 111-113, 238
Mesopotamia, 20, 39
Mexico, 57
Michaelangelo, 61, 238
Midwives, 66, 73-75, 81-83
Modena, University of, 96
Molière, 76, 109, 239
Mongols, 41
Monro, Alexander, 126, 239
Montagu Lady Mary, 103, 239
Montpellier, 44-45
Morgagni, Giovanni, 123, 239
Morgan, John, 86, 239
Morton, William Thomas Green, 155, 239
Moslem Empire, 40

Napoleon Bonaparte, 91, 100, 106, 120, 131, 174, 192, 240
National Health Service (Britain), 216-219
Nelson, Horatio, 100, 110, 240
Nestorius, 39, 240
Newton, Isaac, 83, 240
Nicolle, Charles-Jules-Henri, 161, 240
Nightingale, Florence, 142-146, 240
Nostradamus, 65, 240
Notes on Nursing, 146
Nursing, 139-146

Obstetrics, 81-82

Padua, 44-45, 64, 84, 96
Panama Canal, 177-178
Paracelsus, 46, 59-61, 240
Paré, Ambrose, 59, 240